The New Millennium

Other Books by Pat Robertson

Shout It from the Housetops
The Secret Kingdom
Answers to 200 of Life's Most Probing Questions
America's Date with Destiny
Beyond Reason: How Miracles Can Change Your Life
The Plan

10 Trends That Will Impact
You and Your Family By
The Year 2000

The New Millennium

Pat Robertson

WORD PUBLISHING
Dallas · London · Vancouver · Melbourne

Library of Congress Cataloging in Publication Data

Robertson, Pat.
    The new millenium : what you and your family can expect in the
year 2000 / by Pat Robertson.
        p.   cm.
    Includes bibliographical references.
    ISBN 0-8499-0837-X
    1. Civilization, Modern—1950–   2. Twenty-first century—
Forecasts. I. Title.
    D857.R63   1990
    303.49′09′05—dc20   90–46931
                                                                 CIP

Printed in the United States of America
0 1 2 3 9 AGM 9 8 7 6 5 4

This book is dedicated
to those who sincerely are seeking
to learn the truth of the spiritual megatrends
which are shaping the future of our world.

My profound appreciation goes to Dr. James Black whose indefatigable labor, warm good nature, and vast book publishing experience is responsible for the structure of this work.

I also want to thank two superb newsmen, Drew Parkhill and John Waage, for always being available with the hard-to-find research material and the arcane statistics I always seemed to need at the last minute.

My thanks to editor, Al Bryant, who is this year retiring from a long publishing career.

I would be remiss if I did not mention the help of two key executives at WORD, Incorporated, Joey Paul and Kip Jordon, who made the challenge of writing this book so irresistible that I agreed to do it even though my instincts told me that such a project had to be impossible in light of everything else that I was already obligated to do.

Finally, I owe profound thanks to my wife, Dede, who put up with before dawn mornings, books and papers everywhere, and who faithfully read and discussed every chapter with me as it appeared, then encouraged me on.

Contents

There can be no new world under present conditions. Something dramatic has to happen to alter man and his world. That leaves us with only one absolute certainty about the future: Christ as the Prince of Peace, with the government upon His shoulders.

—BILLY GRAHAM

Preface

As the apostle Paul said, "Now we see through a glass, darkly; but then we shall see face to face . . . Now I know in part, but then I shall know fully." God promises that someday all the mysteries of life will be clear to us; someday all the events of our lives will be revealed and everything will make sense.

But today, there are limits to how much we can know about the significance of the happenings in our daily lives, especially with the rapid pace of the changes taking place in the world around us. Consequently, it is incredibly difficult to predict what lies ahead in the next week, let alone the next year, two years, or decade.

Nevertheless, wisdom has taught us that when we can observe certain trends over a period of time, we can believe that certain other effects and events will probably take place. So as we look ahead at the decade of the 1990s, and toward the year 2000, I would like to focus on some of the things that we can see in our world and begin to analyze some of these trends and their potential consequences.

Absent the violent overthrow of government, or severe economic crisis, or the direct intervention of God in our society, or absent a major spiritual revival, what lies ahead for the United States can be understood to some degree in the light of the trends taking place today in this nation and around the world.

From the vantage point of history, and with a respect for the ethical and moral traditions which have provided the foundation for

Western society throughout most of our history, we can even begin to speculate on what lies ahead.

So, what we will talk about in this book will be a broad range of analysis of the events of the next decade, and how they will affect each individual and his or her family, and what they will likely mean for the United States and our relations with the rest of the world.

We approach these subjects with humility, recognizing that we are fallible human beings; and we recognize that the sudden changes we have already seen in the international arena are clear evidence of the volatile nature of the forces at work in the political world, and in the spiritual world. There will certainly be changes and reversals in some of these events which may shed new light on the issues I will be discussing here.

In some cases, things may in fact turn out quite differently than we had anticipated. Even so, I trust those changes will not invalidate the focus of this work nor its perspectives. I hope, rather, to confirm the volatility of the world situation and affirm other points of focus in this work with greater clarity.

My essential concern has been to reset the pieces on the chessboard of history, to restore a sense of who we are today and how we have come to be where we are.

In the whirlwind of world upheaval, social change, and cultural and emotional restructuring of such tremendous proportions, it is easy to forget the outlines and the context of our experience. We forget where we've come from and how we got here. We even forget that there are definite and unchangeable benchmarks of the human condition.

It is my hope that this book will help to re-establish some of those factors in such a way that we can find a renewed vision of truth and justice, and that we can step out bravely into the new world and the new millennium that waits just ahead.

When we speak from the Bible, we will say "Thus saith the Lord," but otherwise, most of the observations presented here will be my own considered opinion. While I continue to trust the Lord for His wisdom and insight, and while a lot of research and commentary has been included in this work from various professional and scholarly sources, the responsibility for the use and application of these observations rests with the author.

For a world beginning a period of tumultous, exciting, and sometimes frightening changes the words of the prophet Daniel ring clear and true:

> Let the name of God be blessed forever and ever
> For wisdom and power belong to Him.
> And it is He who changes the times and epochs;
> He removes kings and establishes kings;
> He gives wisdom to wise men,
> And knowledge to men of understanding.
> It is He who reveals the profound and hidden things;
> He knows what is in the darkness.
>
> (Daniel 2:20–22 NASB)

It is my fervent hope that each reader will be challenged and strengthened by what follows.

PART ONE

The Clash of Ideologies

Nature abhors a vacuum, and secularism has left a spiritual vacuum in the hearts of all those who once turned to it for freedom and hope. To survive, the humanists will either have to decamp or change their ways, and this is the decade in which one of those two will most certainly come to pass.

1

A New Beginning

This decade will witness "a revolution in the sphere of human consciousness." The Christian church will have an opportunity as great as it experienced at the fall of the Roman Empire.

The media have barely been able to keep up with the rush of world events. Day after day, the headlines of our daily papers and news magazines shout the news of revolutionary changes taking place in every corner of the globe.

Emblazoned across the front page of the *New York Times* Sunday editorial section just a few months ago was a photograph showing a massive portrait of Lenin being erected in Moscow for the fortieth anniversary of the Bolshevik Revolution, in 1957.

After its first forty years, the Revolution still lived in the hearts of the reformers, and the onslaught of communism seemed awesome and relentless to the rest of the world. But by February 1990, the headlines had a very different look. Now they proclaimed the great Lenin "The God That Failed."

After seventy years it is now clear that communism has failed to deliver the great social order and prosperity it promised. Marx and Lenin were wrong, and governments around the world that once pinned their hopes on an idealistic dream—on an economic theory born out of the failures of nineteenth century industrialism—are overthrowing those communist ideologies. As the *New York Times* proclaimed, they are "Renouncing the Revolution's Holy Writ."

Who would have dared imagine over the last forty years that we would live to see the day that the communist empire would fall apart in a single year? Who would have dared to predict that we would see a time when the nightmare of Marxist-Leninist communism would be nothing more than a bad dream?

Would anyone have believed we would see the brutal dictator of East Germany tried for crimes against the state? When the even more repressive and brutal Stalinist head of Romania, Ceausescu, would be executed by a firing squad? Or when millions of people in Poland, Czechoslovakia, Hungary, East Germany, Latvia, Lithuania, Romania, Bulgaria, and the toughest of the lot, Albania, would be demonstrating in the streets for democratic reform?

Communist party after communist party were suddenly dissolving before our eyes—not with revolutionary gunfire, but by demonstrations and public protest, and with remarkably little loss of human life.

We watched stunned as the Berlin Wall crumbled. The nightly news showed us every dramatic detail as the barbed-wire barriers between Hungary and Austria came down. The flow of people and information was suddenly opened up between East and West, and families that had been separated for years by brutal communist tyranny were finally reunited.

Hundreds of thousands of people from East Germany came into West Berlin without restraint. They were shopping, and they were free to stay if they wished. Who would have dared to dream it was possible? And yet it is happening, even now, before our very eyes.

FILLING THE VACUUM

Even more significant than the fall of communism itself is the revival of religious faith in the East Bloc countries. The head of an atheistic system, Mikhail Gorbachev, actually met with the Pope, who is the most visible expression of "theism" and Christianity in the world. And in that historic meeting, the leader of atheism told the world that they needed spiritual truths behind the Iron Curtain. The Kremlin confessed that the Soviet people were perishing from the lack of moral values.

What does this mean for us as we enter into the decade of the 1990s? **Among its many other weaknesses, communism failed to recognize what Pascal called "the God-shaped vacuum" in the human soul.** The spiritual vacuum left by seventy years of communist totalitarianism has created a desperate hunger in the souls of men and women around the world, wherever communism has prevailed. While pockets of Christianity survived by going underground, the majority of these people have been left spiritually and emotionally destitute.

Now they have the freedom to seek nourishment, but what will they find to fill the emptiness? What will satisfy their hunger? In a recent interview, the director of the Center for Strategic Studies at the Free University of Rome, Enrico Jacchia, told the *Wall Street Journal,* "There's a strategic void. Anybody with a concrete design may well succeed."

Beliefs and social structures, both physical and spiritual, are being explored like never before, which means that a "window of opportunity" is open. The need is great. But how will Christians respond?

I believe the 1990s are a "decade of opportunity." There has never been such opportunity in the history of Christianity. As one major belief system crumbles before our very eyes, it is leaving spiritually naked a population of between one and a half and two billion people.

In the process, the crumbling of atheistic communism gives the lie to humanists and atheists and all those who deny the reality of God all over the world, because it says that a system based on atheism, on collectivism, which does not permit people freedom, ultimately will fall. And the reverse of that is also true: "where the Spirit of the Lord is, there is liberty" (2 Corinthians 3:17 NKJV). When you begin to have religious revival in any country, sooner or later that country will move toward freedom.

Who would have dreamed that a television program based on Bible stories, on the discussion of the origin of man, of the fall of man from the garden, of the birth of Jesus Christ, of the crucifixion on the cross, that these very stories would be shown on the communist-run television system? First in Leningrad, then in Latvia and Estonia, then throughout the Soviet Union.

I am proud to report that such a thing did happen because programs we produced at the Christian Broadcasting Network, with the help of our associates in Japan, were available to be shown on those systems at a time when the people were ready to see and hear.

Today our "SuperBook" and "Flying House" animated Bible stories are being broadcast eight times a week inside the Soviet Union, and millions of people are being taught the truths of the Bible on the very vehicle once used for communist, atheistic propaganda inside these communist countries.

That is one small step, but before we take a broader look at the opportunities and the challenges that lie ahead as we approach the new millennium, I think we should look back at our history, to the way these cultures and customs came into being. If we pause to try to understand some of the things that led to this moment in time, we will get a better perspective on what we can expect to happen in the next ten or twenty years.

THE LEGACY OF ROME

At the time of the birth of Jesus Christ, the Roman Empire controlled the then-known world. Through systematic military and political conquest, the Romans conquered all the lands surrounding the Mediterranean and their dominion had grown larger than any previous empire.

The Assyrians, Babylonians, Persians, and the Greeks under Alexander the Great, each created vast and powerful kingdoms in their time. But the Roman Empire surpassed them all. With it had come a universal language, a system of roads, and a stable and orderly government.

The principal religion of Rome at the time of Christ was the Babylonian cult of Ishtar: the so-called "mystery religions" of the erotic goddess known as Astarte among the Canaanites and Ashtoreth among the early Hebrews. These religions were involved with various forms of occult spiritism that had demonic roots. Later the Romans began to worship their emperor as god on earth.

As each emperor died, Roman society began to deify the next emperor and to worship him. By the end of the third century A.D. the corruption and decadence of the rulers made it clear that emperor worship was a fraud. As the people recognized this fraud and the cult gradually disappeared, Christianity emerged as the only logical alternative.

The early apostles had covered all these regions and, despite terrible persecution, the truth of Jesus Christ was spread far and wide. The blood of the martyrs had been the seedbed of the church.

Early civilizations could not have dreamed of the incredible means of communication we take for granted today. Today, thanks to the power of radio, television, jet airplanes, and now satellites, words and ideas can travel across continents and around the world in a split second. But in ancient times, ideas could only move as rapidly as messengers on foot, or in fast chariots, could carry them. By our standards that was not fast at all.

Given the great difficulties of travel and language, and the risks involved in sharing a revolutionary new form of worship, the true scope of what was accomplished by a tiny band of first century Christians is almost inconceivable.

They started out a mere handful, 120 at first, and then a few thousand, and then a few thousand more. But they were valiant and committed even unto death. They burst forth out of Jerusalem, and sailing on creaky old ships or walking torturous journeys, and in constant peril, those men and women turned the world upside down. Within 300 years they had won the Roman Empire for Christ.

THE ASCENDANCY OF THE CHURCH

By the year 320 A.D., the Emperor Constantine had made Christianity the religion of the Empire, and from that point on missionaries began carrying the gospel around the world. Through their efforts, Christianity ultimately replaced the "mystery religions."

The pagan religions also worshiped gods known as the "Baals," which means lords. They had many types of strange gods and goddesses. They worshiped idols of every imaginable sort, which prompted the apostle Paul to say, when he was giving his sermon on Mars Hill, "I see that you are a very religious people." But since they had been created in the minds of men and not in the mind of God, the deities of the Greeks and the Romans were very human-like and fallible creatures.

While the sanctuaries of the Egyptians had been shrines to the ancient pharaohs, their religion was naturalistic and animistic. They worshiped the sun and moon, owls and snakes, and a whole host of imaginary creatures. The pantheons of Greece and Rome, as well as all their temples and shrines, were populated by supernatural beings that resembled human beings much more than gods. They had the same lusts and passions and angers of human beings; they just had a lot more of them.

The priests and scribes credited the various gods with vast powers and with control of the sun, stars and planets; yet Zeus and Apollo and Jupiter behaved like surly, selfish mortals. It was relatively easy by such standards to consider a man, such as the emperor, a god. If no better, he was clearly no worse.

In each of these pagan religions there was always a seed of Satanic root, and even as the various cults failed in the West, those seeds refused to die. As the mysteries began to disappear in the West, they migrated to what is now India, and from there on to China and the Far East.

That particular type of religion which involved the worship of mankind, and deities like man, of many demonic gods and goddesses, and a belief in reincarnation, began to take root in India even as it was being supplanted by Christianity in the Mediterranean world.

From 320 on, Christianity spread throughout the Roman Empire and moved up into Northern Europe. It displaced some of the more primitive religious systems of the Teutonic tribes, and with the growth of Christianity came education, culture, and the genuine enlightenment that inevitably springs from the faithful worship of Jesus Christ.

When the Roman Empire finally began to collapse under the weight of internal corruption, the only power with the strength and authority to replace it was the Church of Rome. Pope Leo the Great personally saved Rome from attack by Attila the Hun in 452, and from a similar fate at the hands of Genseric, leader of the Vandals, in 455.

The spiritual and temporal power of the Roman Church was complete when, on Christmas Day in the year 800, Pope Leo III crowned Charlemagne as the Holy Roman Emperor. This laid the foundation for the designation of Europe—and subsequently the European colonies in North and South America—as Christendom.

This Christian empire combined the might of Rome and the passionate faith of the Byzantine Empire, which had grown strong in Eastern Europe. The church then unified the authority of the European monarch with the authority of the Pope of Rome in what was called a "holy alliance."

From that moment, and for a period of a thousand years— from about the year 500 to the year 1500—Christianity flourished throughout Europe. The civilizations of Greece and Rome had been replaced by a new emerging civilization based on the Bible and the worship of Jesus Christ.

The Christian faith spread to Russia, where there were mass conversions around the year 1000. It spread into England, Ireland, France, Spain, Italy, Germany, Scandinavia, and all over the continent of Europe. There was one religion, one worship, and Jesus Christ was Lord of all: spiritual and temporal.

When any institution becomes that powerful, it inevitably becomes corrupt. "Power corrupts. Absolute power corrupts absolutely," as Lord Acton put it. The seeds of great corruption began to grow within the papacy, and in the Roman Church, and in the government. To get ahead in the government, as in every area of the political and business life of the times, it was necessary to be well connected in the religious life of the society.

Popes began to be popes not because of their allegiance to Jesus Christ, but because of their desire for temporal power. There were feuds within the church—popes and anti-popes, intrigue and corruption, splendor and excess. Therefore, it was not surprising that, about the year 1500, a major challenge was launched against the corruption of the church. That challenge, which we know as the Protestant Reformation, eventually brought about the formation of the Protestant church.

The first expressions of the Reformation came from the teachings of Martin Luther and what, by the middle of the sixteenth century, would be known as Lutheranism. Secondly, through the teachings of the French theologian, John Calvin, came Calvinism, which led to the Presbyterian and Reformed traditions within the Protestant church.

Over the following decades other expressions emerged, such as the Baptists in about 1620. During the next 100 to 150 years, Methodists and the various "holiness" churches came into being through the teachings of John Wesley.

DARKNESS AND THE LIGHT

During the period when the Roman Catholic Church was falling from its place of supremacy, and before the Protestant movement could occupy any comparable degree of authority in Western culture, nonreligious, secular movements began to make their way into European thought through the writings of men like Rene Descartes and Baruch Spinoza. The most pernicious came to be known as "rationalism."

People influenced by these new ideas began to believe that the human mind was more important than the supernatural, and that the aim of philosophy and ethics—and all of life for that matter—was the attainment of god-like human perfection. *Reason, not God, was the center of their universe.*

The philosophers began to speak of God as the great Watchmaker who made the universe, created and organized it after a very carefully defined plan, then withdrew. They suggested He wound the universe up like a clock then turned it loose to run according to the laws He had given it. This belief was known as Deism, and out of Deism came the age of "The Enlightenment," during which the "rationalistic" ideas of thinkers such as Descartes, Rousseau, Voltaire and others had great impact.

Henri Beyle (pronounced baal), who wrote under the name of Voltaire, was essentially an atheist. He loved to poke fun at every type of religious expression. He was a rascal and a lovable rogue with an irreverent and infectious sense of humor. The learned aristocrats of his day found it easy to buy whatever Voltaire was selling.

Jean Jacques Rousseau, though personally a very peculiar and scandalous man, attracted many followers as well. Rousseau did not believe in the original sin of man; instead, he believed that every human being possessed an essential nobility and dignity that needed to be fanned into flame by greater and greater personal freedoms.

Rousseau taught that there was a "noble savage" inside of people who was merely in chains. If the savage in us could be freed, we could have heaven on earth for the enlightened people whose inner deity would come forth without help from (or need of) God, but merely from political freedom.

Out of these new and revolutionary ideas came the horrors of the French Revolution, and the breakup of what was called the *ancien regime,* or the old order. The old order was systematically and brutally dismantled in France through the vehicle of the Revolution, and with it came a turning against the Church.

The Catholic Church had been so closely allied with the old order, with the nobility, with the kings, and with the court, it was discredited in the eyes of the people. The revolutionaries thought that in order to be free politically it was necessary to be free of Christianity. From that time, the central role of the Church in European society was gone forever.

A RAGE OF ANGRY MEN

The rationalist movement swept into the 1800s, an era that brought forth three major figures: Karl Marx, Charles Darwin, and Sigmund Freud. Each of these men—in company with a cadre of German theologians who emerged on the heels of the Revolution—were committed to debunking the Bible, turning against the supernatural, and teaching their own rationalistic theory that man and all the creatures of the animal world are mere products of blind evolution.

Man is *not* made in the image of God, they argued, and if there is to be salvation for mankind it will not be through divine intervention but through scientific discoveries and through the new technologies that were coming about in the Industrial Age. For each of these products of the Age of Reason, the Church was, at best, irrelevant, and Jesus Christ and God were more myth than fact.

It was an age of intellectual rage. The rise of rationalism and the revolutionary spirit led inevitably to the events of 1917. The Bolshevik Revolution of 1917, which came at the height of a horrible, bitter world war (1914-1918), resulted in greater loss of life than any war mankind had ever known. Out of it emerged a country and a government based, not on a religion, but on *atheism*.

So a small band of people, just 17,000 of them, brought forth the tyranny of communism and a new government in the Soviet Union. From the very beginning it was an awesome and terrible force.

The stunned silence in the air during those first years must have seemed very much like what we feel today as we are seeing the evil and the lies of communism exposed.

Who could have dreamed in those days that this atheistic state based on the collective ownership of property, a vicious dictatorship of the proletariat, and the suppression of the desires and the ambitions of every normal person, would sweep the world? But it did, indeed.

First communism was spread by subversive groups in Europe, and then after World War II, by the takeover at the point of the gun in Poland, Czechoslovakia, Hungary, the Baltic States, Romania, and Bulgaria, and in the enormous nation of China.

Almost half of the population of the earth fell under the heel of a system of atheism. And in the rest of the world, Christianity was on the defensive. In Europe today, less than ten percent of the people attend any kind of church. There are state churches in some of these countries, but hardly anyone attends them, hardly anyone cares about religious values and religious matters, or remembers much about them.

Instead of the world being filled by Christianity, and instead of missionaries going out to evangelize in Africa and in Burma and China and all the nations of the world, and instead of the Western countries holding high the light of God's truth, suddenly we have a world where atheism, based on rationalism, has for decades been holding millions captive.

THE AGE OF UNREASON

In the United States of America, key universities, most of which had been founded by Christians, have been taken over by people who are sympathetic with Marxism, some of whom even believe passionately in communism. While only a few label themselves Marxists, almost all identify themselves as "secular humanists."

Virtually all the great universities—Harvard, Yale, Columbia, Princeton, Brown, Amherst, Dartmouth, Bryn Mawr, the various Wesleyan colleges, and many other private colleges and universities in America—were founded by Christians with strong moral values and absolute faith in God.

The humanists, on the other hand, believed in absolute human potential. As philosophical pragmatists, they subscribed to ideas popularized by William James and C.S. Pierce, which denied the existence of absolute or divine truth and held that the true value of any thing or any idea was merely its usefulness.

The leading spokesmen among the humanists—from John Dewey to Isaac Asimov—claim that there is no God, that the Bible is not the revealed Word of God, that mankind should be free of all sexual restraints, that there should be no question of guilt or sin or salvation or redemption, that man is to live out his life here on earth, that he is simply another part of the world he lives in, and that he is just a rung or two above the apes on the evolutionary ladder.

One of the doctrines of *The Humanist Manifesto,* first published in 1933 and signed by John Dewey and the vanguard of leftist intellectuals at this time, was that all humanists should find common cause with socialists around the world. These humanists did not believe in nationalism, they did not want individual countries, and they did not believe in the private ownership of property.

They wanted men to live in a socialist environment where the means of production were controlled by the state "for the common good of everyone." They were not avowed communists as such, but they believed in everything the communists believed in.

The signers of the Manifesto agreed, "A socialized and cooperative economic order must be established to the end that the equitable distribution of the means of life be possible . . . . Humanists demand a shared life in a shared world." In the revised Manifesto, published in 1973, the signers proclaimed their commitment to a one-world government. They write,

We deplore the division of humankind on nationalistic grounds. We have reached a turning point in human history where the best option is to transcend the limits of national sovereignty and to move toward the building of a world community in which all sectors of the human family can participate. Thus we look to the development of a system of world law and a world order based upon transnational federal government.

The document is signed by over 150 intellectuals, scholars, authors, lawyers, planned parenthood activists, social workers, and ministers of the Unitarian church. Notable among them are behaviorist B. F. Skinner, author of *Beyond Freedom and Dignity*; Francis Crick, co-discoverer of the DNA molecule; poet John Ciardi; science fiction writer and virulent atheist Isaac Asimov; Soviet scientist Andrei Sakharov; and Paul Kurtz, editor of *The Humanist* magazine, who drafted the 1973 and 1980 versions of the Manifesto. Most notably, about 40 percent of the original signers were professors and university teachers.

In the universities where they have had so much power, especially during the reign of John Dewey at Teacher's College, Columbia University, the humanists have been teaching what is called "Cultural Relativism." There are no absolutes, there are no rules to follow, they claim, but each society must work out its own rules according to what it feels will be best for "humanity."

This was a very appealing doctrine for the new generation of intellectuals emerging in the 1930s. It looked to science for answers. It put man in charge of his own potential. And while these people were teaching in the schools of America and Britain and other European countries, they believed that the economic and political model to follow was taking shape before their eyes, in the Soviet Union.

Shortly after the Bolshevik Revolution, the American writer, Lincoln Steffens, said on his return from a trip to the Soviet Union, "I have seen the future, and it works!"

Well, the future didn't work and the Soviets were actually failing at everything they tried, but they were being propped up in the public esteem by a press and by an academic elite which was determined that humanism and socialism had to work.

In one of the greatest acts of gall on record, Lenin had the nerve to ask for financial aid from the West to prop up his struggling experimental government even after he had proclaimed the death of capitalism. And to the amazement of everyone, including Lenin, he got it. Such were the times.

A NEW AWAKENING

Today we have come full circle. It has taken us over seventy years to see that bubble burst and the false dream of communism explode. But it has exploded because it is false and it is wrong. People want to marry when they please, they want to travel as they please, they want to work where they please, they want to study what they please, and they want freedom *from* the state.

People want to work out their own destinies as God gives them the wisdom. They want to be accountable to the just laws of an ordered society. They do not want repression. They've learned communism neither works as a framework for economics or government. It never did work, and it never will.

Suddenly the model for the humanistic world view is collapsing before the eyes of the world. In the United States, the educational system founded on humanism is collapsing. Many of the governmental policies founded on humanism are also crumbling.

In an article in *The Humanist* magazine, Isaac Asimov expressed his fear that the construct of liberal humanism based on the socialist worldview has been damaged by the fall of communism. **The death of communist ideology is taking with it the whole facade of liberal, atheistic, humanistic, and deconstructionist thinking, and Asimov is absolutely right. Their side has lost.**

Even though the writer tried to absolve his own fears by attacking Christianity and religious values—saying that religious faith and superstition are the same thing—his point was taken. The mask is off. Communism, humanism, secularism, and atheism have failed, and anyone who can't see that now will find out soon enough.

EXPLODING THE MYTHS OF HUMANISM

The ethics that come from humanism are exploding dramatically before our eyes, with scandal after scandal in politics and business and public life. The free love and unrestrained sexuality they said was to be part of their system has destroyed the lives of young people all over the world.

We have a million teen-agers pregnant out of wedlock each year;

we have a million and a half abortions each year; we have a shocking breakup of homes and families; we have as many as two million children running away from home every year.

There has been a continuous decline of our standard of living before the onslaught of more dedicated, more resolute people of Asia. All this is happening at a rapid pace. It is suddenly clear that beneath all the social failures there has been a fundamental flaw in the world's values.

The humanists who are honest (and unfortunately not many of them are yet intellectually honest) are beginning to say, "We were wrong." Today the press of America is pointing to a religious revival in the communist world and saying to the world that it is because of the religious faith of the Russian people, the Hungarian people, the Polish people and others, that this sweeping transformation is taking place.

The new prime minister of Poland, who was elected by the labor movement, Solidarity, was asked what his belief system was. He said very simply, "I am a Christian." Not a communist, but a Christian, and in his case, a devout Roman Catholic. This is the leader of the country that has been in the vanguard of the movement toward freedom.

THE SPIRITUAL CONFLICT

It is only fair that the American press should pose the battle between communism and capitalism in ecclesiastical language. In speaking of Lenin as "The God That Failed" and the doctrines of the revolutionaries as "Holy Writ," the editors of the *New York Times* recognized the essential spiritual nature of the conflict.

From the beginning, the war of ideologies has been a conflict between the verities of God and the vanities of man. First we had the mystery religions based on the worship of man; then the worship of false gods and animistic beings; then there were religious people consulting oracles, and finally a central church which, even while it had been founded on worship of the true and living God, degenerated into an oligarchy based on greed, temporal power, and corruption.

In earlier times there were cities absolutely full of temples, but they were false temples dedicated to false gods. The dominion of the true Church fell into disfavor when it allowed false ideologies and faulty teachings to prosper. But today all these failures are being swept away by a fresh vision of Christianity. We are seeing the revealed truth of the living God, and the truth of the Holy Bible.

Eastern Europe, the Soviet Union, Communist China, and many other places where darkness has prevailed, are now being exposed to the Light of the World, to man's essential need for a Savior who came to earth, was born as a man, lived among us, was crucified, dead, buried, and rose again. A Savior who lived among His followers and taught them for forty days before ascending into heaven. Then, by the power of His Holy Spirit, He directed them to preach a gospel that had never been heard before in that form in all the world. Along with that incredible message came miracles and works of mighty power. They swept before them everything that was false and everything that wouldn't stand.

When the emptiness and fraud and shame could not be hidden any longer, the false religions of the old world tumbled like dominoes. Suddenly there was nothing left but Christianity to fill the void that a failing political system, a crumbling economic system, and a collapsing religious system left behind.

A DECADE OF CHANGE

In 1990 we witnessed a similar awakening. In his address to the United States Congress in February, the newly elected president of Czechoslovakia, Vaclav Havel, declared the current revolution in Eastern Europe not a war of invasion or retaliation but a "revolution in the sphere of human consciousness." That this European writer, hardly known in the West until recently, and imprisoned for years for refusing to bow to communist ideologies, should now stand before Congress as the leader of his country was an amazing irony. And the irony of his words could not be ignored.

He told his audience of Americans and foreign diplomats, "We are still incapable of understanding that the only genuine backbone of all our actions, if they are moral, is responsibility—responsibility to something higher than my family, my country, my company, my success." The furnace of adversity had prepared this man for this hour, and the truth of his appeal should be an alarm to every man and woman of faith.

The American press printed portions of Havel's New Year's Day speech to the people of Czechoslovakia; but some of the parts they did not print should not be missed. Havel said, "Our first president wrote, 'Jesus and not Caesar.' . . . This idea has now been reawakened in us. I dare say that perhaps we have even the possibility of spreading it further, thus introducing a new factor in European and world politics. Love, desire for understanding, the strength of the spirit and of ideas can radiate forever from our country, if we want this to happen."

"We are a small country," he said, "but nonetheless we were once the spiritual crossroads of Europe. Is there any reason why we cannot be so again? Would this not be another contribution through which we could pay others back for the help we will need from them?"

What a powerful statement from this remarkable man. I can only concur with George Weigel, of the Ethics and Public Policy Center in Washington, D.C., who says, **"If Vaclav Havel is not the 1990 Nobel Peace laureate, then the prize this year has no meaning."**

But the churches of Eastern Europe are small and inexperienced, not yet fully prepared to deal with the sudden freedom of religion and the frenzy of interest in the gospel. In a recent report in the magazine, *Christianity Today,* Bishop Beredi of Yugoslavia, said, "I don't see that we are ready to use all the privileges we have today." The people are hungry and they are coming by the hundreds, but the churches are scarcely able to cope. "We are so small," Beredi said, "we don't have the resources."

Too few pastors, too little training: these are common concerns. Peter Kuzmic, director of the Evangelical Theological College in Osijek, Yugoslavia, said, "We need quality literature that speaks to the man on the street who has never been inside a church, never read the Bible, doesn't understand religious language." But despite the crying need for aid, Kuzmic believes the time is right and the door is open. "There is a vacuum here," he adds, "which needs to be filled with the gospel of Jesus Christ."

Christians from the free democratic nations of the West must acknowledge that they have a clear call to reach out to these people. We have a challenge to encourage and support these aspiring churches and to welcome an entire new generation of Christians into the fellowship of Christ. How will we respond? What an incredible hour for the world. What an opportunity.

"He has loosed the fateful lightning of His terrible, swift sword," says the great Battle Hymn of the Republic, "His truth is marching on!" And we, the children of the true and living God, must carry forth His banner into all the world. This could well be the decade of our greatest challenge.

The fall of communism makes the 1990s truly the decade of opportunity for the Christian church. This is an incredible hope for the world.

2

The Fall of Communism

The world has come to the conclusion that freedom works, not a centralized control economy. Marxist communism will cease to exist as a unifying philosophy for any society.

This decade will witness not only freedom in the formerly communist lands but a dangerous death rattle in the Soviet Union as it breaks apart.

In February 1989 the Soviet Union turned tail and got out of a little country called Afghanistan, and from Riga in the Baltic to Cam Ranh Bay in the South China Sea, the myth of Soviet invincibility was forever shattered.

Who could have dreamed that within a single incredible year we would see the collapse of one communist government after another, and that in Poland, where the democratic revolution actually began, a Christian would be elected prime minister? The collapse of the hard-line government in East Germany and the breaking up of the hated Berlin Wall were object lessons to the world.

The reconstitution of the Communist Party of Hungary into a republican-style Socialist Party; the execution of the brutal dictator, Ceausescu, in Romania; the virtual disintegration of the governmental body, the Communist Party, in Yugoslavia; the declaration by

Lithuania that it was an independent state; the Azerbaijan revolt against the central government of Moscow; and all the incredible events that took place in that twelve-month period brought a new vision of hope to men and women all around the world. Suddenly the regime Ronald Reagan had boldly labeled the "Evil Empire" didn't look like much of an empire anymore.

Even as the Soviets continue to arm at a staggering rate, spending upward of 25 percent of their entire GNP on arms, the ideology of communism has been mortally wounded. Someone has compared the Soviet Union to a crippled old man with a howitzer in the closet. He may be weak, but he's not powerless.

There is a genuine, ongoing danger of an armed uprising by separtist militants, or a military adventure by reactionary elements in Moscow. We cannot allow ourselves to be lulled into a false sense of security. But the events of 1989 and 1990 have given us unmistakable evidence that communism, as an ideology to claim men's hearts and minds, can never again be the threat it once was.

Human beings are creatures made in the image of God, and our hearts yearn to know Him. Any system that denies that yearning, and any ideology that attempts to prove that God does not exist, is destined to fail. God will ultimately find a place in the hearts of people, regardless of their ideologies, and regardless of the political system.

THE TYRANT IS DYING

At the height of its terrible reign, communism has gripped more than two billion people on this planet—at least forty percent of the population of the entire world. While we do not have absolute and final evidence that the seventy year reign of terror has been ended once and for all, the handwriting is on the wall. Today there is no question that Marxist-Leninist communism has failed, and with it has come the failure of atheism as a unifying ideology for a society.

Communism fails because it is an economic theory which does not relieve the suffering of the people, let alone provide for their prosperity. Atheism fails because it does not square with the reality of our world, nor does it address itself to the deepest needs of humanity.

The collectivism of socialism also goes contrary to another very fundamental truth: the innate worth of the individual. While a modern society is a vast organism with widespread powers and responsibilities, it is still made up of individuals who do their jobs each day in communication and in union with many others like them.

The decisions of millions of consumers, business people, factory managers, small entrepreneurs, and owners of large corporations, make up an inter-related network of decisions that affect thousands, millions, and sometimes tens of millions of individual transactions.

That is a fact of life in a busy world. However, the communist system supposed that a small elite cadre of leaders could be responsible for all of those decisions and could, in effect, manipulate and control the way business is done. Never can the decision of any twelve men in a central policy council replace the wonderful complexity and inventiveness of an entire society.

Even the attempt to do so is wrong because it claims for the government a God-like authority. The small cadre of *nomenclatura,* as they were called, saw themselves, in effect, as God's substitutes on earth assuming the authority of God in the lives of people. Any society or any group of people which ascribes such power to itself is doomed to fail. The collective cannot assume the responsibility of the individual, for every individual is called by God to his or her own unique responsibility.

The great truth of this was enunciated in the book of Jeremiah when God said to the prophet, "Before I formed you in the womb I knew you, before you were born I set you apart; I appointed you as a prophet to the nations" (Jeremiah 1:5). Before he was born Jeremiah was called to his unique destiny by God.

Every one of us has a role in life, and the task of government is to provide a framework where each individual citizen can work out in his own way the calling which God has given him.

A FRAMEWORK OF PEACE

Some have a calling for activity, others are called to quiet and contemplation. There is a calling for wealth, and a calling for sacrifice. All the struggles and strivings and aspirations of a society, along with the need to earn a living, make up what we call a free market.

Government should only interfere with that market to keep certain individuals from harming others: keeping certain groups from acquiring so much wealth and power that they threaten the aspirations of others. Beyond that, government should provide a framework of peace and security where the streets are safe and the borders are secure from invasion.

Contrast that with the role of the government under communism, where the government became the enemy of the people, oppressing them in every single thing they did, forcing them to conform in their thoughts, words, and actions to the predetermined government policy and brutally repressing those who deviated from that policy. That system was so contrary to God's will and the basic yearning of people for freedom that it had to fall.

At least five years in advance I predicted that Soviet communism was going to fall. In his book about my campaign for the presidency, Dr. Hubert Morken made note of my prediction along with the reactions of the national media who scoffed that anyone would suggest that communism might conceivably fail in Eastern Europe. But the record stands.

After the Russian debacle in Afghanistan I knew that the myth of Soviet invincibility had been shattered. I was not surprised by the fact that it happened, though I was surprised (as we all were) with the speed at which it happened. Certainly in the East Bloc countries—Poland, Czechoslovakia, East Germany, Romania, Hungary, Bulgaria, Albania—there is a clear move for freedom. And in the Soviet Union itself there seems to be a movement away from communism which is irreversible.

THE BREAKUP OF RED CHINA

Despite the evidences of the massacre at Tiananmen Square, I think the downfall of communism is certain in China. The repression of the popular will by the military and political leadership is merely a momentary setback for freedom in that country. **When the old men like Deng Xiaoping and Li Peng are moved out of the way, I think it is only a matter of time before the full expression of freedom takes place there.**

China is a unique and paradoxical land, known in its own

antiquity as the "Middle Kingdom," the center of the earth. By dint of its sheer magnitude and its long and exotic history, it has proven to be a land where the unexpected can happen. Given that history, I think there is another provocative scenario which could begin to play itself out within the next several years.

Specifically, I would not be surprised if that country did not break up and revert either to a system of warlords similar in many respects to the system that existed back before the Kuomintang and the presidency of General Chiang Kai Shek or to a series of provinces with different economic philosophies and governing units.

I don't know that there is enough strength in the nation to provide a system of free-market democracy to govern more than a billion people. The political and social pressures in such a vast land are simply too immense to contain. I suspect a breakup of some kind is a very real possibility, but if it holds together, a free united China could become an awesome power in the next century.

THE WOUNDED BEAR

The disintegration of a bankrupt system is a natural phase of political change. When empires fall, they crumble. Today many commentators feel that the formal union of fifteen Soviet states will inevitably break up as well. Mother Russia has voted for freedom from the Soviet Union. It seems apparent that the Baltic states and Eastern Europe are destined to go free. Georgia, the Ukraine, Moldavia, Azerbaijan, and the Tashkent-Kazakhstan regions might then form into some kind of autonomous or semi-autonomous states.

The danger of such an eventuality is not the difficult period of transition that would then come about, but the prospect that the Soviet leadership might try some desperate last-ditch effort to prevent the loss of their empire.

We already know that today the Soviets are still spending about as much on arms as they were before the talk of *glasnost*. They have an arsenal that may well be as great as the combined strength of the United States and Europe. The danger to all of us is that as their economy continues to collapse and the empire disintegrates, there might be some kind of military adventure as a means of holding the whole thing together.

Frankly, I think that for the next few years the Soviet Union will be a very dangerous player. The magnitude of their arsenal and their military power is formidable and rapidly growing.

Now, in terms of what has already happened, I think we have to acknowledge that all this is of God. I think the Spirit of the Lord is bringing liberty into these oppressed lands. If we continue the evangelistic work that has been going on in Eastern Europe and continually step up the intensity of our labors, these former communist countries may well be the launching pad for the evangelization, actually the re-evangelization, of Europe.

This is a place where there is great hope spiritually. Without that, Western Europe is lost to Christianity and could easily become the launching ground for a New Age dictator.

Western Europe as a whole is so lacking in any true spiritual roots that I would not be surprised to see the rise of some popular, charismatic leader who could win the hearts of the people by speaking of the noble goals and worldwide aspirations of a renewed Europe, much as Adolph Hitler did in Germany in the late 1930s.

THE PEACE DIVIDEND

Throughout its history, the world has experienced more than 4,000 wars. Therefore, statesmen who have predicted war have usually been correct because they have had the precedent of history on their side. Given the reality of a sinful world, those who really want peace usually attain it only by having a strong military establishment. In political language, "peace through strength."

Nevertheless, I think the United States no longer needs large forces in NATO, nor do we need large forces defending Japan. I think a great empire moves on the strength of its economy before it moves on the strength of its military. If the United States economy becomes bankrupt, then ultimately our military will become bankrupt as well.

The United States must first strengthen its own economy. Then it would not be a great burden to maintain forces adequate for our defense. Having maintained a huge force in Germany for 45 years, we must now turn that task over to the Germans and evacuate our troops.

The same holds true for Japan: the Japanese people can defend themselves. A July 1990 edition of *Business Week* reported that Japan is the world's third largest military spender, after the U.S. and the Soviet Union. The U.S. Defense Department has already announced an 11 percent cutback in military aid to Japan, but that number must increase.

As the Japanese fund more of their own military readiness, we can better balance the federal budget and begin paying off some of the debt, which is imperative. We should certainly do that before we undertake any new social programs. We cannot borrow any more to pay for well-meaning welfare plans.

REAGAN'S CAVEAT

We know only too well that freedom has a high price. Before we allow the media or the reformers to cause us to jump too quickly to the conclusion that we're in for an economic windfall, which they are calling the "peace dividend," we should know where we stand. Returning the defense of Germany and Japan to the people of those countries does not mean we should, at the same time, weaken America's military.

To speak with credibility, America must stand on its strength, and that means we not only speak with authority but that we are prepared to act with authority. A strong voice without a strong military is only a hollow threat.

In what may be his finest public address, Ronald Reagan spoke to the nation of England from the London Guildhall in June 1988. This was at a time when the prospects for reform in Eastern Europe were beginning to seem very real. We weren't sure what Gorbachev was up to, but it seemed as if there might be a realistic hope for peace.

The president reflected on the long and warm kinship between the English and the Americans, and he remembered stories from the Second World War when we struggled together against a common enemy. But, more important, the President warned the English and the world that we must not forget the lessons we have learned in our struggle for liberty. That entire address deserves to be quoted, again and again, but at least some of Mr. Reagan's conclusions are worth citing here. He said,

We have learned the first objective of the adversaries of freedom is to make free nations question their own faith in freedom, to make us think that adhering to our principles and speaking out against human rights abuses or foreign aggression is somehow an act of belligerence. Over the long run, such inhibitions make free peoples silent and ultimately half-hearted about their cause. This is the first and most important defeat free nations can ever suffer. When free peoples cease telling the truth to their adversaries, they cease telling the truth to themselves. In matters of state, unless the truth be spoken, it ceases to exist.

The President told the nobles and statesmen assembled there, and the nations of the world who were listening, that in a sense our actions can be measured by our words. That is, if we really believe in freedom and dignity, and if we are truly prepared to defend our beliefs, then we will not hesitate to say so.

Too often in recent months we have seen our government cave in to foreign intimidation. Too often the diplomats have wanted to maintain their friendly smiles for Gorbachev and Deng Xiaoping and the other tyrants of the world instead of speaking the truth when human rights have been violated and when human dignity has been crushed. Candor and outright honesty, Reagan asserted, do not provoke war: they prevent war. For how else will our enemies know we mean business unless we speak without fear?

Finally in those remarks, Mr. Reagan also expressed the hope that we would one day recognize that our common journey has been a pilgrimage toward honor, love, human dignity, and freedom for all peoples and all nations. He closed by stating his own faith that, wherever the struggle for honor and freedom has prevailed, the hand of God has guided our way and brought the victory of good over evil. He said,

> Here is the strength of our civilization and our belief in the rights of humanity. Our faith is in a higher law. We hold that humanity was meant not to be dishonored by the all-powerful state, but to live in the image and likeness of Him who made us. Let us seek to do His will in all things, to stand for freedom, to speak for humanity.

The issues that confront us today are no less serious than they ever were. The threats to freedom and dignity are no less real.

Smiles and diplomacy and friendly gestures are good for business, but they are also good for treason. Judas betrayed our Lord with a kiss.

The warnings of President Reagan should be a reminder to all of us that we cannot throw down our weapons in the hope the world will suddenly call us friend. Cut back on the defense of Europe? Yes. They are very strong now, and while we will remain a powerful ally, we don't have to pay their bills for them. Cut back our defense of Japan? Yes. But we must never let down our vigilance, our resolve, or our military preparedness. We can best deal with the villains of the world, however much they may smile, when they know we have a mighty saber at the ready.

GORBACHEV

Mikhail Gorbachev, who is he? What is he? Is he the great defender of freedom, the "Man of the Decade," or is he the next great villain? In order to understand this man, it is vital to remember that Gorbachev is a creature of the KGB. He was a protege of Yuri Andropov, who was formerly head of the KGB.

Gorbachev began his rise to power as head of the Communist Youth Movement in Stavrapol. He later succeeded his mentor, Feodor Kulakov, as Central Committee Secretary for Agriculture in Moscow, where he became the protege of Yuri Andropov. He was trained by Andropov, taught by him, and sanctioned by him. He rose to become head of the Communist Party and the nation itself. Clearly, he was the master's prize pupil. There is no other way his incredible rise to power can be explained.

In his book, *Gorbachev: The Path to Power,* C. S. Hauer notes that Gorbachev's direct and speedy rise is unprecedented in Soviet history. He succeeded Kulakov who died, Andropov who died, then Chernenko who died. He took power in the same spot where Lenin declared the Bolshevik victory in 1917, declaring his allegiance to the goals of world communism.

Since his rise to power, Gorbachev has said again and again that his aim is to strengthen and improve communism, not to weaken it. In December 1989, the *New York Times* quoted his speech to Communist Party officials in which we said, "There are attempts to make you believe that I am working on behalf of someone, that I want to tear apart the party, the state, to bury socialism. I reject that. I am a Communist, a convinced Communist. For some that may be a fantasy, but for me, it is my main goal."

From a political perspective, it is clear that there has to be strong backing of his actions by very powerful forces. Seemingly, Gorbachev has undercut the Communist Party, undercut the military, undercut the old guard, and has taken to himself more personal power than any other leader in the history of the Soviet Union, including Joseph Stalin.

He is already a virtual dictator if he wants to exercise his power, and with the expanded powers he lobbied for and won in early 1990 he can even declare war at his own personal discretion.

What does that mean? For one thing, it means that the Soviet President can put through dramatic economic reforms which are critically needed; or he could turn that society very repressive again in order to save his own power.

The Soviet economy is collapsing so fast that either Gorbachev is going to have to use the army to bring people into submission or else he's going to have to permit the Soviet empire to fall apart. But will he do that?

If he should permit the empire to fall apart, it is possible that Gorbachev himself could become the subject of a bloody coup, probably by the army and the radical hard-liners. We saw in the news reports from the 1990 National Party Congress that the old guard are saying they are ready to oust this paradoxical reformer. Only Gorbachev's strength abroad, and the ongoing popularity of dissident leaders such as Boris Yeltsin, seem to stand between the president and the ire of the communists.

The bad news of the Soviet economy is not really news any more. When he came to the West, Aleksandr Solzhenitsyn told us, "communism cannot improve, only die." And now in the aftermath of the economic collapse we are beginning to find out what was really going on behind the Iron Curtain.

We learned that 30 million Soviet citizens do not have pure drinking water, that six million are homeless, 13 million live in communal apartments where two or more couples are forced to share the same bathroom and kitchen, and less than 50 percent of Soviet families can afford a refrigerator.

Instead of the monolithic government touted as the rival of the world's greatest economies, suddenly we see Soviet Russia as a Third World nation. The people are desperately poor, and the idea of collective labor is a colossal failure.

Today we know that 20 percent of Russian crops rot in the field; and over 40 percent of all the machinery in their small businesses doesn't work. People say the sausage sold in the government stores is so bad even the cats won't eat it, and basic necessities such as soap and toilet paper are not even available much of the time.

The average Soviet citizen must work ten times longer than the average American to buy a pound of meat; the infant mortality rate is 250 percent higher than that of Western nations; and the average woman will undergo eight abortions in her lifetime. That's the communist idea of birth control.

All these facts, and many more like them which have surfaced over the past year, are clear evidence that the communist social order has failed on every front. Soviet economists are reporting that over 85 percent of the people live below the poverty line. But apparently none of that has deterred the communists from building their war machine. Nor has it dissuaded the liberals who bet their lives on that godless dream.

The jokes people tell often give a certain insight into national character. A story making the rounds in Eastern Europe these days is about an American, an Englishman and a Russian who ended up in hell. It seems they each got one last chance to call home. It cost the American 1,000 dollars; the Englishman had to pay 600 pounds; but it only cost the Russian one ruble. The first two didn't understand, so they asked the Russian why his call was so cheap. "Local call," he said.

To some, that apocryphal story may not even be a joke. Today it seems that the only people left in the world who still believe in the communist lie are United States college professors caught in a '60s time-warp.

PROPPING UP A DYING REGIME

According to the latest calculations of Secretary of Defense Dick Cheney, reported in *Janes' Defense Weekly,* at least 25 percent, and possibly as high as 40 percent, of the entire gross national product of the Soviet Union goes for arms and military spending.

Soviet support for communist satellite governments or communist insurgencies in Angola, Cuba, Nicaragua, El Salvador, Afghanistan, South Africa, Libya, North Korea, the Philippines, and other Third World nations has been an endless drain on the Soviet economy with no substantial gains in world communism. The Rand Corporation estimates that the USSR has been paying upwards of 15 billion dollars annually in military aid to their dependent regimes.

The Russian ruble is valueless as a currency outside the Soviet bloc. It is useless even in places like Finland, which is closely linked to the Soviet economy. One of the few leaders who seems to be willing to trade with the Soviets, to give approval to them, and to share the latest technological secrets with them is the President of the United States.

During his visit to Washington in June of 1990, President Gorbachev came with no chips and nothing to bargain, but he walked away with a treasure. At the moment when it was clear to the entire world that communism was at last defeated, Gorbachev came to America, and we gave him more than he could ever have dreamed possible.

The arms reduction agreements drafted by Presidents Bush and Gorbachev do not give the West any means of monitoring actual reductions of Soviet nuclear or chemical weapons. We have not insisted that Soviet spy satellites, tracking stations, or antennae be dismantled, as all our defense analysts had demanded.

Despite the warnings of experts, we agreed to share our scientific secrets with Soviet engineers. In effect, George Bush put all the chips in the Soviet president's hands.

A preponderance of our most respected scientists and advisers have warned that we must not give the Soviets our technology, our computer systems, or our financial backing. Now we are shipping IBM PCs and Macintosh computers to Russia by the boatload.

All of the brave dissidents, exiles, KGB defectors, and escaped writers who have fled to the West have reminded us of the way our liberal leaders propped up Lenin's New Economic Policy in 1921; how Franklin Roosevelt propped up "Old Joe" Stalin, the most tyrannical of all the Soviet dictators, between 1946 and 1949. Do not be fooled again by Gorbachev, they warn. We have to wonder if anybody is listening.

A SINISTER NEW SCENARIO

I believe that the fall of communism is real. I believe that the democracy movement in Eastern Europe is real. However, to check our euphoria there have been raised serious voices of caution. Could the entire scenario be nothing but a KGB ruse conceived by the master, Yuri Andropov?

In his book, *New Lies for Old: The Communist Strategy of Deception and Disinformation,* published in 1984, former KGB agent Anatoliy Golitsyn predicted virtually every event that we have witnessed the past three years. The weakness and instability we perceive today, he said, is no more than a massive fraud, a deception being staged by the Kremlin while they attempt to extort aid from the West and implement certain economic changes, on the capitalist model.

Golitsyn cited the exact details of a Communist Party conspiracy to deceive the West into believing that the Soviet Union is falling apart; that its satellites are splintering; that its economy is threadbare. "All warfare is based on deception," they say, therefore "feign incapacity."

"Offer the enemy the bait to lure him; feign disorder and strike him." This military wisdom, from the pages of Sun Tzu's *Art of War,* was adapted by the Soviets in the late 1950s and was being played out for real in the late 1980s. Golitsyn wrote about it in 1984, but of course, the liberals in the academy were not listening. Instead, we have opened our hearts and our vaults to the Kremlin and brought the bear into our midst.

But even our misguided largess may not be enough to save the wounded beast. A new book, co-authored by Moscow correspondent Dusko Doder and Louise Branson, a *London Times* correspondent in Beijing, says that Gorbachev is only a transitional figure in the Soviet government.

Entitled *Gorbachev: Heretic in the Kremlin,* this new book maintains that, like Czar Peter the Great, Gorbachev can see the Russian economy dissolving and the strength of the empire crumbling around him. He knows that his only help can come from the West, so he has made brash overtures to the United States and Europe. But, while he is a hero to many in the West, he is considered a failure and a heretic at home.

Doder and Branson foresee public unrest and riots in the Soviet Union, demanding the ouster of the radical leader. It is obvious that the election of Boris Yeltsin as President of the state of Russia was a rebuff to Gorbachev. Yet, because of his newly granted powers as Soviet President, it would be very hard to oust Gorbachev—it would take an act of the entire Soviet Parliament—and then a strong power would have to succeed him. These authors believe that these events are certain and will lead inevitably to a military dictatorship. Then what?

In another book, *Soviet Disunion,* by Bohdan Nahaylo and Victor Swoboda, two East European authors suggest that there are only four possible scenarios for the USSR at this point in time. Gradual breakup of the empire; creation of a new, looser confederation; federalization; or restoration of the empire through military oppression and a reimposition of control by the hard-liners. Three of those four options would keep the communists in strict control; and even the possibility of a breakup of the empire offers no guarantee that the emerging governments would necessarily reflect Western democratic principles.

So far, everything Gorbachev has done, with few exceptions, seems to be moving toward an open society, free markets, and peace. He has certainly convinced people in the State Department and the White House that he wears a white hat. But that could be an illusion and we would be foolish indeed to put everything we've got into the Soviet leader's basket. The situation is still unclear and, at best, two sided.

THE VIETNAM EFFECT

Vietnam very likely hastened the decline in the United States that was already under way. The Great Society spending of Lyndon Johnson was an enormous failure and no doubt helped push that decline along. It wasted huge amounts of money, but in terms of its impact on reducing poverty its effect has been negligible.

The axiom in war is very simple. There is no substitute for victory. There is no such thing as a limited, no-win war. We should never have gotten into Vietnam; we should never have tried to fight a land war in Asia; we should not have overthrown the Diem regime by a coup and an assassination. We should not have escalated that war the way we did.

The whole thing was a tragic mistake. But if we were determined that a just war was necessary, then we should have moved in with all of our forces as fast as we could and ended it. There should have been no privileged sanctuaries, no targets that were off limits. Except for hospitals and orphanages and that sort of thing, we should have given no quarter.

If we had gone in with military resolve and mobilized our forces, I think that we could have concluded that war, probably in a couple of months. If we had used all of our strength, no nation could have withstood us. Certainly not the Viet Cong. As it is, though, we wasted our strength, demoralized our military, and still lost the war. That loss crippled the conscience of this nation and showed that we are lacking in resolve.

The Afghanistan experience showed the communists how weak they were in a very similar way. More than any other event, it proved that the Soviet machine was not invincible. Without question, Afghanistan started the spiral which made public the apparent decay within the Soviet Union. It was the trigger to the spiral that has been accelerating recently as their powers decline.

The long-term and lasting lesson from both these wars is that no amount of physical force can overrun a people who are determined to resist. It is impossible to kill everyone in a country. The Soviets tried to kill and subjugate, but they were unsuccessful. I think it's true anywhere in the world: brute force can never win over a determined ideology.

The yearning for freedom in the hearts of people, sooner or later, will win out over brute force. There may be suffering, starvation, death, disease, and vast numbers of refugees, and there may be people whose lives are destroyed, whose homes are gone, and whose bodies are maimed, but nevertheless, freedom will inevitably prevail over tyranny. The Soviets learned that lesson in Afghanistan in a dramatic and painful way. At least I hope so.

DEMOCRATIC REFORM

The truth is, except for Chile, no nation has ever voluntarily voted in communists, because the people instinctively understand that communism means tyranny, persecution, death, suffering, and poverty.

With an armed insurrection in Nicaragua and guerrilla insurrections in Guatemala and El Salvador, the communists tried to take over a region which would threaten Mexico and, in turn, imperil the United States. They were never able to get widespread popular support in either Guatemala or El Salvador. And, of course, the resounding defeat of the Sandinistas in Nicaragua's free election showed that those people would prefer almost anything to the desolation that the years of communist misrule in that country has brought them.

The remarkable thing is that in Nicaragua, 17 percent of the people are evangelicals. In Guatemala and El Salvador the total is about 30 percent. Of that 30 percent, about 29 percent attend church on a regular basis. It is not just church affiliation, but very enthusiastic and vocal participation.

I was deeply touched by the contrasts when I visited there in 1989. There was such grinding poverty, the majority of the people had no hope of ever being free again. In Guatemala City the poverty was horrible. The mayor told me if they could just move from misery to poverty it would be an improvement!

You could actually sense the presence of the monstrous evil that was attempting to gain a foothold in those countries. If there was ever a place where God could send a unique spiritual revival, this was it.

On my visits there in 1989, I knew we had to do something to support the believers in that land. Consequently, I instructed our staff at CBN to mobilize all the mass communications skills and all the media that had been put at our disposal—high speed printing, motion pictures and film, television and radio spots, specials, newspaper advertising and billboards, plus church involvement and training of counselors.

Why should we sit around with our hands in our pockets moping about the pathetic conditions in those countries when we had access to the greatest technologies and the most sophisticated promotional concepts in the world? So we decided to blitz those countries with the gospel and see what God would do. We organized campaigns in all three countries to make it possible for a majority of people to hear the gospel and come to the Lord. And it is now clear that this is just what happened.

We had a massive campaign, with something like 73,000 radio spots; 3,300 television spots; 50 film teams equipped with portable generators, projectors and screens, showing a feature film on the life of Jesus 5,200 times. We had 20,000 trained counselors; 10 million pieces of literature; hundreds of billboards; 400 tons of food and medicine given to the poor; and then prime time television programs on what is called a "roadblock."

We essentially took all the air time on all the stations in the country during one evening. After the blitz, we commissioned six surveys to be done by secular agencies. They reported that these were the most-watched programs in the histories of those countries. In just Guatemala and El Salvador, some 2,090,000 people prayed with the television host to receive the Lord; in Nicaragua it was over one million.

That campaign was successful beyond all our expectations. It shows the tremendous receptivity of people to accept Jesus as Savior in these countries which have been under the intense assault of communism. They have now freely chosen to go another route.

THE FUTURE OF CAPITALISM

No system of government is ultimately perfect, and no government of men can truly solve all our problems or bring ultimate good. In our own country we can see that capitalism, without a foundation of moral and ethical principles, is capable of terrible greed and corruption. I talked about this in my book, *The Secret Kingdom.* Without moral enlightenment, any secular system will lead to exploitation.

The headlines of the *New York Times* and the *Washington Post* shout the news that capitalism without ethics is exploitational and unscrupulous and ultimately self-serving. The most dramatic expression of the new face of capitalism in Moscow these days, as it is throughout Europe, is McDonald's and Coca Cola and blue jeans and plastic cups and all the traditional symbols of commercialism and consumerism.

While it may be colorful and even funny to see these things against the rather grim backdrop of Soviet communism, there is also the suggestion that there is a potential for exploitation in any economic system.

But over the past 50 years we have observed the results of communism and socialism and the planned "Welfare State." We have been able to compare the results of free market capitalism with the best communism could offer, and the world has come to the conclusion that freedom works, not a centralized control economy.

There is only one system of economics in the history of mankind that truly makes sense and leads to the prosperity and well-being of the people, and that is the free-market profit-motivated economic system we know as Capitalism.

Jesus said, "Do unto others as you would have them do unto you." In that statement He recognized individual self-interest as being a very real part of the human makeup, and something not necessarily bad or sinful. The desire of an individual to improve his lot in life, to provide a dwelling place for himself and his family, to put food on his table, to save something for retirement, and to have some joy in life is very natural: it is the way we are made.

It is also reminiscent of the comment of Paul in his letter to Timothy in which he said, "To God who gives us all things richly to enjoy. . . ." The enjoyment of life was God's plan. Enlightened self-interest was also obviously His plan. So the profit motive, *per se,* the desire for economic betterment, is not at all contrary to Scripture.

There was some primitive communism in the early church, but it resulted in poverty. Everybody gave up what they had, but they did it voluntarily. It was a communal existence but it was based strictly on personal benevolence.

If you remember the story in the book of Acts, Ananias sold some land and, secretly holding back a little for himself, he told everyone he was giving all the money to the church. But Peter knew he was lying and told Ananias to look at the land. "When you had it, wasn't it yours? And when you sold it, couldn't you have done with the proceeds what you wanted to? So why did you come here and lie to us and pretend that you're more holy than you really are?"

Ananias dropped dead on the spot. That was his reward for lying. But there was never a demand from the apostles that all the early Christians give up their money and live communally. They did it voluntarily because they had such love for each other and such zeal for the Lord.

Later on the apostle Paul went around the Mediterranean world taking up money for the poor saints in Jerusalem. Possibly one of the reasons they were poor was that they had given up all their money in this first burst of love and zeal. Some scholars believe they sold everything in the belief that the Messiah would return very soon. Perhaps they truly wanted to live in a communal relationship with other believers; but in the long run, it made them lacking in the means of self-help.

The thing that must make capitalism humane is the corollary teaching of Jesus that said, "Unto whom much is given much will be required." It is the concept of *noblesse oblige,* that nobility (or privilege) obligates. If you have privilege you must use that privilege for others. The Bible has striking examples of those who had great material wealth but did nothing to help their brother in need.

How can the love of God reside in their hearts? Capitalism— the accumulation of capital, the placing of money to the exchangers, individual self-initiative, all this kind of thing—was taught and encouraged by the Lord. But at the same time He said, "A man's life does not consist in the abundance of the things that he possesses."

Jesus told the Roman governor of Judea, "My kingdom is not of this world," and He taught His disciples, "seek first the kingdom of God and his righteousness and these other things will be added unto you." He said, "Don't be anxious about what you should wear or what you should eat. Your heavenly Father knows you have need of these things."

Jesus said—and His apostles taught—to give to the poor and the needy, to give to the work of the Lord, and to lay aside generously. Christians were to be stewards. I am not master of 90 percent and steward of 10 percent. I am steward of 100 percent: all of my spending, all of my life should be lived in relation to what God wants me to do.

If I believe what He taught, I am to be considered a bond slave of Jesus, bought with a price, and therefore my money and possessions and capital are, in turn, His, not mine. I am merely a life tenant of the wealth placed at my disposal.

Only when given the nobility and responsibility of the Christian view of property can free market capitalism, however successful, rise above the dangers of greed and exploitation.

THE GOD OF THE GODLESS

The other forms of economic organization violate so many of the principles of God, they actually deny the rightful place of God in society and raise up idols in His place. They do not permit the individual to be blessed by God. They don't let the individual receive what God wants to give him. They don't let him express compassion for his fellow human beings by giving money as he would like to give.

Under the socialist forms of government, the individual is not a steward of God but a steward of the state. He works for the state, is paid by the state, his salary and wealth are regulated by the state. His emotions are regulated by the state, and therefore he is not a servant of God but of whomever happens to be the governing party, whether it is communist, socialist, Labour, or whatever.

This false religion substitutes the state for God, and the creed is that the state will care for my needs. The citizen cannot then say, "The Lord is my shepherd, I shall not want," but, "The Government is my shepherd, I shall not want." The government says, "In turn, we will take care of your needs, we will give you work and money and take care of you after you retire, but in exchange for that you must give up your freedom and liberty and make us your God."

That is the most horrible life I can imagine. Yet, it was an experiment in improving the lives of people who had been crushed by the ravages of the industrial revolution, and by the other damaging forms of exploitation which industrialization brought with it in its early stages.

But today we know that the people who have lived under communism have now rejected it and have risen up to expel all remaining vestiges of that abusive system. I believe in a very short time we will see the last of those systems.

The greatest irony now is the lingering presence of the all-encompassing welfare state in the United States Congress and the continued presence of tenured Marxists in America's schools and universities. We still have a coterie of misguided intellectuals in the church who are preaching a so-called "Liberation Theology," which is nothing short of communist repression dressed up as social reform. Perhaps now even the most progressive thinkers will begin to see these fellow travelers for what they are and either reform the reformers or cast them from the temple.

THE CHALLENGE OF EASTERN EUROPE

The greatest challenge for Christians standing at the threshold of Eastern Europe today is to fill a vacuum. Everyone knows that a vacuum sucks in air. It doesn't stay around in suspended animation for very long; it consumes whatever comes near. That's what we are facing in Eastern Europe right now. It is an enormous spiritual and cultural vacuum, and that vacuum is going to be filled very quickly.

Recently we heard that fully half of the money spent by the East Berliners who crossed into the West to shop during those first exciting months of 1989 and 1990 went for pornography. We also learned that within two weeks of the opening of the gates, when the Berlin Wall was flattened and the unification of the two Germanys was complete, *Playboy* magazines were being sold on newsstands in Leipzig and Dresden and East Berlin.

Now the fact that Christian worship and ethical values have been forbidden for so long means that entire generations have grown up without a system of applied moral values. The heady exhilaration of personal freedom suggests to these young men and women that now everything is possible, and the warfare of ideologies has clearly already begun. But will they merely trade the slavery of communist tyranny for the slavery of sin and carnality and materialism?

The need for Christian literature is very clear. Number one, the people of the East Bloc need Bibles in their own languages. There has been very little printing of Bibles. Number two, they need Bible helps. There has been very little of that. They need evangelistic literature, and they need the simple type of literature that explains to the new believer what he or she is supposed to do after a decision for Christ.

They also need books and teaching on the inner relationship of God to government, society, family life, and the events of their everyday lives. How does Christianity apply to my society?

The trouble is that in America we have been woefully lacking in that kind of teaching ourselves. There are very few Christians in America who have an intelligent concept of citizenship or of the way that God would have us interrelate to the body politic. So we have allowed alien ideologies to fill the vacuum in America, so much so that Christian values have virtually been crowded out.

Clearly, America is struggling with its own moral identity, but at least we have the benefit of an ethical tradition. If it were not for the incredible reservoir of Christian beliefs and customs which we have inherited from the precepts of our founding fathers and the framers of the Constitution, I have no doubt that we would have lost our own moral vision years ago.

Sadly, there is no such reservoir in Eastern Europe. Everything is being written on a blank slate, right now. The questions concerning the relationship of public policy and personal beliefs are incredibly urgent. As laws are being drafted, positions are being filled. As parties are being organized, leaders are being chosen. Who is going to be in those parties? What philosophy is going to be enshrined in the government?

In our founding documents here in America we enshrined Christian beliefs. The State of South Dakota, for example, has a wonderful motto, "Under God the People Rule." Our Declaration of Independence paid homage to a Creator and spoke of the fact that our freedoms came from a Creator.

The Constitution, rightly interpreted, was clearly a document based on Christian concepts of sin and justice. We believe that all men are born sinners and even the best of them cannot be trusted with absolute power. So in framing the nation, our founding fathers circumscribed the leaders with a great many checks and balances so no one group could dominate our government.

Unfortunately, some people want us to forget that Christian heritage. Even the World Council of Churches, who should be on the side of Christian faith and tradition, voted recently to censure Christopher Columbus for bringing racism, bigotry, and exploitation to the New World.

What a warped view of reality! Liberals of that ilk would have us believe that the Pilgrims who settled in this continent were secular dissidents, and not men and women who left Europe for religious freedom. But that is simply not the case, and those who say so are either woefully ignorant of their own history or patently dishonest.

More and more historians and scholars are coming forth with the proof of our Christian heritage. Dr. Gary Amos, a historian and lawyer who teaches at Regent University, has compiled conclusive historical evidence in his book, *Defending the Declaration,* which clearly refutes the anti-Christian hypothesis.

In a study on Federalism, Dr. Amos says that the secular historians have never understood the degree to which our founders were trained and schooled in biblical thinking. He shows that there is a direct, logical, and historical connection between the Protestant conception of scriptural truth and the American constitutional form of government.

The colonists had 150 years in this country to learn how to govern a society by a "written standard," preceded by 150 years among their Protestant ancestors in Britain, France, Holland, Germany, and Switzerland. They knew the Bible to be "the one infallible rule of faith and practice," and they built schools wherever they went so every man, woman and child could read and understand the Bible.

In his book, *Independence and Involvement,* another scholar, Rene de Visme Williamson, points out that the early settlers were steeped in biblical wisdom:

> They read and reread it, meditated upon it, memorized large portions of it, argued about it, listened to innumerable sermons expository of it. They were so filled with it that their vocabulary and their literary style bore an unmistakable biblical stamp. In colonial Connecticut the Bible was accepted as a basis for decisions by civil courts. In their churches they were accustomed to living under written confessions of faith and written church constitutions.

Their knowledge of covenant law and of the teachings of the New Testament gave the founding fathers an innate understanding of God's plan for mankind. The *Magna Carta,* published in 1215, embodied these same principles, making provisions for freedom of religion, protection of individual rights, free trade, unity for the common good, and protection of the people.

The first Americans obviously understood the nature of original sin as well as the means of structuring the documents of government with wisdom and compassion. Even if secular historians deny those facts, the truth remains. The genius of the American constitutional government is proof of that wisdom.

The doctrine of original sin doesn't exist in Eastern Europe these days. At least it is not very well defined. So when framing documents are set up, will they have the wisdom our forefathers did to write enduring constitutions and pieces of founding legislation?

Maybe. At least there seems to be a strong Christian faith in many parts. We know that Czechoslovakia became a Christian nation before the year 1000. Poland has a strong Catholic tradition, and even under persecution and adversity that nation produced the current Pope. Hungary, Czechoslovakia, and Romania were also strongly Christian at one time, but whether these nations hold any of the concepts our founding fathers brought with them to America, we cannot yet say.

There is a clear mandate now for concerned Christians in the West to support the growth and development of Christian principles in these emerging governments. We must get the Bible into the hands of the people. Christian principles have to be taught, and the people need to understand the kinds of institutions that should naturally come from a Bible-based faith.

THE WIND FROM THE EAST

It has been refreshing to see the influence of the Christian faith returning to us from lands which just decades ago were only mission fields. We have seen the gospel return from Korea, from China, and from Africa with wonderful vigor and enthusiasm, and now we are seeing the same things coming from the churches of Eastern Europe.

The American press, which is notoriously cold to Christianity and hardened against conservative Christian values, was forced to report on Romania, and those reports were highlighted by the comments of Christian leaders who told of prayer vigils, of the faith that sustained them through the dark years of communist repression, of believers meeting in ancient churches to pray for freedom.

But the other side of that story is that in many papers, and other media as well, the American press quickly began to edit out those declarations of faith and to report only the purely political statements.

A press corps that screams for freedom of speech when it comes to pornography, vulgarity, and blatant anti-religious forms of expression, and a national media that lambasts censorship of every kind, has done its best to censor out all references to Jesus Christ or to Christianity or to the profound faith that has kept Eastern Europe alive these many years.

When Vaclav Havel spoke to the American Congress he mentioned that Czechoslovakia was the crossroads of Christianity in Europe. He mentioned the first coming of Christianity; he talked about God. But according to a report in *USA Today,* those comments were expunged from his address in the reports in the *New York Times* and the *Washington Post.* That tells you that the American liberal media is predominantly anti-religion and is going to do everything it can to prevent the favored expression of faith in God from coming through to the people.

They will make fun of those who claim to stand for God if they can show them in some moral dilemma. But for a world leader who is becoming a hero, as Havel is doing, they don't want him to have Christian words coming from his mouth if they can help it. The first time many Americans could read for themselves the unexpurgated text of Havel's speech was when Philip Yancey quoted those parts in his column for the magazine *Christianity Today.*

But the truth will not be restrained. Those nations are going to show us something remarkable. But more than that, they may well be the future for the potential revitalization of the faith in Europe.

This is the great hope, and the great irony, that Europe, which has been so terribly secular, will rediscover the Word of God. The land where, at best, less than 10 percent of all the people attend church, may rediscover the vision and the spirit of Christianity through the awakening taking place in Poland, Hungary, Czechoslovakia, and Romania. **Those who survived a half century of persecution may awaken in us the force and the conviction that will lead us all back to faith in Christ.**

There is a revival taking place there even today, and there is the very real hope that those men and women who have endured decades of repression and humiliation will someday hear their fellow Europeans saying, "We believe in Jesus Christ, and He has given us new life!" That hope is one of the key reasons why it is vital that the church over there be strong and that revival continue.

It is so vital that on their blank slate we write large the words of our Lord. Especially in a country like Romania. They are so open it just touches the heart.

A HUNGER FOR THE WORD

I spoke in a church in the city of Timisoara, Romania, in the spring of 1990. The place was packed. It was meant to hold 2,100, and they had somewhere between five and six thousand people, standing up all the way down the front aisles, along the walls, in the balcony.

I gave what was for me a fairly long message, and when I sat down the pastor said, "Brother, you didn't talk enough. These people are hungry for the Bible. They want to hear more about the Word of God."

They had stood in this hot place for a couple of hours but they wanted more. There is an unbelievable spiritual hunger among these poor, suffering people, but I am convinced they can be the revival spark for all of Europe.

Wouldn't it be one of God's supreme ironies that just as America, once the stronghold of faith and religious freedom and a beacon of hope to the entire world, loses its faith and falls from power very much like the once-great Roman Empire, that the once-communist nations of Eastern Europe, where Christians have been persecuted, should be the ones to bring revival and renewal?

There's no question that American and Western Christians have a dynamic challenge. Despite being persecuted today in our own land, we also have the challenge to help make this vision of rebirth of faith in Eastern Europe a reality as well. There are hundreds of immediate and dramatic opportunities for Christian service in these emerging countries.

In Czechoslovakia and Hungary they are begging for teachers of English. American young people could go by the thousands. President Havel wants 12,000 English teachers in Czechoslovakia. There is a marvelous openness to any kind of belief, so there is a critical need for Bible teachers, for those who would work in Bible schools to train pastors.

There is also a vital need for talented professionals to teach Christians in those countries the principles of business administration. With everything so very primitive, the Christian church can rise very rapidly if the people are taught more advanced principles of management. They need to know about management procedures, business systems, accounting practices, computer applications, and all the other business skills that can contribute to financial independence.

I think it will be very important to go into these countries and support the church. Frequently the evangelicals have been the church of the poor. They have been regarded by the leaders as people who are not really relevant to what's going on since they are generally among the poor and downtrodden.

I would like to see those churches advance the roles they have had in feeding the poor, in helping with social problems, especially in educating the masses. But I would also like to see the coming generation of young Christian leaders trained for law and government, for economics, and for the media, so that the emerging elite in these countries will be evangelical Christians.

I think that is very possible right now. Now is the time to begin implementing a long-range strategic plan which will ensure the preservation of the Christian faith and of personal freedom in the emerging democracies of Central and Eastern Europe.

Unless there is immediate action to instill the principles of Bible-based constitutional government and individual self-restraint, the specter of chaos looms over the nations of Europe recently freed from communism.

3

The Rise and Fall of Secularism

Along with communism, secular humanism has failed. In this decade the believers will stand firmly astride the failed and crumbling ruin of the secular colossus.

As we observe the failures of communism in Europe and Asia, it seems as if we may have finally come to the end of an era, to the conclusion of one of the long cycles of history. From the publication of the *Communist Manifesto* in 1848 to the collapse of the Berlin Wall in 1989, the world has witnessed a long and bitter warfare of ideologies that has engulfed entire continents and cost tens of millions of lives. Could the warfare suddenly be at an end?

It seems obvious that communism has failed as a practical system of economics. But there was always more to communism than the practical side; there was an emotional and intellectual side as well. While the practical seems to have failed, it is more certain today than ever that the ideology, the intellectual side of the nightmare, lives on. Not just in Cuba and Angola and North Korea, but in America, and especially in our universities.

First and foremost, communism sprang from a secular hypothesis. It was based on the belief that man can live without faith in God, that man is the master of his fate and the captain of his soul. Framed on the rudiments of G. F. Hegel's dialectical hypothesis, Marxist-style communism proposed that society is necessarily in a constant state of revolution and that the goal of society must be a classless state and a world without boundaries. In other words, the genuine aim of communism is one-world government.

A TALE OF TWO REVOLUTIONS

In recent years, secular historians have written about the affinities between the American Revolution of 1776 and the French Revolution of 1789, as if both were merely incarnations of the same dynamic force. But that is not true.

While there was a thriving commerce between the United States and France during the eighteenth century, both in goods and in ideas, the aims of the patriots in America and the ideologies of the revolutionaries in France were two very different forces.

The American Revolution produced a constitution and a government based on biblical principles of Christianity. The French revolution was, at its core, anti-Christian. Motivated by rebellion against the Church, and influenced by the ideas of the deists and free-thinkers such as Rousseau and Descartes, the revolutionaries in France sought to remove God from His throne and to crown Reason in His place.

The French Revolution was a product of the Enlightenment. It was based on the glorification of man and the exaltation of wisdom and learning. While the colonial patriots in America humbled themselves before a wise and loving God, Rousseau proclaimed, "Man was born free, but everywhere he is in chains!"

One of the most touching stories of the American revolution was that of a British officer who somehow got separated from his unit and was trying to make his way back to camp, silently, through the trees. As he approached a clearing, he was startled to see an American general on his knees, hands clasped before his face in deep and fervent prayer.

As the Englishman looked on, his heart sank and tears came to his eyes, for he saw that the praying officer was General George Washington, commander of the American forces. "When I saw that sight," he said later, "I knew we were defeated. For any army whose commander was so humble before Almighty God could never lose the war."

THE FRAMING DOCUMENTS

The authors of the American constitution did not lack for self-respect, but they also understood that without appropriate checks and balances any government of men would inevitably grow corrupt. They had seen it in England, and they had lived under it in colonial America. So they framed a document that limited the power and authority of government.

The Declaration of Independence proclaimed "it is self-evident" that all men are created equal and are "endowed by their Creator with certain unalienable rights. . . ." But those rights did not, by any means, suggest absolute license. James Madison, generally recognized as the father of the constitution, wrote, "If men were angels, no government would be necessary." So the American documents of government protected the rights of the individual while they also imposed certain responsibilities and limitations. That is the true genius of the Constitution.

The revolutionary government of France took a very different turn. It became the goal of the revolutionaries to dismantle the European heritage of civilization and the Christian heritage of faith. According to Ben Hart, author of *Faith & Freedom,* "Rousseau did not believe in original sin or private property. He hated European civilization precisely because he saw it as a product of Christianity."

Voltaire had once said that the only way to have good laws was to burn the existing ones and start all over again. In essence, that was what the revolutionaries sought to accomplish.

At one point the revolutionaries wanted to throw out the Christian calendar and start fresh, from year one of the revolution. Ultimately it was not moral outrage that stopped them but European nationalism. The nations on either side felt no such esteem for the French Revolution; if anything they feared and resented it, so they wouldn't support that arrogant notion. They simply refused to go along.

Another curious mark of the revolution's antagonism toward God was manifested in the way they labeled themselves as left-wingers.

When the National Assembly split into factions, the conservatives sat on the right side of the hall and the revolutionaries chose the left.

James Billington, historian and Librarian of Congress, writes, "The subsequent equation of the left with virtue dramatized revolutionary defiance of Christian tradition, which had always represented those on the right of God as saved and those on the left as damned."

Toward the end of his ministry on earth, Jesus told His disciples parables of the end times, and among those was the story of the Judgment. In Matthew 25:41, Jesus described how He would one day bring all the people together, separate the righteous from the unrighteous, and then pronounce judgment.

To those on the right He would say, "Come, ye blessed of my Father, inherit the kingdom prepared for you from the foundation of the world." But to those on the left He would say, "Depart from me, accursed ones, into the eternal fire which has been prepared for the devil and his angels."

So great was their hatred of Christ and His Church, the radical reformers chose to be identified with those on the left as evidence of their rage.

These revolutionaries sought to acknowledge man as God. They believed each individual had the power of the divine within himself and that he could do whatever he believed to be right, short of harming another. Today that precept is enshrined in the French Declaration of Rights, Article Four, which states "liberty consists in whatever does not harm another."

The aftermath of the Revolution of 1789 remains one of the bloodiest and most outrageous blots on history. The idealism of the early patriots quickly degenerated into terror and chaos. They executed their king, even after he had sworn allegiance to the new constitution. Then, under Robespierre, tens of thousands of merchants, tradesmen, landowners, and nobles were executed; and the rioting and bloodshed provided a pretext for slaughtering one's enemies, for whatever reasons, throughout France.

Eventually Robespierre, himself, was guillotined, and after a prolonged period of anarchy, Napoleon Bonaparte came forth from the rabble and crowned himself Emperor. It was a classic pattern; after the collapse of empire, a bloodthirsty dictator rises to power.

THE VIEW FROM THE SHAMBLES

The English statesman, Edmund Burke, had seen early what would come in France. After a trip to Paris in 1773 to see what was afoot, he warned the British Parliament that the political theories of the philosophers could only produce tyranny. Burke predicted it would be ". . . the most horrid and cruel blow that can be offered to civil society through atheism. . . ." After the fall of the Bastille in 1789, and the Reign of Terror that ensued, Burke placed the blame for France's miseries on the philosophy that denied God.

Ironically, that revolution actually proved the humanists' faith in man to be unfounded and unwise. James Hitchcock writes, "The Terror, an orgy of hate and revenge, was strong disproof of the Enlightenment belief that man, left to himself, would inevitably behave in a rational and just way. The dark side of human nature asserted itself with a literal vengeance in the mid-1790s." He continues,

> The Terror was the first example of a familiar modern phenomenon: a movement to remake the world in the name of humanity gives birth to a murderous and destructive fanaticism. Every modern revolution has borne the same witness. It is one of the strongest arguments against total reliance on man and his goodwill. It has also given rise, among thoughtful people, to a strong distrust of all movements which proclaim that they have the welfare of "humanity" at heart. Time and again, this has meant the crushing of individual human beings in the name of a political abstraction.

The Terror and its outpouring in France was the true outpouring of what Rousseau had called "The General Will" as expressed through what John Locke had called "The Social Contract." That is, a moral consensus among men for the good of man. What it actually proved to be was one of the first and most poignant examples of humanism unchecked, and man given unlimited power apart from God.

Among the first items on the agenda of the revolutionaries was the debunking and the desecration of the Church. It was fashionable to scoff at religion. Hitchcock writes, "The intellectuals of the time portrayed the churches as reactionary enemies of progress." Sound familiar?

How often have we heard the charge in recent years that conservative Christians want to "turn back the clock" on progress to a "better time," before the great social advances of abortion on demand, homosexual liberation, no fault divorce, and the dissolution of the nuclear family?

Historians point out that all pretense of religious toleration among the French revolutionaries quickly turned into religious persecution. "Soon the government embarked on a systematic 'de-Christianizing' campaign." Hitchcock writes,

> Churches were closed and converted to profane uses, like stables for horses. Religious schools were destroyed. The religious press was outlawed. All religious services were forbidden. Priests and nuns were rounded up in large numbers and sent into exile, imprisoned, or executed. The aim of the government was to wipe out every remaining vestige of Christianity.

Our American forefathers had worked diligently to avoid these very things. They knew, as John Adams said, "The people, when they have been unchecked, have been as unjust, tyrannical, brutal, barbarous, and cruel as any king or senate possessed of uncontrolled power."

Another patriot said, "Whatever may be conceded to the influence of refined education on minds of peculiar structure, reason and experience both forbid us to expect that national morality can prevail in exclusion of religion." The speaker was George Washington, and you can be sure that he wasn't talking about just any religion. He wasn't speaking of cults, or Eastern religions, or humanist ideologies, for he also said, "It is impossible to govern rightly without God and the Bible."

TURNING THE CORNER

The motto of the French Revolution, as enshrined today on the national coat of arms, was "liberty, fraternity, equality." Author James Billington has suggested that the revolutionary egalitarianism of the French idea of liberty was the progenitor of modern communism. The "common happiness" idea in the French Revolution was "proto-communist."

And according to Hitchcock, "Although its full fury was found in France, similar ideas and practices spread to other parts of Europe where the Revolution itself spread. It became, in time, a permanent feature of European life."

In that sort of intellectual climate where man is supreme and God is irrelevant, society will ultimately sink to the level of expedience and self-centeredness. If there is no moral absolute; if I am the arbiter of right and wrong and the ultimate judge of worth; if I am all there is, then why shouldn't I have whatever I want? It is not hard to see where that line of thinking can lead. Courtesy is no longer a duty or a virtue but a way to "grease the wheels" so that I get what I want.

Jesus Christ taught that we should esteem our neighbor more highly that we do ourselves. In the section of Matthew quoted above, Christ told how He would say to the righteous, "I was hungry and you fed me; I was thirsty and you gave me to drink." And it was not what they had given to Him directly, but what they had given to "the least of these." The righteous had given selflessly to the humble, the downcast, the frightened, the helpless. How contradictory that view is to the humanist ideology!

It was in just such a godless environment that Karl Marx formulated his ideas of communism. This man, a German Jew who had once been a pious Christian, had grown bitter and angry. He had been an activist in Germany during the 1840s and was eventually tried by the state for treason in the same year he published the Communist Manifesto. But he escaped to England and, from his cold, drafty dwelling in London, Marx systematically conceived his theories of dialectical materialism, which would ultimately threaten the entire world.

Communism succeeded in Moscow and, again, the king and his family were slaughtered. Tens of thousands who disagreed with the Bolsheviks were butchered in the streets and on the farms and in the villages. Today we know that Stalin murdered more than 20 million of his fellow countrymen and buried them, unceremoniously, in unmarked graves from one end of Russia to the other.

The humanism that lies within communism has not been a very noble theology. Tens of thousands of citizens who have committed the heinous crime of seeking travel permits, emigration papers, passports, or who have simply been in the wrong place at the wrong time have been sent for "retraining" to Siberia. Others have simply been murdered in cold blood, and who could question the executioners?

THE BOLSHEVIKS IN AMERICA

Relentlessly, communism spread throughout Europe and across to the United States where the firebrands of the Labor Movement eagerly championed the doctrines of Marx and Lenin in the 1920s and '30s. **While most of the ordinary Americans who had suffered greatest from the Depression years determined to get back on their feet the old-fashioned way, by hard work and sweat, the urban intellectuals in America gravitated to the Marxist ideologies with incredible fervor.**

Among them, Edmund Wilson, John Dos Passos, Malcolm Cowley, Theodore Dreiser and many others were singing the praises of communist ideology, and a new genre of "proletarian fiction" was born. John Steinbeck wrote it in *Grapes of Wrath.* Carl Sandburg wrote it in *The People, Yes.* Richard Wright wrote it in *Native Son.* There were poets, painters, musicians, and philosophers, and, as we shall see, more and more professors in major universities who have now passed their theories along to three generations of American scholars.

In his book, *Since Yesterday,* historian Frederick Lewis Allen wrote that in 1932, at the depth of the Depression, communism was notably gaining strength, not only among the unemployed but among the intellectual elite. "Ideas were in flux," he writes. "There was a sharp upsurge of interest in the Russian experiment. Lecturers of Russia were in demand; Maurice Hindu's *Humanity Uprooted* and *New Russia's Primer* were thumbed and puzzled over."

The editor of Hearst's "usually frivolous" *Cosmopolitan* magazine had gone to Moscow to sign up Soviet writers and, on his return, threw a lavish, capitalist dinner party. Allen writes, "Gentle liberals who prided themselves on their open-mindedness were assuring one another that 'after all we had something to learn from Russia,' especially about 'planning'; many of the more forthright liberals were tumbling head over heels into communism."

By 1932, 52 writers, critics, and college professors signed an endorsement of communist presidential candidate William Z. Foster.

Marxism was in the air. However, as Paul McElvaine, author of *The Great Depression,* points out, Americans didn't buy the idea of collectivism so much as the belief that socialism would provide "the economic security necessary for people to be truly free to express their individuality." But wasn't that the dream behind the French Revolution as well?

In the 1940s, less than five million Americans actually completed four years of college; however, by the mid-1960s that number had swelled to twelve million. That increase is tied in to the social transitions taking place in America, the change from a rural to an urban society; but it also reflects a steady rise in the number of intellectuals and theoretical thinkers in the nation.

According to Stanley Rothman and Robert Lichter, in their book *The Roots of Radicalism,* the increasing numbers of intellectuals also reflects a greater spread of liberal and socialist influence. In the early years, that did not make as much of a difference as it would in the 1960s and '70s when the radical revolution truly hit home.

Rothman and Lichter report that "in 1944, college faculties voted only 3 percent more Democratic than the general public; in 1952 they voted 12 percent more Democratic; and in 1972 they gave George McGovern 18 percent more votes than did the general public."

But these authors also point out that if the universities were having an impact on the behavior of the American middle class, their influence was greatly magnified by the revolutions taking place in communications and transportation.

Now ideas could move freely. Theories learned in the colleges in the East were broadcast throughout the land, from coast to coast, and from the Northern steel mills to the Midwestern Bible belt. Now, more and more, the media was in the hands of college-educated liberals who were attracted to the whole range of liberal thinking, ranging from free speech to communist activism. And the gospel of socialism was blossoming in America and around the world.

AMERICA'S CLOSED MINDS

Today we are reaping the whirlwind of the academy's experimentation with communism and secularism. The educational collapse we are seeing in America's classrooms today is nothing more or less than the playing out of those flawed theories. The idea of a value-free culture is nothing but a humanist fantasy. Translate "open-mindedness" for "empty-headedness" and you have the real meaning of the socialist dream.

Today we are seeing that America's dalliance with experimental education has been a monumental failure, that people are beginning to wake up to the fact that it's not money, or buildings, or computers that we need but a new pedagogy.

For the first time, the intellectual establishment is saying that they are also fed up with the ignorance and anarchy of deconstructionist thinking in America's universities. Many were stung by Allan Bloom's monumental bestseller, *The Closing of the American Mind,* which pointed out the predominance and the folly of so-called "value neutral" thinking in our schools.

Bloom's book shows how generations of students have been so well trained to be so open minded, their minds are essentially empty. *Tabla rasa.* The subtitle of Bloom's book, *How Higher Education Has Failed Democracy and Impoverished the Souls of Today's Students,* really says it all. Secularism in the classroom, supported by socialist ideology, has raped the minds of America's young.

Millions of college graduates don't even have the mental tools to make basic decisions. It is no wonder they can't form lasting relationships, they have been brainwashed since kindergarten to be "open minded" and "non-judgmental." They may not have faith, and they may have no convictions, but they're open minded. And that is supposed to be a virtue?

Since Bloom's work first appeared in 1987, others have come along to add kindling to the fire. Most recently, Roger Kimball's book, *Tenured Radicals: How Politics Has Corrupted Our Higher Education,* depicts in detail the inglorious failures of university administrators and the systems of political manipulation within the academy; and Page Smith's *Killing the Spirit: Higher Education in America* adds another indictment to the charge that our students have been indoctrinated by Marxists, atheists, and skeptics who have robbed our children of values without offering anything of value in return.

Dr. Bruce Lockerbie's brilliant address to the Chautauqua Institution in New York in 1989 capsulized the contradictions of America's "moral neutrality" and the educational mediocrity of the last forty years. Throughout the history of education—at least since the time of Socrates—there has never been a serious quest of any kind for which Truth is not the objective.

Yet in absolute defiance of that fact, today's students have been taught that "truth is relative." Teachers and students in our universities hold the view that "truth" smells of "absolutism," and for them there is only one absolute: that is, "truth is relative."

Lockerbie told his audience that the kinds of absolute truth American college students know for certain are as follows:

1. "I think, therefore I am." (René Descartes)

2. "God is dead. God remains dead. And we have killed him." (Friedrich Nietzsche)

3. "There are truths but no truth." (Albert Camus)

4. "We have neither behind us, nor before us in a luminous realm of values, any means of justification or excuse. We are left alone, without excuse." (Jean-Paul Sartre)

5. "Life is hard, then you die." (bumper sticker)

For students, and their teachers, who have such a mind-set, the worst accusation you can make against anyone is to say that they believe strongly in anything other than everyone's right to his own opinions. Their greatest moral virtue is "openness," but in becoming so, they have become vacant-minded and empty-headed.

However, Lockerbie, who is Scholar-in-residence at the Stony Brook School, understands that there is no truth which does not recognize that the "the fear of the Lord" is the beginning, and even the end, of wisdom, and the criterion of all legitimate knowledge.

"Of course, we recognize that some human beings differ concerning our need to acknowledge a Supreme Being's existence and sovereignty over the affairs of the cosmos," said Lockerbie. The Psalms twice describe such persons. "The fool has said in his heart, 'There is no God.' To ignore or reject as fundamental truth the existence and sovereignty of God, in search of some alternative, isn't 'open-mindedness' but folly." In unison with Bloom, Lockerbie says that the university must stand for something: and that something must be Truth.

It should not be an altogether new revelation to most of us that the educational theorists have failed. In the early 1960s we first heard that "Johnny Can't Read"; then in 1981 Rudolph Flesch told us that "Johnny Still Can't Read," and not only that, he doesn't even know the basics that Americans have believed to be foundational for generations.

E. D. Hirsch's brilliant bestseller, *Cultural Literacy: What Every American Needs to Know,* outlined vast areas of ignorance of the average American and described the gulf America's educators must span in order to restore sound teaching and values to the classroom.

The official reports of former Secretary of Education William J. Bennett, and the recent public addresses of current Secretary of Education, Lauro F. Cavazos, have handed out stinging reproof of the policies of the National Education Association (NEA) and the methodologies of the education establishment. The scores of high school students on the Scholastic Aptitude Test (SAT) continue to drop year after year.

While liberals prefer to attack the surveys and to claim prejudicial language and bias, students are learning less and less and reports from university campuses all across this nation prove that entering freshmen are incredibly ignorant and apathetic. Many have lost faith in the system and in their ability to gain anything of value from education.

On the latest reports, American students have dropped to fourteenth place in educational achievement, ranking somewhere between Togo and Chad!

THE ONRUSHING TIDE

In 1983 the National Commission on Excellence in Education published its *Open Letter to the American People* with the subtitle, *A Nation at Risk: The Imperative for Educational Reform.* It was that report which, more than any government study before or since, helped to portray the crisis that confronts us in the ominous phrase, "the educational foundations of our society are presently being eroded by *a rising tide of mediocrity* that threatens our very future as a nation and a people."

While it is demoralizing to see what the colleges have done to our youth, the legacy of failure in the elementary and secondary schools is even more heart-rending. In his excellent work, *Changing the Way America Thinks,* Regent University President and former *New York Times* editor Bob Slosser chronicles the collapse of the educational process with many pointed examples. Slosser writes that,

> Illiteracy is so pervasive in American schools today that it is no longer limited to crumbling cities, nor even to rural shacks. Illiteracy has become an equal-opportunity disgrace. The city of Boston, once the literacy capital of America, was described recently by a disgusted businessman as "not only second rate, but a disaster, a waste basket."

In *Illiterate America,* Jonathan Kozol pointed out that 25 million American adults are so illiterate they cannot read the warning label on a bottle of poison. Another 35 million read only at a survival level. This is the result of educational experimentation, and we have the principles of Dewey and the socialists to thank.

Marxists and socialists who have burrowed into the schools are going to have to be rooted out if we're going to change the way America thinks. They're going to be so discredited that nobody who's intellectually responsible is going to accept the Marxist view of life any more. Sadly, that has been the prevailing doctrine in America's schools for the better part of 40 years.

In 1989, Chester E. Finn, Jr., former Assistant Secretary of Education and now a professor at Vanderbilt University, reported in *Commentary* magazine that only 5 percent of 17-year-old high-school students can read well enough to understand technical documents, literary essays, or historical documents; barely 6 percent can solve multi-step math problems and use basic algebra; and only 7 percent are able to draw conclusions from scientific knowledge.

Finn said that 60 percent of eleventh graders do not know why the *Federalist* papers were written; three-fourths do not know when Lincoln was president; and just one in five knows what "Reconstruction" was about.

Furthermore, high school students are essentially ignorant of geography or international affairs. But lest we argue that the tests are prejudiced or unfair, Finn points out that in head-to-head comparison with teen-agers in Europe and Asia, Americans are clearly outclassed in all categories. He writes,

The most recent [study] reported by the Education Testing Service in January [1989] compares the performance of thirteen-year-olds in mathematics and science in six countries. In math, ours came in dead last. In science, American girls and boys were tied for last place (with Ireland and two Canadian provinces). Korea led in both subjects, and the United States was also bested in both by England, Spain, and three other Canadian provinces.

But, Finn reports, another part of the problem is denial. For example, even though the American students ranked at the bottom, the same study shows that the American kids had the highest self-regard. Fully 68 percent of the American 13-year-olds believed themselves to be "good at mathematics," while only 23 percent of the high-scoring Korean youngsters felt so. And while 91 percent of American mothers said their schools were doing an "excellent" or "good" job, only 42 percent of Chinese mothers and 39 percent of the Japanese surveyed rated their schools at those levels.

Complacency, denial, and divisiveness are rampant in all sectors, but the behaviorism and secularism of the '60s and '70s is still a prime ingredient of public education, and some of our educators are still actively engaged in the process of destroying schools.

We had a guest on the 700 Club television program who had been involved in some of the experiments where they literally made California schools into experiments for their so-called "social studies." They call it social science, but it is not science at all. It is pseudoscience, built upon very faulty statistics and untenable assumptions.

It is a game of educational experimentation and a mechanistic form of behaviorism straight out of Pavlov and B. F. Skinner. The social scientists hold a view of human beings which does not take into account the fact that our children are made in the image of God, or that God has anything to do with them.

BACK TO BASICS

Ironically, the government's destructive programs of the past decade are part of what was termed the "Back to Basics" movement. But whatever it was, it wasn't basic and it didn't work. The evidence is only too clear.

The results of a ten-year study of schooling in America and the various systems for financing public education concludes that the only way our schools can be made responsive to the legitimate educational needs of children is by eliminating bureaucratic control over education and returning the decision-making power to the parents.

The report, entitled *Politics, Markets and America's Schools,* is the work of John E. Chubb, a senior fellow at the Brookings Institution, and Terry M. Moe, a political scientist at Stanford University, who analyzed the experiences of more than 20,000 students, teachers, and principals in 500 public and private schools all across the country. It is important to see that these researchers, by taking a straightforward, objective look, discovered the inevitable truth that the natural way is the best way.

Bureaucracy is unnatural and ineffective. The institution created by God for development and nurturing is the family. Government's task should be to empower the family—whether through a system of vouchers for education or through substantial tax relief—and not to interfere in the natural order established by God.

The secularizing of education and the destruction of the natural order has served as the springboard for a vicious vendetta against religious values in the schools of America. The horror stories abound. Jay Sekulow, of CASE, a lawyer who defends cases of religious persecution, along with John Whitehead and attorneys at the Rutherford Institute, has told many of them; and we gathered others at the Freedom Council a few years ago.

One of the most shocking examples was the story of a student who was suspended from school in DeKalb County, Georgia, for "the possession of Christian literature." Not drugs, not alcohol, not firearms: but Christian literature! He handed a piece of paper to a friend inviting him to come to a Fellowship of Christian Athletes meeting, and it may have said something about Jesus.

The assistant principal was apparently in the hall and demanded to see the note. He read it, then suspended the boy for possession—possession of Christian literature! That is just one example of the kinds of antagonism toward Christian faith and values that has flourished in this country over the past two decades. And in some places that sort of prejudice and bias is still growing worse.

Somehow the secular establishment doesn't perceive the irony that the very same school that suspended this student for possession of Christian literature had Satanic literature on its bulletin board! When confronted with that fact, they said, we're not interested in talking about Satan; we're just interested in keeping Christianity out. At least that was their message. If this is worship of the true God, their actions implied, we won't tolerate it. Worship of a false god is okay.

You can't put the Ten Commandments on the classroom wall, but apparently there's nothing wrong with having gurus come in to lecture, or having seances and meditations. Those practices are going on right now in many schools. We know of schools where they are teaching astral projection in the classrooms. Students are taught that they are going out of their bodies into space, meeting with creatures in space, and bringing spirits back to earth with them.

We reported on television that in some schools in New Mexico, children are told to lie on the floor and meditate into a trance. At best this type of thing is absurd; at worst it is demonic, and opens up these innocent children to evil powers and spirits. But the school boards of America see nothing wrong!

Still, the handwriting is already on the wall, and I predict we will see dramatic changes in the coming decade. I believe we will see this nation moving away from rationalistic and atheistic thinking very quickly. There is going to be an openness of faith, and people all across this land will be taking a stand for their faith.

For many we trust it will be faith in Jesus Christ, but for others it will no doubt be faith in some other power. Whether it comes from the New Age or Hinduism or Buddhism or Islam or some other Eastern-type religion, there is going be a sudden and overwhelming rise of religious belief in this country. We are going to witness a spiritual awakening of inconceivable proportions, and it will be a spiritual awakening ready-made for a post-Christian Europe as well.

THE ALLURE OF SECULARISM

From its inception, secularism has focused intently on the overt de-Christianizing of America. It starts with dialogue about "pluralism" and "tolerance" and "relative values," as it did in France 200 years ago, but it always ends with an outright assault on Christianity and the Church.

In the beginning, the intellectual allure of secularism is intriguing. Educated men and women are tantalized by the ideas and promises of the humanist dream, and it seems no great leap of faith to swallow the absurd logic of Darwinism, or Freudian psychology, or even of Marxist-Leninist social theory.

The mind becomes a playground of ideas. **It is the hunger for the apple all over again; the lust for the knowledge of good and evil; the desire to attain what Satan promised, "you shall be as gods."**

The idea of evolution has been taught as gospel truth in America's schools now for at least forty years. Except in Christian schools and a few small community schools where Christianity is still considered a virtue, the biblical account of creation is not even taught today.

The central idea of evolution is that there is no God; things occur by chance, which leads directly to the belief that values and mores are purely functional. "If it feels good, do it." Social scientists, from Carl Jung to B. F. Skinner, suddenly gained a new stature in the secularized society. Jung told us the collective conscience of the human race determines our values and our beliefs; Skinner taught that we practice norms of right and wrong by simply learning the natural behavioral patterns acceptable to the greatest number of people.

Human law, we then conclude, need not be based on eternal truth or the revealed Word of God, but on the basis of consensus, pluralism, relativism, and social determinism. And if we lose the promise of eternal life and a personal walk with the Lord God in the process, we at least gain the freedom to be fully human and masters of our own fate.

How ironic that in freeing himself from all moral restraint, mankind has become a slave to his own pride and immorality. By casting off his soul, he has put himself on the level of the animals. By disowning the family of God, he has alienated himself from God's most sacred institution on earth, the family of man.

It has become great public sport in the 1990s to scoff at Christians and Christianity. As film critic Michael Medved points out, "If someone turns up in a film today wearing a Roman collar or bearing the title Reverend, you can be fairly sure he will be crazy or corrupt—or both."

In the film, *Monsignor,* Christopher Reeve plays a priest who seduces a nun and invests Vatican money with the Mafia. In *Agnes of God,* Meg Tilly plays a nun who murders her own baby and stuffs it into a trash can. Others, from *True Confessions, Mass Appeal,* and *The Mission,* to the scurrilous and thoroughly artless *Last Temptation of Christ,* set out to prove the corruption and hypocrisy of Christianity and the Church.

In his lecture at Hillsdale College, quoted in *Reader's Digest,* Mr. Medved wondered why Hollywood is so intent in its hatred of religion that it produces one box office fiasco after another, like those named above, while the films which have portrayed the positive values of the faith have scored so well.

Chariots of Fire was a "worldwide box-office smash," he says. Robert Duvall won an oscar for his part in *Tender Mercies,* in which he played a washed-up country singer whose life is transformed by religious faith. "In one scene," says Medved, "he is baptized and most convincingly born again. The movie confounded the experts with its strong audience appeal."

There was a time when Hollywood seemed to understand and appreciate the deep religious faith of this nation. *The Ten Commandments, The Robe, Ben Hur,* and *The Greatest Story Ever Told* were sensational film successes. Actors such as Pat O'Brien, Bing Crosby, and Spencer Tracy made a tradition of playing "earthy, compassionate priests who gave hope to underprivileged kids or comforted GIs on the battlefield."

The film-makers have forgotten that tradition, however, and they are completely out of touch with what faith in God is all about. Medved said,

> A 1982 survey analyzing the attitudes of key figures in the movie business showed that only four percent regularly attend church or synagogue. In the country at large, by contrast, over 40 percent flock to services on a regular basis. If most big-screen images of religious leaders tend to resemble Jimmy Swaggart or Jim Bakker, it's because evangelists on TV are the only believers who are readily visible to members of the film colony.

Except for the cable networks and religious programming, television is essentially a desert. The implied morals of so-called family shows such as "My Two Dads," "Family Matters," "Empty Nest," "Roseanne," and all of the network soap operas suggest that American viewers have lost all sense of propriety or shame. Deviant sexual behavior is out in the open; sex outside of marriage is the norm;

anger, bitterness, and exploitation are everywhere; and there is an outright glorification of carnality and brutality and godlessness. One can only wonder, where will it all end?

On network television and in the print media liberal, socialist, humanistic, and promiscuous values prevail. Those who stand for restraint, for religious values, or for moral codes are often branded extremists, fundamentalists, and reactionaries.

What outcry comes from the secular press when newsfilms document the images of riot squads breaking the arms of pro-life demonstrators? And even as the news readers recite the lurid evidence of drugs and violence in the streets of America, no one seems to make the connection between the loss of Christian values and the spiraling increase in crime.

For the time being, secular humanism is still held somewhat in check by America's long tradition of Christian values. Though it is a pale shadow of its former self, America's tradition of morality still ascribes some worth to the Ten Commandments and to the principles of compassion Jesus taught in the Sermon on the Mount. But for how long?

THE FRENCH WITNESS

About 40 years after the French Revolution—still troubled by the devils the Reign of Terror had unleashed at home—the French government commissioned Alexis de Tocqueville to journey through America to discover what it was about the American experiment that had made it such a conspicuous success. Like the French, the Americans had gone through a bloody revolution; yet, unlike the French, they had come out of it basically loyal, law-abiding citizens, charitable and respectful, and remarkably tranquil. Why?

In his book, *Democracy in America,* de Tocqueville told his countrymen it was their faith in God that made the American experiment unique. "I do not know whether all Americans have a sincere faith in their religion," he wrote, "for who can know the human heart?—but I am certain that they hold it to be indispensable for the maintenance of republican institutions. This opinion is not peculiar to a class of citizens or to a party, but it belongs to the whole rank of society."

America is, he wrote, "the place where the Christian religion has kept the greatest power over men's souls; and nothing better demonstrates how useful and natural it is to man, since the country where it now has the widest sway is both the most enlightened and the freest."

THE COMING COLLISION OF BELIEFS

Despite the apparent collapse of world communism, America is still wrestling with the specter of the humanists and socialists in our own midst. The advocates of the secular society, both inside and outside the established church, are preaching "separation of church and state."

By misconstruing the "no establishment" clause of the Constitution, which states that Congress must keep its hands out of matters concerning the church, the secularists have tried to throw out the last remnants of Christianity in America.

The spokesmen and gurus of popular society have been trying for 30 years to shove the church into a mold made in the shape of the Ku Klux Klan, Nazism, and racial bigotry. The perpetrators of that fraud say they simply want the church to restrict itself to ecclesiastical matters and to leave the running of society to the government, but their ambition is much larger than that. They want to destroy Christianity.

Under communism the church was not allowed a voice in secular affairs, in education, or in the policy issues that affected the welfare of the citizens. Bred from the same stock as the atheists, the rationalists, and the pragmatists, the communist leaders were in a war against God and His kingdom on earth. To silence God in society, they first had to silence the church and the men and women of faith who believed in Him. Today's secular humanists are their heirs.

The fact is, the church must always be able to speak out on anything of a moral nature. That includes the family, the bond of husband and wife, sexual relationships, the origin of life, the rearing of children, the education of the young, the welfare of the poor and needy, the faithful worship of Jesus Christ, and all the other issues which are the time-honored concerns of Christianity in Western society. **We simply will not let secularization crowd us out. After all, our forefathers founded this country, and we're not about to give it up!**

Today it is clear that secular humanism has failed. Like communism, to which it has been allied from the beginning, it is a bankrupt system without moral guidelines or reliable safeguards to protect the people from its own corruptions. It has degenerated into carnality, sensuality, lawlessness, and disease, and it has left millions of men and women all over the world adrift, without purpose, and emotionally crippled.

Nature abhors a vacuum, and secularism has left a spiritual vacuum in the hearts of all those who once turned to it for freedom and hope. To survive, the humanists will either have to decamp or change their ways, and this is the decade in which one of those two will most certainly come to pass.

Now after their half-century rampage through the pages of history, I am not holding out much hope that they will simply admit their folly and give up. I am not betting that they will suddenly see the moral and emotional carnage in their wake and reform, but I am betting they will change.

In *Megatrends 2000,* John Naisbitt and Patricia Aburdene forecast a mammoth boom in spirituality in this country in the years ahead: "a worldwide multidenominational religious revival" they call it. Reciting how American society has passed from genuine faith to a belief in science, passing through the "God is dead" movement at mid-century, these authors write that "Science and technology do not tell us what life means. We learn that through literature, the arts, and spirituality."

So the decade ahead will offer a supermarket of spirituality for the discriminating palate. Basic Christianity? Yes. New Age? You bet. Channeling, holistic healing, tarot, ancient lords, ascended masters, and alien visitors, all these will be readily available, packaged attractively and marketed tastefully for the perceptive consumer, and every one of them worthy of serious worship in the coming decade. These authors don't care which you choose.

Fundamentalists—that is, those who actually believe the Bible is the Word of God and that it contains truth which must be believed and followed—may now seem a nuisance to the humanistic power brokers. But in my judgment, after a period of intense struggle the believers will stand firmly astride the fallen and crumbling ruins of the secular colossus.

From the rise of secularism to the fall of communism, the world has now endured a 300-year assault on its very soul. Now the tide is turning. The year 1990 will be remembered as the beginning of the end of secularism. For today we are standing at the threshold of a massive collision of beliefs.

From the French Revolution on, the secularists have tried to destroy the Christian religion. They are still entrenched in the schools, the courts, and many parts of government. The warfare between secularism and religious faith will conclude in this decade with the clear victory of faith.

4

The Rise of the Supernatural

During this decade we will witness a crumbling of the power of prevailing intellectual elites in the United States and Europe.

The 1990s will not be a decade dominated by rationalism or science, but a decade of religious faith. We are entering the age of the supernatural.

As the decade of the 1980s was coming to a close, a keen observer could detect some clear trends. The traditional church in Western Europe lay prostrate before the centuries old attack of rationalism, humanism, and secularism.

Clearly the high ground of society in Western Europe and the United States—the universities, schools, media, think tanks, courts, and to a lesser extent the parliaments—had been captured by the forces of anti-Christian rationalism. The "Christendom" that had held sway since 500 A.D.—what Winston Churchill in 1940 had termed "Christian Civilisation"—was dead.

The Christian church behind the iron and bamboo curtains was alive but lacking influence. Persecuted, hunted, imprisoned, ridiculed, the church in these lands lacked trained priests, Bibles, basic literature, Bible schools and seminaries, and even places to meet. Most of all, they lacked freedom.

71

For over two billion of the earth's inhabitants, their gods were Marx, Lenin, Stalin, or Mao Tse Tung. The only heaven held out to them was the oppressive, stultifying "worker's paradise" of communism.

Then in a few electrifying months, the gods of East and West began to tumble. Marx, Lenin, Stalin, and Mao all came crashing down. Communism was revealed as the empty lie many of us have always known it to be.

The fall of the Berlin Wall, the execution of Nikolae and Elena Ceausescu, the election of Vaclav Havel, the political disintegration of the Soviet Union are all highly visible events. We can watch pictures of these events on television. We can see the leaders and hear the debates in their assemblies.

What we cannot see on television is the dismantling of the humanist philosophical superstructure that saw its hopes and dreams for a communist one-world utopia suddenly dashed by the emerging reality of faith in God, love of freedom, and the superiority of free-market economics.

During the next few years, particularly in the United States and to a lesser degree in Western Europe, a fierce, intense, and sometimes ugly battle is going to be waged to seize the control points of society away from the advocates of anti-Christian secularism.

When communism lost, the secularists lost. The problem is that they hold entrenched positions of power and, like the World War II Japanese defenders of Iwo Jima who holed up in caves and bunkers in the hills, they will have to be taken out of their strongholds one at a time.

In the United States, the skirmishes over abortion, government-funded obscenity, and parental rights are just part of the larger battle to take back education, the courts, governmental agencies and, indeed, our culture from the intellectual heirs of the French Revolution.

During this decade we will witness a crumbling of the power of prevailing intellectual elites in the United States and Western Europe. Atheistic communism is dying. Rationalism and atheistic humanism are also dying.

In my judgment, the 1990s will witness an intellectual and spiritual renaissance that can only be compared to that of the early days of the Christian Church or the emergence of the power of the Church after the fall of Rome.

The 1990s will not be a decade dominated by rationalism or science, but a decade of religious faith. We are entering the age of the supernatural.

What we don't yet know is what form the religious faith will take. Will the world embrace the claims of Jesus Christ and the truths of the Bible, or are we to expect the world to turn to an "Age of Aquarius" dominated by the Hindu religions and led by mystic holy men in touch with demonic spirits known as "ascended masters"?

AWAKENING IDEOLOGIES

Europe is a spawning ground for ideologies. They received the gospel from the apostle Paul and the early missionaries of the first century, and from then on through the Middle Ages until fairly recent times Europeans have been involved in evangelizing the world for Christ.

But now the direction may be changing, and I suspect we will see a new era of missionary activity in Europe as we move toward the new millennium. But in this case, the missionaries will be coming in to them from the Orient, bringing a new kind of religion.

The confrontation of Eastern and Western religions on the soil of Europe may well be the great struggle of the decade, and the new millennium is going to be shaped somehow by the spiritual forces that have been let loose in this age. Faced with the dismantling of the old ideologies of Marxism and atheism, the logical conclusion would be that the European people will begin to champion democratic ideals and the doctrines of love and brotherhood taught by Christianity.

They should say, "In the past we rejected Christianity, but now it is clear that Christianity is the answer. Therefore, we will turn to Christ." But I'm afraid that is not going to happen. Those people aren't going to do that. That would be too difficult, too self-effacing. It would mean loss of pride and prestige.

So what they will do, little by little, is to introduce another religion. They can't go with traditional Christianity which they rejected, so they will choose to embrace the secular religion of self-actualization, self-realization, and other New Age-type religious concepts born out of Hinduism.

Obviously, that sort of belief system is entirely compatible with the worship of Mother Earth, with the concept that we are all gods, we all come out of some universal consciousness. The philosophy of Carl Jung talks about a great universal sense of right and wrong, and the pre-existent consciousness of man. It is God-free and sanitary, and the whole concept of reincarnation fits so nicely with that.

Nobody is really responsible for his actions; after all, we each have a Karma attached to us that goes back to some grandparent, some debt that has to paid because of some former life. What a convenient theology for a post-Christian world in a desperate search for values.

FALSE PROMISES OF THE NEW AGE

The promises of the New Age are so radical and subversive of everything Christ taught us, it seems to be tailor-made for a secular elite looking for a philosophy. Among the various cults and mysteries, there are those which promise unlimited wealth to anyone who wants it.

The Unity Church, for example, is a theology of prosperity which promises that the believer will accumulate wealth and prosperity as he or she accepts the divine nature—the Christ consciousness—within. "Be all that you can be," they say. "Achieve everything you've dreamed of"; but none of these cults has the slightest thought of repentance or the need for a Savior or a Cross. Even the concept, to these people, is foolishness.

When I look at the book of Revelation, I have to wonder if these kinds of cults might not be the origin of the Anti-Christ? It certainly seems that way. Things could already be in place for some kind of a world dictatorship based, not on communism or socialism or fascism or any of the man-made, mechanical, ideological systems we have known in the past which focus on government, but based on a one-world religion.

If you will recall, it was the religious vacuum caused by divisions in the Church that allowed the anti-Christian heresies and the secularization of the sixteenth century to begin. By the same token, the vacuum caused by the collapse of communism could create a very similar environment in this century in which a counterfeit religion could emerge, and it would be such a subtle counterfeit that people who are spiritually motivated would receive it. Especially those who have rejected Christianity.

I believe that is another major trend, and I believe that this is what we're going to be facing in the next decade. The manifestation of satanic power is going to come at us—that is, at Bible-believing Christians—in such a way we would not have believed it possible. But I also believe that during this decade there will be a counter-balancing Christian revival of the power of God's Holy Spirit.

In the coming decade there will be evangelism we could never have dreamed of at any other time. The power of mass communication will revolutionize the way we present the gospel, and millions all over the world will be exposed to the ministry of Jesus Christ who might never have heard the name before.

During April of 1990, our evangelistic teams saw 2,090,000 people accept the Lord in Central America in one week. That's more than we saw in 30 years of previous ministry. And I believe it's going to be that way in country after country after country. But, right now, the world is in the balance and it's going to be a spiritual struggle more than anything else.

If the communist political values have collapsed; if the atheistic, humanistic philosophy is in a state of collapse; and if the only other ready-made form of worship we have is materialism and there's a worldwide depression—which I believe there well may be because of the mounting debt crisis—that would mean the collapse of another materialistic god.

All of that would leave people desperately longing for something, somebody, some way, some philosophy to get them out of their mess. I suspect some will find it quite easy to put their faith in a bold New Age leader who offers them the world.

INSIDIOUS ALLEGIANCES

If you take a look at the full-page ads for the guru god, "Lord Meitreya," paid for by Benjamin Creme in the *New York Times* and other international papers, you can see what absurd ideologies people will accept and what lengths their false prophets will go to in promulgating them.

From his office at the Tara Center, a British cult organization, Creme told the world that the Lord Meitreya is the true Messiah. He said he is already here and is merely waiting the moment to arrive when he will lead the world into a glorious millennium.

Creme did not mention, however, that the name "Meitreya" is Sanskrit for the name Buddha, since the aim of the movement is to mislead those who would be more open to a Western concept of Messiah. Nevertheless, someone identified as Meitreya has reportedly made appearances in Europe and Africa and is only waiting for his followers around the world to help bring about his "Declaration Day," when he will declare himself the new Christ.

These people are clearly talking about a one-world government that will solve the problem of war, depression, famine, poverty, and bring an end to the cycles of suffering that are afflicting mankind. They are promising a new era of peace, and they describe it as the fulfillment of the Age of Aquarius.

In 1949 L. Ron Hubbard was a failed science fiction writer who authored a presumptuous book called *Dianetics, the Modern Science of Mental Health.* For whatever reasons, the book became an instant bestseller and virtually overnight a movement was born.

By 1952 Hubbard founded the Church of Scientology and, surrounded by drug addicts, teeny boppers, and movie stars, this "chain-smoking enigmatic bundle of contradictions" built a massive empire, including an entire ocean-going fleet, out of a desperate search for love and power.

Over the past forty years the Church of Scientology has become a multi-million dollar operation—some say a billion-dollar operation. In 1972 the *Encyclopedia Brittanica,* quoting Peter Rowley's work, *New Gods in America,* called it the largest new religion in America.

Werner Erhard, founder of EST, called Hubbard the "greatest philosopher of the twentieth century." For more than 25 years the rich and famous beat a path to his door, and celebrities such as John Travolta, Karen Black, Sonny Bono, Chick Corea, Stephen Boyd, Gloria Swanson, William Burroughs, Priscilla Presley and many more, worshiped at his shrine.

In the powerful expose written by Hubbard's oldest son and a collaborator, a man who had worked at Hubbard's side for many years, the father of Dianetics is shown to be a fraud, a pathological liar, and a deceitful manipulator who masterminded break-ins, theft, extortion, blackmail, revenge plots, murders, and many other felonies.

The book, *L. Ron Hubbard: Messiah or Madman?* shows how Hubbard identified himself with Meitreya, "he whose name is kindness," the god with the golden hair prophesied to appear in the West 2,500 years after the death of Buddha. And it cites Hubbard's lyric, "Address me and you address/Lord Buddha/Address Lord Buddha/And you then address/Meitreya."

Even though Hubbard died in 1986, the empire continues and the leaders of the militant cult claim the spirit of this "cosmic outlaw" still directs them from the astral plane. He leads them from his higher-level being. Accordingly, the bestsellers continue to pour off the presses, and each brings in multiplied millions of dollars to support the brain-washing, terrorism, and fraud which fuels the madman's empire.

Just knowing that hundreds of thousands of Americans, and hundreds of thousands more on all five major continents, are actually reading and believing—and more, joining and following—such outrageous ideologies should convince anyone that the dangers of the New Age are neither innocent nor benign.

Such cults are insidious and evil. Having styled himself on cultist Aleister Crowley, who calls himself "Beast 666," it is patently clear that one of Hubbard's chief aims was to eradicate Christianity from the face of the earth, to destroy the credibility of Jesus Christ, and to bring Christians into submission to the spirit of the Beast. Sooner or later, all false religions which deny the deity of Christ come back to the same satanic root.

INSIDE THE NEW AGE

The human potential movement may seem trendy and full of pop psychology, emotional therapy such as Silva Mind Control, the Forum (formerly known as EST), and high-priced bearded gurus chanting mantras over well-known rock and roll musicians. Actually, it is nothing new.

It was first found in the Garden of Eden when Satan whispered to innocent Eve, "you shall be as gods." At its core is a simple message: human beings who are able to develop their full potential of mystic and psychic powers can gain access to the hidden mysteries of occult knowledge and power and, thereby, be as God.

To the idealistic, the New Age offers a universal brotherhood of man, a one world government, no war, no heaven, no hell, only everlasting peace. The words of the song "Imagine," written by the late megastar, John Lennon, clearly set forth the New Age agenda for mankind. No church, no preachers, no need for repentance, and no salvation in Christ.

The message of the New Age is just as beguiling as the message of the serpent in the Garden, and it is every bit as insidious. It is not surprising that the New Age religion is spreading like wildfire into the spiritual vacuum that now exists in the world.

In his book, *Understanding the New Age,* Russell Chandler, a religion writer for the *Los Angeles Times,* says that the New Age movement is "a hybrid mix of spiritual, social, and political forces, and it encompasses sociology, theology, the physical sciences, medicine, anthropology, history, the human potential movement, sports, and science fiction."

It is not a single cult but an entire spectrum of beliefs, and although New Agers often disagree among themselves about what the essential precepts really are, the underlying proposition is a belief in the transcendence of mankind. It is prompted by a belief in an essential divinity.

Marketing savvy has a lot to do with the success of the movement as well. When George Gallup reported in 1978 that ten million Americans were involved in some form of Eastern mysticism and another nine million were into spiritual healing, that news seemed to trigger a feeding frenzy on Madison Avenue.

Suddenly television shows such as *Star Trek* and *Battlestar Galactica* were all the rage. Hollywood scored phenomenal hits with movies like *ET, Star Wars, Close Encounters of the Third Kind,* and the *Star Trek* series. In every case, revenues from the sale and licensing of products, toys, T-shirts, puppets and dolls, along with unlimited product endorsements, was many times greater than the box-office take alone.

Movies such as *The Exorcist, Poltergeist,* and *Rosemary's Baby,* and later *Alien,* along with the somewhat fluffier *Cocoon,* exposed specters and fantasies in the public imagination, but the new wave of space thrillers seemed to be an opening of the American soul to alien powers.

Most invoking was the paradoxical spirit George Lucas called "The Force," which has been variously described as a blending of biblical teachings and Eastern lore, along with a large dose of pop psychology and psycho-kinesis, which involves demonic forces.

THE MORONIC CONVERGENCE

In his book about the Hollywood film world, Lloyd Billingsley called the movement a "*gazpacho* of Eastern ideas and assorted nostrums, which the *New Republic* has called 'Moronic Convergence.'" It is true that many people have joked about the absurd claims of Shirley MacLaine and J. Z. Knight, who supposedly channels a 35,000-year-old warrior, Ramtha, from the lost continent of Atlantis. But it is much more than a joke. It is a multi-million dollar industry which boasts tens of thousands of converts and is having a tangible impact in virtually every city and town in North America.

In addition to all the show business celebrities associated with the New Age movement, from MacLaine to Sylvester Stallone, an increasing number of business and political leaders have identified themselves as New Agers.

At a conference in Denver, Atlanta broadcaster Ted Turner called for a New Age president to transport America into the new millennium. He said America needs a new moral code to give us a sense of order and dignity and he offered money to anyone who could come up with a document superior to the Ten Commandments which, in Turner's opinion, is hopelessly flawed and outdated.

In the United States Senate, Rhode Island Democrat Claiborne Pell, a dabbler in the occult and a New Age convert, introduced legislation in Congress in 1989 to fund a National Commission on Human Resource Development. Fortunately, Pell's efforts to legitimize the New Age movement and to funnel millions of taxpayer dollars into the hands of so-called "Mind-Body" experts failed, but just barely.

The national New Age policy lobbied by Pell would have set up a commission of 25 advisers and a full-fledged administration department. It was rebuffed largely through the protest of Senator Dan

Coats, who reminded the Senate that they had already rejected a similar measure in 1988.

CHANNELING THE CORPORATION

In 1986 the *New York Times* reported on the increase of New Age mind control in the corporate world. The story showed how large corporations, under the misguided pretext of increasing efficiency and productivity, are pushing meditation, hypnosis, channeling, biofeedback, psychic manifestations, and other components of Eastern mysticism loosely built on Maslow's principles of "self actualization."

These "human potential" seminars and "mind control clinics" are still very much in vogue and are being required for employees in companies such as Ford, Chrysler, General Motors, Westinghouse, IBM, RCA, Boeing, TRW, Proctor & Gamble, Polaroid, and other industry giants. In some cases, refusal to participate can mean loss of a job, harassment on the job, or denial of advancement opportunities.

Some of our largest airlines currently require all their flight personnel to undergo "psychic training" based on New Age concepts at least twice a year.

A survey of 500 California firms conducted by *California Business* magazine showed that fully half were already employing some kind of "consciousness-raising" techniques. And graduate schools of business, from Stanford to Yale, are experimenting with "creativity" training involving everything from witchcraft to primal therapy.

In her February 1990 newsletter, Phyllis Schlafly reported on many of these activities and described further the Department of Education hearing on "protection of pupil rights" which revealed that many of these same occult practices, along with many examples of outright Satanism, have been used in public schools to "retrain" our sons and daughters and to indoctrinate children into the New Age.

ROOTS OF THE OCCULT

New Age is another term for occult which became prominent as booksellers, in particular, discovered the growing appeal of metaphysical and occult books dealing with what the authors termed "a coming new age of spiritual enlightenment."

Simply replacing the "Occult" label on the bookshelves with "New Age" escalated sales on everything in the section, from books on herbal cures to the Satanist Bible.

The idea of reincarnation, which is characteristic of many of the New Age religions, is a Hindu belief which has gained great popularity in this country because it offers a concept of eternal life. But it is very different from the doctrine of death and resurrection taught by the Bible.

Hindu beliefs offer a view of the world that is cyclical. The idea of *karma,* the Hindu wheel of fate, is a central concept. It is the belief that people continue to come around until their *karma,* or debt, is purged; but the *karma* never does get purged, unless they attain Nirvana, which is nothingness.

It is a chilling and joyless vision of life, but these beliefs are spreading like wildfire. We recently learned that a new Hindu temple goes up in the United States every 21 days. Swamis, Yogis, Gurus, and Zen Masters seem to be multiplying everywhere, particularly on the West Coast.

SALVATION FROM THE STARS

If that weren't enough, belief in UFOs is also growing rapidly. The movie *ET* was an immediate success in this country because it allowed a lot of people to hope that there might really be salvation for mankind from the stars. At the same time, the concept of Extra Sensory Perception (ESP) has become as commonplace as horoscopes. Author and sociologist Andrew Greeley reports that 70 million Americans have had ESP experiences, and a study done at Northern Illinois University suggests that nearly the same number follow their horoscopes on a regular basis.

Beyond that, there are a vast number of popular forms of spiritism, from Ouija boards to palm reading, and other things which are very much in vogue because people want to believe that the spirits guide them. I even heard recently that some psychics, including Jeanne Dixon, are advertising their services on television with a toll-free 800 number for call-in customers.

The sad irony is that spirits can and do guide them; but they are not the spirits the seekers are expecting. They are not innocent and benign spirits but evil ones who prey on the weak and ignorant. Those who dabble in the occult and who have rejected the atonement of Jesus Christ become the victims of demonic forces whose sole aim is to use up and destroy their victims.

It is pathetic to see mediums and gurus claiming to possess some magical combination lock to the unknown. There is no mystery to summoning up evil spirits. The Bible says, "Your adversary the devil walks about as a roaring lion seeking whom he may devour" (1 Peter 5:8). Satan roams the earth in search of victims, and his demons and minions of evil are constantly prowling in our very midst. Frank Peretti's book, *This Present Darkness,* portrays this reality so very forcefully, it is no wonder the novel has become a national bestseller.

The only thing easier than becoming a willing victim of Satan is renouncing sin and becoming a child of God. Yet, despite the promises of Jesus Christ and the essential simplicity of His message, the New Agers appear to be intent not only on leading millions astray but participating in their own self-destruction.

The leading mystics and seers of the movement have tried to incorporate some of the basic teachings of Christianity with the "all is one" ideology of the Eastern tradition to create a new image of god in man. Their theology is a hodgepodge, at best, but it is a heady mixture for those who have no roots and for those who have an openness to the occult.

The essential heresy of the entire movement is the denial of God's authority and the promotion of man into the role of God. Shirley MacLaine has written, "We already know everything. The knowingness of our divinity is the highest intelligence. And to *be* what we already know is the free will. Free will is simply the enactment of the realization you are God, a realization that you are the divine free will is making everything accessible to you."

Only the ignorant or the deceitful could ever accept such a twisted vision of God, but there are millions of ready converts among us. The Bible also says we should be strong in faith and resist evil. More and more, resisting that evil means we must endure the scorn and abuse of those who call us names, but it is not the laughter or even the violence of the scoffers that we should fear but God Himself, who will certainly judge the unfaithful witness.

SIGNS AND WONDERS

Already the false gods of the movement are gaining power, a power which comes straight from Satan. Accordingly, I believe we can expect to witness Satanic miracles, signs and wonders, and a host of demonic manifestations in the not-too-distant future. None of us should be surprised if during this decade we begin to see many more supernatural events taking place in our world.

Just as Christ foretold, demonic forces will be raging against the church of God, but the power of God will be alive in the church and we will also see incredible signs and wonders through the power of the Holy Spirit.

The clash we will experience, then, will not be between belief and unbelief, but between one form of belief and another. It will be faith in God versus faith in the Devil, and it will be very clear where the people of God will have to make their stand.

At the same time, cults which claim to be Christian will be blossoming among us. Jehovah's Witnesses, Unity, Christian Science, the Way, the Worldwide Church of God, and many others, are actively proselyting in this country and abroad. In every case, the fallacy of their claims is in the denial of the absolute deity of Jesus Christ and His lordship over mankind.

Either by watering down the gospel message or by adding false teachings and false writings to the Word of God, these false doctrines commit the sin of Revelation 22:18 by adding to this record and thereby bring down the wrath of God upon their own heads.

THE STAMP OF SATAN

Communism is also a religious belief, though it is more of a belief in the mechanical determinism of history than in any kind of supernatural force. But within the umbrella of the New Age there is room for a plethora of beliefs—not just the ones mentioned here, but all kinds, from Indian gurus to those who claim to be possessed by disembodied spirits who pass along messages.

There are those who claim to have had out-of-body experiences, some who claim to have been visited by beings from outer space, and others who believe in some kind of occult faith or luck. There is an enormous variety, but they all bear the unmistakable stamp of Satan.

Many of these phenomena can only be explained by reference to demons. So far the Devil and his demons have been hidden. Very few people in America believe in the Devil. They say they believe in God, but they don't believe in these things which are satanic manifestations.

It seems fairly clear that in the next ten years the manifestations will coalesce more and more into a unified whole and their satanic origins will become more and more visible. I think Satan is going to be showing himself.

Of course, there are satanic groups in this country who are nothing more than pornographers in disguise. They are using satanic rituals to make kiddie-porn and to engage in sadistic rituals that really have nothing to do with Satan except the name. Nevertheless, they are there and there is hardly a city in America where there have not been instances of ritual torture and repeated abuse of little children in the name of Satan. There is sexual abuse, physical torture and many instances of dismemberment and death—not only of animals, but of people. This is the work of Satan, and it is on the rise in America.

In some cases, Indian drugs such as peyote have been used in these rites. The Satanist group that murdered the American medical student in Matamoros, Mexico, is one such case. They were engaged in ritual sacrifice, but there was also drug involvement. Unfortunately, there are dozens of these kinds of cults, and they all come under the heading of Hindu thought and structures.

THE RISE OF ISLAM

We will also see a rise of militant Islam in this country during the coming decade. Islam is very active in America; its adherents are building mosques in hundreds of cities and towns. In a special report on the growth of Islam in the *Bible Baptist Tribune,* Dr. James

Combs says that "In the 1990s there will be more Moslems in America than Jews! One out of every five persons on earth is a Moslem."

Money has a way of allowing people to propagate their religious beliefs, and since there is so much oil money flowing into the Arab world, it is being manifested in the spread of Islam into America, especially into the Black community.

The spread of Islam among African-Americans is such an incredible irony. It was the Arab and Muslim merchants in Africa who were the main proponents of the slave trade. They created it. Although English and American ships transported the slaves to the United States, it was the Arab Muslim traders who went into the heartland of Africa, captured the people, brought them to the coast, and sold them to the slavers.

Now to see Black Americans forsaking their Christian heritage, which has produced some of the most beautiful and godly people on earth, in order to turn to Islam—as if that were a way of bringing some sort of national deliverance to them—is utterly absurd and, frankly, heartbreaking.

But Louis Farrakhan and his ilk are pushing a militant and rabidly racist form of Islam which is growing dramatically on the pretext that somehow Islam offers Blacks in the inner-city a chance to express their heritage. That never was the case, and it is a fraud and a lie, but thousands of Blacks are buying it. Farrakhan's anti-Semitism is a matter of public record, yet he draws audiences of tens of thousands whenever he speaks.

There is a large Arab population in America, especially in Michigan and other industrial regions. In its militant, nationalistic form, Islam is a very powerful force. The Arab Brotherhood murdered Anwar Sadat, and fanatic Shiites were responsible for the kidnapings and murders that took place in Lebanon and Iran.

Whether Islam can break out beyond the boundaries of the Middle East into Europe is doubtful, but their continuing growth is still surprising. There is a huge population of people who believe in Islam. If Dr. Combs' estimates are correct, as many as a billion people on earth are Muslims.

The good news is that the Muslims share many common beliefs with Christians. It is a monotheistic religion, and the Allah of the Muslims is essentially the same as Jehovah. Only Christianity, Judaism, and Islam reject an evolutionary concept of man and therefore reject the doctrine of reincarnation. But from there the differences far outweigh the similarities.

It is my feeling that Islam is actually a Christian heresy. It was born at a time when the church was weak, when there was squabbling between Rome and Constantinople and when the theology of the church had degenerated into needless fantasy and speculation. The Christian church had lost both its fervor and its spiritual hold over the people of the Mediterranean world.

When Mohammed appeared on the scene in 622 A.D., he proclaimed himself a new prophet of the historic faith of the Bible. He wrote the books of the Koran very much as Jeremiah and Ezekiel had written the prophetic books of the Old Testament.

When his successors began to launch repeated Islamic Jihads, or holy wars, neither the Christian churches nor the Christian governments in the very cradle of Christianity could stand before them. What was taken has never been recovered. Only tiny Lebanon remained as a Christian enclave in the midst of a Muslim Middle East.

Followers of Mohammed believed in the idea of one God. They also believed in Abraham and Isaac and Ishmael and Jesus; the principal problem for Christians—and it is a very serious problem—is the role assigned to Mohammed as the last prophet and the fact that he did not recognize Jesus Christ as the Messiah, or the Mahdi.

Nevertheless, there is within Islam a tone that can respond somewhat to Christianity. Islam may be considered a Christian heresy, but at least it springs from the Bible. It is not a totally alien religion as is Hinduism.

OF ALIEN GODS

Although dangerous men like Saddam Hussein have called for unification of Muslim nations—what he calls the "Pan Arab World"—Islam is not the spiritual threat that Hinduism will be because Hinduism comes at us much more subtly and has, as its origin, demonic power.

There is really no common ground between the beliefs of Hinduism and the beliefs of Christianity. It is the product of a totally

alien culture and an alien concept of religion which cannot be reconciled in any way with the Christian faith.

The Bible says that it is appointed once for man to die and after that the judgment. There is no possibility of coming back in different forms. Christians believe in the idea of original sin, in the possibility of redemption through faith in a sovereign God. We believe in the unique life of each human being. The Hindus really don't have any concept of a personal God or of sin or redemption by a God-sent personal Savior.

They believe that each human being lives this life then returns as a dog or a cow or a dung beetle, or even as the rain or another human being. Each stage in the transmigration of the soul is, to them, determined by karma. As for social justice, there is no necessity to improve the lot of the poor untouchables because their karma determined their status in life.

For a Westerner brought up according to the compassionate teachings of Jesus Christ, it is virtually inconceivable to behold the misery, the suffering, and the degradation that the Hindu beliefs bring about in a nation like India.

We should also be aware that the genius of the Buddha was to create some escape from the fiendish hell of Hinduism. The salvation he offered, unfortunately, was unattainable. Escape from karma to Nirvana, or paradise, was only possible to those who had ceased all human desire, and that any right-thinking person must realize will never happen short of death itself.

In the rigors of their worship and the attempts to change their karma, Hindus seek physical transcendence through out-of-body experiences, ecstatic trances, and the visitation of alien spirits. Hindu worship is aimed by and large at bribing the angry spirits and buying off the gods with gifts of appeasement, mortification, endless self-degradation, and humiliation. This totally alien system of beliefs can only lead people to poverty, anguish and, ultimately, to demon possession.

Nevertheless, as we have seen, many cults born out of Hinduism will emerge as rivals to the Christian faith during the coming decade. They will come with all the trappings of the New Age, with promises of sensuality and mystical transcendence to rush into the spiritual void existing in our world today. They will offer a host of bogus promises, and millions will believe.

FALSE MESSIAH

Lest anyone dismiss the New Age philosophy and its Hindu roots as too bizarre for serious consideration, we should recall the full-page advertisements announcing the appearance in the world of a new messiah, the Lord Meitreya.

In these advertisements we were told that this messiah figure would come to lead the peoples and governments of the world out of their problems because he would have at his disposal the spiritual wisdom of the ages.

From the time of people like Alice Bailey on, those at the heart of the New Age movement have promised solutions to the imponderable problems of the world through wisdom given to them from beings described as "ascended masters." Obviously these beings are calling for a one world government, the end of national sovereignty, and the elimination of those people who would resist their all-encompassing plans for the world.

I have twice interviewed Tal Brooke, the author of a fascinating book entitled *When the World Will Be One.* Brooke was in India as a disciple of the famed guru, Sai Baba. Sai Baba was in turn reputed to be a disciple of "ascended masters." Brooke told me that when he drew closer to Sai Baba it was evident the human being was no longer present. Sai Baba was completely inhabited by another being: a powerful demon which was giving him the concepts and plans that his disciples so eagerly followed, as well as the miracles which astonished his followers.

It is reasonable to believe that many of the present Western intellectuals and thought leaders who have fought Christianity so vehemently will not now turn to Christianity for their solutions. Instead, they will seek wisdom by becoming disciples of those who offer what appear to be eminently practical solutions served up by the emissaries of Satan himself.

The worldwide struggle in this decade will not be temporal but spiritual. As the apostle Paul put it, "We wrestle not against flesh and blood, but against principalities and powers, against spiritual wickedness in high places, against the rulers of the darkness of this age."

In this decade and beyond, how much more important will it be to weigh every public policy initiative and every church initiative to identify its true source and where it will eventually lead. When leaders speak of "one world" and "a new world order," what do they really mean? Where will their counsel take us?

THE COUNTERBALANCE

Before we succumb to the fear that these various cults, heresies, and New Age counterfeits will totally overtake us, we need to recognize that there has also been a groundswell of Christian renewal throughout the world during the past ten years, and the evidence suggests that trend will accelerate during the coming decade.

I believe that, irrespective of the apparent reason for glasnost, perestroika, and the collapse of communism, the momentum toward freedom was brought about by God as an occasion for evangelism.

As this book is being published, CBN will be in the process of distributing 13 million gospel booklets in Romania, eight broadcasts of Bible stories each week throughout the Soviet Union on Soviet television, the printing of 100,000 Bibles and 100,000 copies of a key Christian book in Poland, the licensing for printing four major Christian books in Hungary, the distribution of 15,000 Bibles in Bulgaria, and the donation of 100,000 dollars to evangelical churches in Czechoslovakia for the paper to print Bibles for that country.

Only two years ago, in Budapest, Hungary, Sandor Nemeth was conducting underground church services in fear of arrest. Now his Sunday services are so huge that his church is forced to meet in a sports arena. During the past year he has established 35 fast-growing satellite churches throughout Hungary.

Reports have reached me of powerful spiritual revival in the Ukraine. The move toward God is so strong in the Soviet Union that people are actually kneeling in Red Square to receive Jesus Christ as their Savior.

Everywhere that I went the message was clear. A spiritual revival of unprecedented magnitude is coming about in the former communist lands. Their reasoning is simple. Communist oppression is equated with atheism, freedom is equated with faith in God.

The needs are immense. There is a crucial need for pastors, for seminaries, and Bible training schools, for programs to train lay leaders, and to give them the tools to assist new converts just coming to the faith.

Even in communist China the religious revival is strong. In 1979, I spoke on the streets to friendly crowds in Guangdong (Canton Province) and Kweilin. Their voracious hunger to receive copies of the Bible and their warm-hearted willingness to receive salvation through Jesus Christ were as intense as anything I have witnessed anyplace in the world.

Although church statistics coming out of mainland China are unreliable, reports reaching me indicate that there are between 50 and 75 million professing Christians in China. Some sources estimate as high as 100 million. A powerful religious revival has been in progress in coastal Fukien Province with demonstrations of faith reminiscent of the New Testament church.

A particularly touching account of revival concerns the resisting students following the brutal suppression of their pro-democracy demonstrations in Tiananmen Square. Reports indicate that entire dormitories of students were renouncing communism and becoming Christians.

THE WORLD OF FAITH

My visits to Eastern Europe, to Central America, and to China have made one thing very clear to me. Communism and war have broken down the entrenched religions and social oligarchies which were opposed to Christianity. In mainland China, Buddhism was suppressed by the communists, and through them, one dialect, Mandarin, is now the only language suitable for conversation throughout the entire nation.

In the Soviet Union, Eastern Europe, and in Nicaragua, the communists repressed all religions and all classes of entrenched privilege. Once communism has been removed, there is now no impediment between the simple gospel of Jesus Christ and the hearts of deeply religious people.

Although North Africa is still hostile to Christianity, past colonial Black Africa is remarkably receptive to the Christian message. Some observers feel that a majority of Africa will be Christian by the end of the decade.

The ministry of German-born evangelist Reinhard Bonnke throughout Africa has been nothing short of phenomenal. In South Africa, Kenya, Burkina Faso, Mali, Malawi, and Nigeria, crowds numbering in the hundreds of thousands have come out to hear Bonnke preach. Sometimes the attendance at his meetings is equal to the entire population of the city in which he is speaking.

The population of the world has now exceeded five billion. Half of that number is made up of people under the age of 18. The total, we are told, exceeds the combined populations of the world from the time of Jesus Christ until now. Certainly this can be the church's finest hour as it experiences a spiritual harvest that could easily number during this decade between 500 million and a billion people.

GROWTH AND RENEWAL

One of the most exhaustive studies ever conducted of church growth in America was developed by Dr. John Vaughan, publisher and editor of the newsletter, "Church Growth Today," and his associates at Southwestern Baptist University in Bolivar, Missouri. The study completed in early 1990 shows that the churches which are growing the fastest are those which are preaching the gospel and sharing the love of Jesus Christ in their communities.

The denominational statistics are especially interesting. Vaughan reports that, of the 512 fastest growing churches in America, 117 are Southern Baptist, 79 are Assembly of God, 37 are independent charismatic, 36 are United Methodist, 29 are independent non-charismatic, 29 are Independent Baptist congregations, 19 are Lutheran Missouri-Synod, 18 are Evangelical Free Church, 14 are Church of Christ, 14 are Presbyterian Church USA, 14 are Presbyterian Church in America, and 10 are Foursquare Gospel.

Atlanta, Los Angeles, Houston and Dallas/Fort Worth topped the list of most spiritually dynamic cities while California, Texas, Florida and Georgia topped the most-dynamic states list.

What we are seeing are churches—such as Calvary Chapel in Costa Mesa, California, and Church on the Rock in Rockwall, Texas—which are not only dynamic congregations themselves, but are spinning off churches in their own cities and sometimes in far-flung communities.

The fastest growing church in America in 1989 was Calvary Chapel in Albuquerque, New Mexico, pastored by Skip Heitzig, a church planted by Chuck Smith's church in Costa Mesa. Congregations are emerging with ten to fifteen thousand people and a tremendous passion for service. They are growing, reproducing themselves, and they are changing the landscape of Christianity in this country.

A few years ago no one would have believed this kind of church growth was remotely possible, but the trend of the '80s is continuing into the '90s and appears to be growing stronger. Part of the reason it is happening now, I suspect, is the fact that Christian broadcasting has been accelerating all through the '80s.

Between 1980 and 1986, CBN recorded some 600,000 decisions for Christ during that time, hundreds of thousands of whom were referred to local churches. We found that the number of decisions were growing dramatically year by year. In 29 years of ministry, we have recorded 1.6 million decisions for Christ and our counselors have received over 35 million telephone calls for help.

Almost all of the new converts and many of those seeking counsel have been referred to local churches. How many thousands more have come from other similar ministries?

THE TURNING POINT

One of the critical points in America's spiritual life during the 1980s was the event called "Washington for Jesus," which Bill Bright of Campus Crusade for Christ has called "the turning point of our century." It was the largest inter-denominational gathering of Christians in the history of the country.

It was estimated that somewhere in the neighborhood of 500,000 people attended that conference, people from every corner of America. There were 45,000 people from the state of Massachusetts alone. There was a trainload from Florida. People flew in from Hawaii. They were from all over, from all races, and they represented every kind of organization, from Cops for Christ, to Catholic outreach ministries and Protestant bishops.

The event featured a tremendous time of prayer for revival in America. Clearly, that had a profound impact on the elections of 1980, on the presidency, and on the shift of influence in the United

States Senate. Washington for Jesus was not in any way a political movement; it wasn't intended to influence politics. It was intended to fulfill 2 Chronicles 7:14 which says, "If my people, who are called by my name, shall humble themselves, and pray, and seek my face, and turn from their wicked ways; then will I hear from heaven, and will forgive their sin, and will heal their land."

It was a time of fasting and prayer and crying out to God for revival in our nation. The country was in a state of malaise, confusion, and drifting moral values. Washington for Jesus was a manifestation of Americans seeking the face of God.

Out of that conference, we believe, came a new sense of national purpose, a new strength of vision, and a new pride in this nation. Two years later there was a sense of national pride we hadn't seen in years. There is no question that God heard and answered prayer.

THE EVANGELICAL RIGHT

Time magazine's cover story, "The Year of the Evangelical," focused on the fact that evangelicals were on the move. Not only did we have a man in the presidency who called himself "born again," but evangelicals were instrumental in bringing in another man into the White House who professed most of the beliefs of the evangelical Christians.

Subsequent to the success of his book, *The Naked Public Square*—which told secular America we could not function as a society without religious and moral values—Richard John Neuhaus penned an article for *Commentary* in which he described "What the Fundamentalists Want," and informed liberal America that, like it or not, "the country cousins have shown up in force at the family picnic.

"They want a few rules changed right away," he said. "Other than that they promise to behave, provided we do not again try to exclude them from family deliberations." The book and the article merely voiced what was already becoming quite clear. Evangelicals had grown sick and tired of being sick and tired, and they were on the move.

Every time a great victory like that happens, it is natural to expect a counterattack. Every victory in battle, until the enemy is totally crushed, will bring forth a counterattack. Unfortunately, the counterattack in this case took place to coincide with my run for the nomination of the Republican Party for the presidency in 1988.

The secular press and those who are anti-Christian in our society were looking for any opportunity to discredit this enormous movement of renewal and revival in our country which was beginning to impact the secular order. They placarded the story of Jim and Tammy Bakker and Jimmy Swaggart on every television network and in the headlines, and they played it over and over again for the better part of two years. And with that they were successful in discouraging evangelicals from giving to all kinds of worthy causes.

Financial support for Christian work dropped dramatically, across the board, whether to the Wycliffe Bible Translators, to interdenominational mission work, or to the various Bible societies. It also had an enormous impact on the local churches and small ministries.

SHAKING THE CHURCH

But the truth is, this assault and regrouping was merely a lull to prepare for something greater. **The Bible makes it clear that judgment begins at the house of the Lord.** Those of us who were looking at what God was doing realized two important things.

First, there could not be a continuation of revival as long as there was spiritual rot in the church: it had to be cleansed and cleansed publicly. But the second thing was that God as a righteous God could not judge the secular world for its evil if He permitted comparable evil within His church. So He first did a work of cleansing and purging.

Now we see that this wasn't bad, it was good. That period of purging laid the foundation for a decade of evangelism which is going to exceed anything we have known in the history of the world. **By shaking out the church, God actually prepared it for the greater challenge to come.**

Using the incredible tools that we have available to us through radio, TV, film, video, high speed printing, and all the various skills that we have accumulated over the past 30 years, it is literally possible to blitz an entire nation for Christ and to bring about a spiritual harvest of unprecedented magnitude. It can be done through the existing church structure so that our churches will be revitalized, trained and equipped, and given the opportunity to become leaders in the education, social welfare, and spiritual life of our communities.

RECLAIMING THE LAND

It is interesting that just as this decade dawned, the Lord enabled us at CBN to start a spiritual blitz into the three major countries of Central America: Guatemala, El Salvador, and Nicaragua. We called it *"Projecto Luz"* (Project Light). Our goal was to see two million decisions for Christ through a massive media blitz that would guarantee that every home throughout these three countries would hear the gospel. We were not disappointed. The response of the churches was overwhelming.

The church in Guatemala applauded our efforts. The ministerial head of the evangelicals in Guatemala told me that he wholeheartedly endorsed the campaign because it did not exalt any man; rather, it exalted Jesus Christ. He said, this was the most unifying thing that had ever happened to those churches.

It was strictly an interdenominational activity to bring people to Christ and to enable the churches to take advantage of the opportunity in accordance with their own spiritual desires. If the local church chose to be active, they could see their church membership tripled or quadrupled in a year's time. And even those who were less diligent could still add a few more members.

In every church there was equal opportunity to reach out as far as they were able. We made available to them a climate in which people would listen to the claims of Christ, and actually receive those claims.

This kind of outreach can be repeated, and I assure you it will be repeated in the East Bloc countries, in the Soviet Union, all over Africa, in parts of the Middle East, in vast areas of Asia, and throughout Latin America. I have heard statistics which indicate that, in Latin America, if the gospel is clearly presented, one out of every two people who hear it will receive Christ on the spot. In Asia, that figure is more like one out of four; and the same figure holds for the United States!

To date, CBN has either initiated or taken part in outreach programs in 85 nations around the world. Our broadcasts have been carried throughout mainland China. In the Middle East, we are beaming the message to a potential audience of some 10 million people, both Arabs and Jews. In Argentina we are preparing a fresh media blitz. One month after this book reaches the bookstores of America, five million Argentinians are expected to have made decisions for Christ.

All that is necessary at the present time is to have a sense of spiritual awareness and revival within the church, and a sense of diligence, and then to take the resources we already have available into the traditional channels of the marketplace of these nations.

The object is not to broadcast on early Sunday morning when very few are watching, but to go into prime time with major spot announcements on the most popular programs on the most popular television and radio stations. We must go where the people are, to be where they're looking and listening. Having done it once in Central America, we now see that the potential harvest is beyond calculation.

THE MINISTRY EXPLOSION

I am convinced the coming decade will see an explosion of ministry, which means the number of people who will hear the gospel in the next few years will be greater than the total number of all those who have heard it, collectively, from the time of Jesus until now.

That means that our evangelistic activities can be more fruitful now, in terms of mass numbers, than at any time since the time of Christ. So the final harvest—and this may well be our final harvest—will be the most glorious in the history of the church.

Logistics became a major factor in the evangelical explosion of the 1980s. Some churches were having to go to three and even four services on Sundays to accommodate the crowds. In one church in Dallas, people literally ran to church to get a seat. You could see them hurrying into the church building to be assured of a place to sit.

Willow Creek Community Church, north of Chicago, has added a Saturday night service as well, and Bill Hybels is preaching to standing-room-only crowds. From a group of just 150 dedicated believers 15 years ago, Willow Creek grew to more than 14,000 members in 1990. That is a far cry from what we used to think of as typical church growth.

There is a real explosion of faith going on in the hearts of believers. But while we see the evangelical faith thriving as never before, we also see that the intellectual theology of doubters and equivocators is dying of self-inflicted wounds. Jesus told the Jews of His day, "The kingdom of God will be taken from you and given to those bearing the fruit thereof."

There is no question that the mainline churches—the Episcopal, Presbyterian, Methodist, Lutheran and other historic denominations—have been hemorrhaging members for the past 25 years. The reason is that, by and large, they have moved away from the clear proclamation of Jesus Christ, Who declared, "I am the way, the truth, and the life. No one comes to the Father but by Me."

In mid-1990, UPI reported on a study by the Lilly Endowment which indicates that doctrinal and political divisions in the mainline churches are eating away at these congregations. Episcopalians, Congregationalists, and Presbyterians were the dominant institutions in this nation for more than two centuries, since long before the Declaration of Independence.

Today, the UPI article suggests, it looks like the mainline has headed to the sidelines. After holding a near-monopoly on government in this country, the Presbyterians have lost fully a third of their membership in the past 25 years, along with much of their clout.

On January 29, 1990, Bishop Maurice M. Benitez, of the Episcopal Diocese of Texas, told the Church Club of New York, "Over the past twenty years the Episcopal Church dropped from 3.5 million baptized members to 2.5 million members." He then added,

> St. Paul and the other apostles did not barnstorm the Mediterranean world preaching social justice, preaching abolition of slavery, or calling the Roman Empire to provide housing for the homeless and a more equitable economic system. They preached Jesus Christ, crucified and raised from the dead for our salvation. They called all who would listen to repent, to turn their lives around . . .

The denominations that have permitted the secularization of their seminaries and the liberalizing of their theology have lost their grip on the core of the faith. They have forgotten the words of Christ when He said, "Except a man be born again, he shall in no wise see the kingdom of heaven." Instead, they have chosen to preach a "social Gospel," to dwell on the so-called "higher criticism" of scholars such as Bultmann, Heidegger, and others who cast doubt on the authenticity of the Bible, the miracles, and on Jesus Christ Himself.

THE LIBERAL AGENDA

As Jim Reapsome, editor of *Evangelical Missions Quarterly,* pointed out in a recent series, "Liberals claim that the world sets the agenda for the church. God's kingdom, they say, is not established by proclaiming the unique salvation message of Jesus Christ, but by restructuring the world's social, political, and economic order."

In the National Council of Churches, these people have further allied themselves with leftist movements in America, the most shocking of which was perhaps the contribution of 10,000 dollars by the Presbyterian Church to the Defense Fund of the Marxist radical, Angela Davis.

When I was in Colombia in the 1970s, a Presbyterian missionary told me of a 75,000 dollar gift that was going to support a rebel group seeking the overthrow of the democratically elected government of Colombia.

University of Oregon sociologist Benton Johnson, in his study of the Presbyterian Church U.S.A., reports that less than 55 percent of Presbyterians confirmed in the 1960s are still active in churches. Between 1970 and 1987, the denomination lost more than a million members.

Even though hard times have forced the social churches to rethink some of their policies, the Presbyterian General Assembly which met in Salt Lake City in June 1990 announced that the environment would be a major thrust of the denomination for the '90s and that the liturgy would now profess the female as well as male attributes of God.

It appears the people in the pews just don't want any part of that. They want their souls to be fed, and they want to have the faith proclaimed by men of God who know God and who are willing to teach that faith and to build them up in the faith once delivered to the saints. And when they don't get it, they leave.

God removes His hand from those churches which refuse to serve Him. The money dries up, and the churches inevitably fall into disrepair. And the pundits proclaim that God is dead, but God is not dead. He will not submit His Spirit to churches that *are* dead. God is very much alive and He is looking for men and women who believe it.

A DECADE OF OPPORTUNITY

The church is booming in America. Certain expressions of it are dying on the vine, but that can change. There are signs of revival in the Anglican and Episcopal churches. There are pockets of revival in the Methodist and the Presbyterian churches, but only in those congregations where Christ is being preached and the truth of Scripture is being proclaimed. God's Spirit will not remain in an atmosphere of compromise; but where Christ is preached, He lives.

In the inspired words of Bishop Benitez,

> I declare that people are looking for something, someone in whom they can believe, for a faith on which they can bet their lives . . . People in our world, people in our pews, are hungry for spiritual renewal, hungry not for more meetings, or more social issues, or more turmoil, they are hungry for God, and yearn to know His presence and power in their lives. People will go to a church that believes that Jesus Christ is the Way and the Truth and the Life and says it.

If there is to be revival in the land, it will not come through compromise and equivocation but through that kind of fervent faith in and passionate commitment to the gospel.

> **Today the world is poised for a spiritual revival. This is an incredible decade of opportunity for the Christian church.**
>
> **Age old barriers to missionary activity have fallen and billions of people are open to receive the claims of Jesus Christ.**
>
> **But if the Christian church fails, or if we fail to reach out with the genuine nourishment of God's Word, the world's present spiritual hunger will most certainly be filled with the Hindu-based spirituality of the New Age.**

PART TWO

The Tri-lateral World

The United States borders two oceans, one facing Europe, the other facing Asia. . . . American people and American business can no longer comfort themselves by crowing over our superiority. All of us from now on are on a course of continuous gut-wrenching change and fierce competition from East and West. We will no longer be insulated from any development in our world whether it takes place in Brussels or Berlin, Moscow or the Persian Gulf, Tokyo or Beijing.

5

The Unification
of Europe

Long weak and divided, Europe will soon unite as a powerful equal of the United States.

Unification should mean trade, investment potential, and jobs for Americans. Together we should share a rapidly growing world economy. But dangers exist.

Are powerful forces pulling strings to fold Western Europe, Eastern Europe, Japan, and the United States into a one world political system?

When the final documents are signed and the official oaths are sworn, the world will experience an event reminiscent of that Christmas day in 800 A.D. when Charlemagne was crowned by Pope Leo III as emperor of a United Europe, then termed the Holy Roman Empire. For on December 31, 1992, in furtherance of what is called "The Single Europe Act," a European community will be formed as an economic and quasi-political federation of the twelve nations of France, Germany, Great Britain, Italy, Spain, Holland, Belgium, Ireland, Luxembourg, Denmark, Portugal, and Greece.

With its parliament in Strasbourg and its executive offices in Brussels, the single Europe will encompass a population of 323 million and a gross national product which at 4.274 trillion dollars will be about 19 percent smaller than the United States GNP and roughly equal to the combined output of Japan and the fast-growth economies of the Pacific Rim.

The current arrangement leaves more questions than answers. Will this be a loose customs union, or will there emerge a United States of Europe similar to the United States of America? Will the single Europe be a responsible trading partner for America, or will it erect barriers to shut out our products?

Why is the demise of communism in the Soviet Union occurring as if on cue to coincide with the 1992 European Union? Is this mere coincidence, or are powerful forces pulling strings in order to fold Western Europe, Central Europe, and Eastern Europe into some one world political system yet to be unveiled?

Of particular interest is the issue of a single European currency and a single European Central Bank. A European-style Federal Reserve Bank setting interest rates and regulating money supply would effectively negate national sovereignty among the twelve member nations. Why was Margaret Thatcher of Great Britain set upon so thoroughly by the establishment press when she chose to defend British sovereignty by opposing a Central European Bank?

What will happen to the freedom of every American if a European Central Bank were to combine with the seven-member American Federal Reserve Bank and they, in turn, were to combine its efforts with a seven-member Japanese or perhaps Japan-Asia Central Bank?

Such an arrangement might make the world's finances neat and tidy, but it would also mean that as few as twenty-one non-elected officials would control the money of the world! We can hark back to Lenin who declared that if he could control the world's money he would not care what else others controlled.

Regrettably, the time has already come when the interest rates paid by every American family or business are not being set just in Washington but by investors and bankers in Tokyo, Bonn, London, and Hong Kong. A group of powerful world leaders meeting under the auspices of what is known as the Tri-Lateral Commission—which is directly linked in turn to the New York-based Council on Foreign Relations—has repeatedly called for a "new world order" based essentially on a one world government.

This means a diminished role for national sovereignty, especially for the United States of America. It means that the destiny of every American family would be taken from their hands, from the hands of their own elected officials, and given to some yet-to-be-determined supra-national governing body.

It hardly takes a genius to see that a closely coordinated world monetary policy between only three powerful central banks could bring about a de facto one world system long before the average man on the street knew what was going on. It could happen long before any elected official was even given the opportunity to vote on it.

The book of Revelation warns of a time in history when economic control will be so tight that no one could buy or sell without the identification number of the worldwide dictator.

Such gloomy thoughts aside, when most of us think of a United Europe we think of burgeoning markets to buy American goods. We think of prosperous Europeans visiting America and investing in our businesses, our securities, our real estate.

We see exciting opportunities to participate in an ever-growing world economy with those nations that produced our ancestors and many of our Western institutions, and with whom we as a nation have shared common ideals for centuries. We see in Europe those nations whose freedom we defended in two bitter world wars and whose economies we helped rebuild with the Marshall Plan.

We think of historic towns and cities that we have visited. Of universities where many of us have studied. Indeed, Western Europe's prosperity should be our prosperity, and a single Europe should mean jobs for Americans, a greater variety of goods for our consumers, and tremendous investment opportunities for our businesses.

Yet lingering in the back of the mind of every Christian should be one other question. A United Europe in 1992 will not be a "holy empire." Western Europe is probably the most cynical and irreligious part of the entire world. One stroll through the red light district of Amsterdam or Hamburg would shock even the most jaded.

Paul Henri Spaak, one of the primary post-World War II architects of a United Europe is reported to have blurted out the following: "Give us a man to solve our problems, and be he a god or a devil, we will follow him."

Could the bright hope we share for the future of a United Europe be dashed in the new millennium by the appearance of a charismatic leader who, like Adolf Hitler, resembles the Anti-Christ of the Bible?

Only time will tell.

HOW IT HAPPENED

For many years, political power in Western Europe has been controlled largely by its Christian Democratic parties. The tradition that began after World War II under the leadership of an Italian priest, Luigi Sturzo, has included such illustrious leaders as Konrad Adenauer of Germany, Robert Schuman of France, and Alcide de Gasperi of Italy. West German chancellor Helmut Kohl, of the Christian Democratic Union (CDU), is probably the best known of today's Christian Democratic leaders.

The founders of all these parties had deep Christian convictions which gave a focus and purpose to their political beliefs. The principles of their faith conformed their commitment to their culture. Furthermore, as reported by *The Economist* in March 1990, the founders of the movement were also the true founders of the European Community. As early as 1920 they were meeting to discuss the possibilities of a unified Europe based on principles of faith and service.

One of the unifying factors of these various national groups was French philosopher Jacques Maritain's concept of "personalism," which is the belief that mankind fulfills his innate purpose through service to others, particularly to his family and his community. Their idea of personalism was, therefore, strongly opposed to the competing beliefs of "liberal individualism" and "social collectivism" which have begun to dominate European political thought in recent years.

Even though many of these parties—in Italy, France, Germany, Holland, and Belgium—have continued to hold power, they have tended to do so over the past three decades by compromising with more liberal positions, by sacrificing principles for votes.

Fernan Herman, a member of the European Parliament and former Belgian minister of economy, claims "Christian Democracy has lost its soul and should go into opposition. The leaders now," he says, "accept anything to stay in power and they disregard our principles and traditions."

Herman scolded his colleagues, reminding them that they were the first federalists, "but now we focus too much on domestic politics and leave it to socialists like Delors and Mitterrand to push forward European integration."

LOOKING BEYOND THE WALL

The collapse of the Berlin Wall has done more than create new commerce in Europe, however, and conservative leaders among the Christian Democrats are pointing to the marriage of faith and political power that has brought new life to Poland, Hungary, Romania, Czechoslovakia, and all the rest of Eastern Europe. In those countries, they say, "50 years of persecution have made the new or revived Christian political groups unashamedly forthright."

Even the Soviet Union has a rapidly growing Christian Democratic Party whose chairman, Victor Aksyuchits, told *Forbes* magazine for its August 20, 1990, issue,

> Social democracy, when it looks to the West, only sees material wealth. We, on the other hand, understand that the concept of Western liberalism (in its traditional sense) could only arise as the heir to Christian Civilization. Only the conviction that man is created in the image of God makes the individual inherently valuable.

To add evidence to their outcry, the Christian Democrats also cite the example of a group in Italy, called Communion and Liberation, which claims more than 100,000 active members and whose aim is "to put Christ at the centre of life and society." The party operates radio stations, businesses, publishing houses, and "solidarity centres" which offer training for the unemployed. *The Economist* reports that the group's most recent annual festival and political debate, in Rimini, Italy, drew more than 700,000 attendees, "most of them young."

The Christian leaders say there is no reason to cower in the shadows of the political arena when these others have proved that courage and dedication can give them authentic victory. The communists have failed, they say, and there is a window of opportunity today for Christian Democrats who will dare to hold fast to their convictions.

But the challenge is apparently not being taken up. Most spectators are predicting that the secular socialist position will continue to grow more rapidly than the conservative position in Europe and, consequently, the more secular parties, such as Kohl's CDU, will likely become the new model for European politics.

OF EMPIRE AND IDEOLOGY

The Unification of 1992 will be the final culmination of a plan signed into being in March 1957 at a conference of six European nations, which has come to be known as the Treaty of Rome. That document established the Common Market as the administrative headquarters of Europe for trade and trans-national dialog. Further, the treaty set forth the principles of an integrated market system based on "the four freedoms": free movement of goods, services, capital, and people.

Over the past thirty years, the European Community (EC) has grown to a league of twelve nations and has gone through periods of strife and compromise followed by periods of slow and painful consolidation some have called "Eurosclerosis."

During that time thousands of principles and policies have been enacted, most of which have required that delegates of the Community return to their homes and ensure that their respective nations make whatever changes may be required in their internal policies in order to bring all these disparate nations (and baroque bureaucratic systems) into accord before Unification Day in 1992.

Needless to say, it has not been an easy process. How do you get Italians to agree with Frenchmen? And how do you get Belgians to accept a policy introduced by the Dutch? Politics has played an enormous role, but time and determination seem to have made a difference and, today, it does look as if the unification will take place as planned.

Part of the jockeying in the EC has been due to both perceived and real differences in character and worldview. For example, most of the member nations still admit to fear of the German state, since that nation was responsible for the two greatest conflagrations of this century. On the other hand, Germany's administrative and economic programs are as polished and efficient as their machinery, and the other European nations realize they very much need leaders with those traits.

ISSUES OF NATIONAL CHARACTER

Germany's role is already beginning to loom large in the unification game. The re-unification of the two Germanys in October 1990 will have economic consequences in the near future, but it is already having political and emotional consequences.

An accord in 1979 gave Germany's Bundesbank dominant influence over the European Monetary System (EMS) and its Exchange Rate Mechanism (ERM). That more than anything else has caused concern for Britain's Prime Minister, Margaret Thatcher, who has refused to submit the British pound or the English economic system to the EC or the Bundesbank.

Mrs. Thatcher disagrees with the protectionist-isolationist tendencies of the EC and its president, Jacques Delors, and favors a market-driven economy which would encourage the current open exchange with world nations, such as the United States. *Forbes* magazine quoted one American observer, Stanislav Yassukovich of Merrill Lynch, as saying that "The Continentals expect an institution-led approach. Her approach is more American; theirs reflects the influence of Catholic socialism. You have two fundamentally opposed political traditions."

Jacques Delors, in particular, has helped to foster the strongly socialist institutional policies of the EC. In fact, the blueprint for the Unification of 1992, frequently called the "Delors Report," calls for uniform economic policies imposed upon member nations by the EC. It calls for a *"transfer of decision-making power* from Member States to the Community," which means that the real power of the twelve independent nations of united Europe would actually rest in a single body, or worse, in a single man.

Along with that, Delors is big on social programs such as minimum wage and maximum work-week restraints. He would do away with the availability of "cheap labor" which (as in Asia, or the American Southwest) has given many smaller, poorer nations a distinct economic advantage in an increasingly competitive marketplace.

Having barely fought her own (and Britain's) way out of the depths of the socialist quagmire, Margaret Thatcher has no interest in going back into the pits. She inflamed her liberal opponents by saying so in a brilliant speech in Bruges, Belgium in September 1988. At that meeting she said, "We have not successfully rolled back the frontiers of the state in Britain only to see them reimposed at a European level with a European superstate exercising a new dominance from Brussels."

Her critics at home and abroad accuse Mrs. Thatcher of denying Britain a chance to compete fairly in the new Europe. They say she is obstinate and obstructionist. Ironically, *Forbes* also reports that Mrs. Thatcher's government has really been the most effective in actually implementing the various EC policies handed down by the administration in Brussels. Of the 88 directives, Britain has enacted 69. Italy, by comparison, has enacted 35. Only Denmark has enacted more.

Most observers of the ongoing debates and negotiations say it is also clear that the Delors economic model is exclusionist and protectionist, and that his trade plan specifically militates against free trade with the United States. That is another limitation Margaret Thatcher will not abide.

In concluding her remarks in Bruges, she made an appeal for a united Europe "which looks outward—not inward—and which preserves that Atlantic community—that Europe on both sides of the Atlantic—which is our noblest inheritance and our greatest strength." Clearly, she was referring to the United States.

THE TRI-LATERAL WORLD

Europe's unification finally brings into alignment a three-way division of world power than has been predicted for some time. The EC will quickly become the dominant force in the European sphere, surpassing NATO, the defunct Warsaw Pact, the communist economic organization, COMECON, and other agencies and organizations which once gave focus to the multinational interests of Western and Eastern Europe.

A world away, Japan, despite its troubles with a faltering stock market and sporadic economic readjustments, continues its plans to unite with China and its neighbors throughout Asia and the Pacific

Rim. The combined economic impact of a trading block which includes the major nations of Asia will be staggering, and the Japan-Asia league will be a mighty player in the coming tri-lateral world.

Finally, the ongoing economic and diplomatic consolidations between Canada, Mexico, and the United States, part of a North American Free Trade Zone, will form the third leg of the triangle which may set the tone for the world of the future.

According to the statistics of the International Monetary Fund, for the period 1981-1987, the three economies already stack up as generally equal competitors for global markets. Without the input of figures from China, Korea, or any of the other Asian partners, Japan's Gross National Product (GNP) is 2.9 trillion dollars. Comparatively, the combined GNP of the 12 EC nations is 4.3 trillion while the United States GNP just tops 5.2 trillion dollars.

On the same scale, Japan's population base is 123 million, while the EC reports 323 million and the USA 270 million. Perhaps the most interesting relationship of those numbers is the Per Capita GNP of the three. This time, Japan's tally is 23,600 dollars per person while the EC's is 13,300 dollars per person and the United States is 19,300. Suddenly the relationship comes more into balance.

Analysts project the EC's overall GNP to rise about 4.5 percent after unification, compared to a projected rise of about 2 percent in the United States. During the coming decade we will see those figures fleshed out with greater precision and, doubtless, we will see a greater parity between these three rivals.

INTERPRETING THE SIGNS

So what is the real consequence of all these matters for us in the decade ahead? For one thing, the way the European Community develops may have just as much historical and social impact on the world in the next ten years as the collapse of communism. The forms established now will determine the EC's role in world affairs well into the new millennium.

Europe's unification will give these 12 nations enormous clout in the increasingly competitive and complicated world economy. However, in a purely economic sense, the union of Europe has many complex implications for the United States, as it does for all the other players in the world economy. Many are good; some are bad.

While we once dealt with Germany or France or Italy as separate nations—with separate currencies and separate trade policies—unification will change all that. Now there will be a single currency, a uniform trade policy, very likely a single banking community, and twelve nations will deal effectively as one global superpower.

Unification has given these countries a feeling of "European" nationalism and an *esprit de corps* previously unknown to them, and it comes at a time when national pride was flagging badly. A 1989 Gallup Poll reported that only 41 percent of Italians, 33 percent of French, 21 percent of Germans, and 19 percent of Dutch express pride in their nationality. In citing this report, *Business Week* concluded that the idea of a powerful united Europe may appeal to citizens of these nations in search of some sort of "higher nationalism."

Germans in particular seem to find some relief in broadening their national identification. Haunted by the ghosts of their past, many would agree with Hartmut Ruge, managing editor of a German newspaper quoted recently in *Time* as saying, "We are part of the rubble generation, a generation of moral disorientation and guilt. Now there is normality."

The generation that lived through the last war has had to endure the recriminations and reprisals of a half century. Many, like Manfred Poeck, also quoted in *Time,* find remembering painful. "I have real problems with our past," he says, "a sense of deep shame." All agree that their new identity as "Europeans" mandated by unification helps to exorcise the demons of history.

WE ARE EUROPEANS

I recognized this attitude on my recent trip to Hungary. I thought it was striking that young political leaders I talked to said to me, "We are Europeans." They are not just Hungarians any more, but Europeans. And I think this attitude of European pride is going to be felt more and more, in Germany, but also in Austria, in the Benelux countries, as well as in France and Spain. More and more people are going to say, "We are part of Europe. We are a world superpower. Now you will have to take us more seriously."

Beyond a certain nationalistic arrogance, the promise of world power can create certain expectations in government and business leaders which are not altogether healthy.

As I suggested above, perhaps the greatest immediate concern to American interests abroad is the initiative for currency control being put forth by Jacques DeLors in his attempts to create a European Central Bank. This central bank would level, effectively, the national interests of all the various countries.

While it might centralize and simplify many complex procedures, solve exchange rate problems, and provide certain other advantages for businesses involved in international trade, it would also be in control of all the currency of those twelve countries. It would, thereby, have enormous financial leverage and could manipulate markets and economies on a grand scale in order to improve its own financial position or perhaps to discriminate in favor of its own industries and holdings.

If we think the recent scandals on Wall Street are bad; if we're afraid of a few men who can drive the stock market up or down for personal gain; or if we recognize the legitimate dangers of the S&L collapse we are going through in this country, just think about the dangers of giving a handful of men the power to control the entire economic resources of a dozen nations.

If it chose, the European Central Bank could bring about inflation or deflation on demand. And if linked with the Federal Reserve Bank of Washington and the Central Bank of Japan—which has already been discussed—it would put absolute economic control of the world in the hands of 21 or 22 people.

AN ECONOMIC CARTEL

Frankly, that's a frightening prospect. These would be non-elected representatives who would effectively control the money supply of the entire world. They would be involved in hundreds of billions of dollars in transactions every single day, and could, thereby, affect the ultimate destiny of the entire world.

This is the thing that is most worrisome to me about the "New Europe." I am concerned that somehow the real power would fall into the hands of a few bankers. However honest or reliable they may be in the beginning, or at any point for that matter, the potential for corruption and mismanagement is just too great.

The thrust of the thinking in Europe now is that the banking community would not be autonomous as it is in the United States, but that it would be responsive to the European Parliament in Strasbourg. But that parliament, in turn, is unapologetically socialistic, generally militant against traditional Western-style capitalism, and some of the delegates are quite radical in their personal beliefs.

We know only too well from our own experience, and from the recent experience of Eastern Europe and the Soviet Union, that socialism will destroy a free market economy and lead to enslavement of the people. We have lived that nightmare, and we can't afford to fall into that trap again.

THE ATLANTIC ALLIANCE

Because of its enormous strength, the European Community has the potential of being a very valued ally to the United States. We have a deep, long-standing relationship with Great Britain, and we have great affection for our allies and trading partners throughout Europe. Even though they have often deserted us—even scorned us—in our efforts to defend Western Democracy, we recognize our common heritage and destiny with them, and we want the best for them.

But at the same time, if Europe continues its flirtation with socialism and secularism, and particularly if it closes its doors to the influence of the United States, it could conceivably become the foundation for some type of dictatorial regime based 100 percent on a humanistic system, whose values are not only very different from our own, but threatening to them.

Despite the efforts of the Christian Democrats, and especially the Catholic Church in many countries, Europe is a post-Christian society and a thoroughly hedonistic culture. We can only pray that the flame of Christianity which has emerged from Eastern Europe—unextinguished and more powerful than anyone ever dared to imagine—may be the spark that ignites a great revival throughout Western Europe as well. But that is still just a hope and a prayer at this moment.

If the united Europe continues to develop as it has, there is always the possibility that those who have resented us in the past because of our economic or military power might discover the new-found power and unity of Europe as some means of redress.

There are many in Europe who resent the United States because of what they may have perceived as our meddling in their national affairs. There are some who resent us for our part in World War II.

The formation of a new, more powerful league of nations could give those voices a means of settling old scores. At the present moment they are our friends and our allies, and it is obviously a place where American business needs to be. But all these relationships are in some jeopardy until we can see better how it will develop. I believe this will be an area of great concern for Americans over the next decade.

FORTRESS EUROPE vs. FORTRESS USA

Charges have flown back and forth between business leaders in the United States and Europe over the last few years, Americans charging the EC of having a fortress mentality, excluding the U.S. and everybody else from their country club, and the Europeans saying they're just trying to get into position to deal with giants like America and Japan on an equal basis. There seems to be a lot of insecurity on both sides, but the formation of the European Community is going to bring about great advantages to its member countries.

It is clear that the EC will offer some type of associate memberships for countries outside the immediate European Community but still within the European land mass, but it is equally clear that there will be walls set up against the United States and Japan.

The creation of trade barriers and other restrictions of one kind or another will definitely change our current relationships, and in the beginning that will probably hurt us economically. But in time, I suspect that for its own self-interest the EC will have to make some accommodations for a more or less open market between the world's major trading nations.

To ensure their right to participate in the European market, many American companies are already rushing to get in on the action. They are buying European companies, opening plants and facilities in Europe, and creating various kinds of subsidiaries so they can get products produced and marketed inside the EC.

In the newest comprehensive study of the unification compiled by the Brookings Institution, Gary Hufbauer reports that the percentage of United States foreign investment stock placed in the EC rose from about 18 percent in 1960 to nearly 40 percent in 1988. Our trade balance with Europe fell substantially during that period of time, but some sources report that U.S. exports have climbed into surplus with Europe in the last two years.

Hufbauer reports in the book, *Europe 1992,* that U.S. firms already doing business in Europe see the coming unification as a bonanza, and they are not so much concerned about trans-Atlantic relations as they are about improved relations within Europe.

It is not surprising, he writes, that the principal organizations which speak for American business—the Business Roundtable, the U.S. Council for International Business, and the U.S. Chamber of Commerce—are enthusiastic about Europe 1992.

Although the community could be a great benefit as an ally to America in the years ahead, chances are it's going to wind up being a formidable rival. Combining the industrial and economic strength of the twelve European nations will change the face of the world as we know it.

These are ancient and proud countries with a deep sense of history and culture. They have been down—economically, militarily, and spiritually—for a long time, and now they are glowing with a sudden burst of entrepreneurial vigor. That chemistry cannot help but produce a gigantic impact.

RECONSTRUCTION IN THE EAST

In dramatic contrast to the growing prosperity in the West, Eastern Europe is extremely primitive in terms of economics. Their factories are hopelessly out of date. Their labor force is unskilled. They are choking in pollution. The Vistula River is essentially dead. Southern Poland, the Silesia area, is choked with filth.

In the cities of Romania, especially where there is heavy mining, the people are gasping with lung diseases and birth defects and other serious illnesses caused by pollution. This seems to be endemic in nations such as Poland which have been under the iron heel of communism for so many decades.

What happened at Chernobyl is merely one example of the communist system's callous disregard for the health and safety of its people. The explosions at the atomic energy plant at Chernobyl and the massive radiation exposure and resulting murders of untold thousands of people (as a direct result of the government's attempt to cover up the magnitude of that disaster) only prove what we already knew: that communism is not concerned with the life of the individual.

The big thing in any "socialistic" system is to produce, to get something out of the laborers, and to keep the wheels of industry rolling, regardless of what it does to the ecology or how much it may devastate the lives of individual men, women, and children.

It will cost multiplied billions of dollars to clean up the environment in that entire region of the Soviet Union. Recent evidence from studies in northern Europe indicate that Finland, Scandinavia and the Baltic countries may be contaminated by the nuclear fallout from that disaster and entire generations are doomed to suffer cancers, leukemia, and other radiation-related diseases.

Apparently the shocks to the ecology from the Soviet Union are still not over. Intelligence expert, Jack Wheeler, reports that in May of 1990 thousands of tons of rocket fuel leaked out of a storage tank at the nuclear submarine facility at Sverodvinsk. *Pravda* reported that one third of all marine life in that area of the White Sea, including five million fish and 100,000 seals, died as a result of the spill.

In the Siberian oil fields there have been 1,100 pipeline breaks and subsequent leaks causing the staggering loss of 700,000 tons of crude oil by August of 1990. Wheeler expressed his amazement that not one mention of these huge ecological disasters has ever appeared in the Western media.

It's going to cost the emerging communist nations billions more to overcome the infrastructure's deficiencies and to upgrade or replace their antiquated plants and equipment. But what the Eastern Europeans do have is a literate population and a tradition of high-quality workmanship that goes back centuries. At this point in time, though, they are still poor, underpaid in relation to the West, and they don't produce as much.

The Eastern European countries are like economic babes in the wilderness. Yet, from a spiritual standpoint they are much stronger than their counterparts in the West: they have been persecuted for their faith and have endured. They have been willing to fight and die for their freedom, and they have come to appreciate freedom so much more than anybody who has always taken it for granted ever can.

The men and women of Eastern Europe are willing to make sacrifices for the important things of life, and that depth of character and courage won't go away—at least not among the Christian people—any time soon.

On the one hand the West can infuse the East with the latest advances their technology can provide—computer skills, accounting and marketing expertise, manufacturing knowhow, and all the things needed to upgrade the standard of living—but the East has the potential to bring to the West a level of faith and dedication that has been unknown there for decades.

TECHNOLOGY'S GODS

It just could be one of God's wonderful ironies that the impulse to bring Europe back to Himself and to give them a chance at revival will come from these former strongholds of communism.

Even if that is to be the case, it will still be a struggle. Western Europe has been thoroughly secularized over the past forty years. In Germany as few as one percent of the people go to church. There is a type of thinking there that is totally anti-Christian and post-Christian, and the people have no understanding of even the most basic spiritual foundations of Christian life and behavior. That type of ignorance in Western Europe may well be harder to overcome than the mere technological ignorance of the East.

I was in Bavaria recently, in the Garmisch-Partenkirchen area of the Bavarian Alps, when a young man who had seen me on my television program came up to speak to me. He was a bright, handsome young man who had been with the Unifil forces on the border between Lebanon and Israel and had seen the 700 Club broadcast on Middle East Television.

When I asked him about his concept of God, he told me he didn't know much about God. "Actually, I don't believe in God," he said. "But if there is a God, He is certainly not the one you talk about on television. I don't know, maybe God is a computer."

Needless to say, I was saddened by his casual concept of the Creator, but even more, I was staggered by his apparent willingness to accept a computer as an object of worship if it simply possessed enough intelligence to take care of people's basic demands.

If there were a computer smart enough—and I have no doubt there will be some very sophisticated and intelligent machines in the not too distant future—this young man would worship it as his god. If the computer says, "I have the answers. I have unparalleled science and technology at my disposal. I will see that there are no more wars, and I will give you the means to have prosperity and a happy life," many would follow. This young man was willing, essentially, to deify intelligence, whatever kind of intelligence manifested itself. And I fear he is not unique.

That isn't too far away from what we read in the book of Revelation. John's prophecy indicates that there will be some incredible intelligence who will know where everybody is and will have great power for good as well as evil. And through the power of this super intelligence, there will be economic controls, so that the people can buy and sell only with the authority of the state, or with some kind of a mark or token of submission to the state.

But to think that this intelligent, college-trained Austrian would say, "Whoever God is, maybe he's a computer," just absolutely astounded me. And I'm afraid that he is much more typical of the emerging young generation in Europe today than we dare to think possible.

THE INSTITUTIONS OF COMMUNISM

It appears that the Warsaw Pact is finished as a military alliance, and what has been called COMECON, the economic alliance of Soviet satellites and communist-led countries, is essentially dead because the Soviet Union doesn't have anything of value with which to pay for its imports.

The United States and Europe will not take Soviet rubles, and all the Soviets have to export is gold and oil, and they don't have very much of them. So they desperately need Western support.

East Germany has already effectively joined West Germany as one nation. That big, powerful nation is going to set the tone in Western Europe. Before anything was signed, West German industrialists raced into the East to grab up everything of value while they still had an enormous capital advantage.

The big manufacturing plants, trading companies, and retailers have moved in to establish beachheads and to buy up East German companies as fast as they can. As the merger uniting East and West Germany as one nation takes final form, those frontrunners will be in a controlling position.

The same thing is happening—though perhaps to a lesser degree—in Poland, Hungary, and Czechoslovakia. There is a tremendous movement of capital into those countries from Western Europe.

Once that happens, corporations in Germany, Austria, Italy, France, and other Western European nations will begin to put pressure on their governments to make concessions for goods coming out of the Eastern countries. In fact, in lieu of gigantic direct subsidies to East Bloc countries which will end up creating debt and dependency, the best way Western Europe can help the Eastern Europeans come back to economic health is through trade concessions and private investment. It looks as if that may be happening now.

It is not likely that East Bloc countries will be allowed to be members of the European Community, but they will most likely be accorded a favored trading relationship as associate members with full economic privileges for their goods, and a close relationship with the rest of Europe.

THE MORAL DILEMMA

Beyond political considerations, the moral collapse in Western Europe has reached epidemic proportions and, unfortunately, West Germany seems to be leading the way.

Even *Time* magazine seemed shocked by its own report in July 1990 that West German theater has sunk to the "vilest displays of the body onstage" along with the "vilest displays of the mind." In the article, *Time*'s reporter in Berlin offered a revolting inventory of crude and vulgar displays.

"Onstage vomiting, with visual effects, four times, including a mass upheaval by a dozen actors at once. Excretion, with sound effects, three times. Full frontal nudity, three times, plus two lavish displays of dildoes. Onstage copulation, involving every imaginable combination of genders, countless times in seven separate works. Plus incest, transvestism, self-mutilation, murder." And that is only a partial tally.

Now in Munich, Hamburg, Bremen, Bochum, Schwerin, and stages in East and West Berlin, such degradation is becoming common public fare. And to make matters worse, it is being supported at taxpayer expense. As much as 1.5 billion dollars a year is doled out to theater groups to bathe their audiences in obscenity.

But the public goes to these performances, and while a handful scoff or walk out of the theater, there is wild and exuberant applause from the majority. One can only wonder where it will lead. If this is public morality in West Germany, generally acknowledged by most Europeans as the most likely leaders of the forthcoming unification, what can be in store for the rest of the Continent?

For centuries men and women have considered such graphic display as immoral, degrading, and dehumanizing, for it sinks to the lowest and basest form of human experience. Since Plato, the aim of Art has been to present images of life and nature which are "elevating," not "degrading."

The masochistic absorption with filth and vulgarity displays a depraved state of the soul. The degradation of "art" to "pornography" proves that the soul of Europe may well be on its way to utter dehumanization.

When the first Westerners crossed the Berlin Wall in late 1989 and early 1990, they saw the stunned looks on the faces of the East Berliners coming out, as it were, to the light of a new day. One American pastor asked some of them how they felt about the possibility of reunification with the West, and he was shocked at their answer.

"We are happy," said one young woman, "but we are scared."

Pursuing that answer, the American asked why she felt both those emotions.

"We're happy for freedom," she responded. "We haven't much money, but we can buy in the stores now, and goods in the West are much better. We can also see our loved ones. But we are afraid for our country, afraid now we will be exposed to your Western materialism, to much greater crime, and to drugs and pornography."

What a sad, wise answer. For forty years the socialist government had denied the noble aspirations of its people; ironically, it had also shielded them from those aspects of Western culture of which we should be most ashamed. But how sad to see that, already, that woman's fears are being recognized. Consumerism, excessive self-indulgence, and the freedom to wallow in filth and pornography will certainly have an impact on these naive and oddly protected peoples from the East.

There is only one hope in such a situation, and that is the deep faith in Jesus Christ which has been growing strong under persecution. Again, we pray nourishment for that faith will come quickly.

THE POPULATION DILEMMA

While the Club of Rome, the environmentalists, the pro-death movement, and all those who support the Malthusian hypothesis that the world is being over-populated continue to hold forth, Europe has begun to realize that it is in a serious population dilemma. Not from over-population, but from under-population.

In his book, *The Birth Dearth,* Ben Wattenberg pointed out that during the first half of this century, the Western nations made up roughly 30 percent of the world's population. Today that percentage is in rapid decline and Europe in particular cannot keep up with the death rate.

By 1990 the percentage of people of European stock (including those in America) has fallen to just 15 percent of the world's population. By the year 2035, if the present trends continue, these nations will constitute an insignificant 7.5 percent.

It is generally accepted that a modern nation must have a minimum of 2.1 births per woman to simply maintain its population at a constant level. Today, however, West Germany and Denmark have curbed the birth rate so sharply they are now at 1.3 births per woman and still declining.

The Netherlands and Italy are at 1.5, Britain 1.8, and the United States has fallen from 3.6 in 1955 to a low of 1.7 in 1976, and has recently leveled out at about 1.8.

Little has been reported in the American press, but the world's birth crisis—labeled by some now as the "Depopulation Bomb" (in response to Paul Ehrlich's book of the 1970s)—is beginning to raise eyebrows in Europe. Sorbonne professor Pierre Channu calls it the "European cancer" and correctly identifies the crisis as "a refusal of life itself." Others say, as reported by Allan C. Carlson in his book *Family Questions,* that the West is signing its own death warrant.

Oddly enough, French families are given substantial welfare assistance and tax incentives to have more children, but the plan has not worked. The Italian government is so concerned about their falling population they are trying to woo Italian emigrants back from Latin America.

One of the implications of the population crisis is the impact on the labor force. More and more companies are discovering they cannot find qualified natives to fill the jobs they have available. Most are being forced to hire immigrants, or in many cases, to actually import immigrants from Eastern Europe, Africa, and the Middle East.

Needless to say, these policies merely complicate the lives of the Europeans even further and lead to racial and social tensions most of these nations have, until now, never really experienced.

The decline of Europe's population is not just a function of abortion, but of a general unwillingness of Europeans to have children. Many believe the quality of life is unsuitable, and they offer many reasons for deferring or denying child-bearing.

In European Russia, where the average woman has eight abortions, the wretched condition of life under communism makes parenting an unwelcome option. In Western Europe, it may be the high cost of living combined with the post-World War II despair caused by lack of faith and lack of hope.

Between the United States Supreme Courts's Roe v. Wade decision legalizing abortion in 1973 and the year 2000, there will be 40,000,000 abortions in this country. The number in Europe is conceivably even higher. If so, the total number of abortions in Europe and America could reach an unbelievable 100,000,000 by the end of the decade. The nations of the West have literally committed genocide on themselves.

REGAINING THE STATUS QUO

In their addresses to members of the EC and the other major decision-making bodies in Europe, both President Bush and Secretary of State Baker have tried to encourage restraint and sound judgment, and a continuing role for the United States in Europe.

Speaking to the Berlin Press Club, Secretary Baker pressed for continuing support for NATO and its role in keeping the peace. He said the new "architecture" of Europe should help to preserve the link between Europe and North America, "politically, militarily, and economically." He also stressed the importance for cooperation in science, industry, environmental policy, and "a host of other fields."

Surely one of the key areas of cooperation and dialogue should be with regard to the social and moral issues that will confront the European Community and its growing sphere of influence in the coming decade.

Europe first became aware of itself as a unique entity and a force in a larger framework when Emperor Constantine united Europe in 320 A.D. under the Roman Empire and the cross of Jesus Christ. The dynamism of that union expanded and retracted over many centuries until today when, once again the Continent is being united under a powerful central authority.

But only one thing is missing: the hand of God.

Clearly the hand of God will not come from within, for the church has fallen on hard times throughout Western Europe. It will have to come from outside, and both Eastern Europe, with a new vision of faith and freedom, and the United States, with its legacy of Democratic freedom and a Christian Constitution, could possibly offer the vehicle of reform.

But will it be enough? Can it be done? Will there be time?

At the death of a star, it first implodes then bursts out in a fiery display. We call such stars "supernovae."

I believe that Western Europe is beginning one last bright burst of fire before it sinks into a major cycle of decline lasting for centuries.

Western Europe is now the most irreligious part of the world. Europe united under the control of a New Age dictator would menace the globe.

Will Christian Democratic ideals win out? Will there be a new influence of Christianity throughout Europe, flowing from the newly liberated communist countries?

6

The Rise of
the East

The oil price shocks of 1973 and 1979 signaled the beginning of a 500-year cycle of Eastern ascendancy in the world.

Japan is the economic forerunner of the East Asian world powers.

The new millennium may see a post-communist, free-market, Christian China become the world's dominant power.

In early 1990 the land surrounding the Imperial Palace in Tokyo, Japan, was reportedly appraised at 70 billion dollars, a price equal to the total market value of all of the real estate in Florida.

Then we were told that the market value of the land in the tiny islands comprising the nation of Japan was five times that of the market value of all of the land in the United States from Maine to California.

Then a list of the world's largest banks was published. At the top was the Dai-Ichi Kangyo bank with assets approaching 400 billion dollars, twice those of Citibank, America's only entrant in the top ten of world banking. Of the top ten world banks, eight were Japanese.

When J.D. Power and Associates publishes various studies of consumer satisfaction with automobiles sold in the United States the

Japanese built Acura tops the list year after year. In the latest study of reported automobile defects, a new Japanese luxury car, the Lexus, comes in with the fewest reported defects. Now the Lexus advertisements joke that owners of the highly regarded German made Mercedes Benz can actually step up in quality at half the price by buying a Japanese Lexus.

The only American car in the top ten is Buick, which is enthusiastically promoting its fifth place standing. We are no longer surprised to learn that by 1992 Japanese car makers will have a share of the United States automobile market equal to once mighty General Motors.

There are no broadcast television cameras manufactured today in the United States. The Japanese-built Sony Betacams have become the industry standard, as are Japanese home television sets, VCRs, camcorders, walkman audio recorders, and a host of other electronic products sold in America.

Japan has enjoyed an annual trade surplus of some 90 billion dollars, of which as much as 50 to 60 billion dollars comes from the United States. The money has been recycled to America by the Japanese, who have been purchasing up to 30 percent of all United States government debt securities, and in the process a sizable chunk of California banking assets and such choice parts of America as Rockefeller Center and Columbia Studios.

The Japanese are surpassing the United States in total share of world markets. In the semiconductor industry, which the U.S. pioneered and developed, the Japanese share of the world market rose from 33 percent in 1982 to 50 percent in 1990 while the U.S. share in the same period of time plummeted from 57 percent to 37 percent.

Now the Japanese are planning in the 1990s an industrial and financial thrust of such magnitude that we can only conclude its intent is to make Japan the dominant economy of the world. This thrust will be fueled by a hoard of cash unprecedented in world history and according to an American economist based in Tokyo, "It is literally frightening to contemplate the effects, within three or four years of the gigantic increase in exports" that the new Japanese capital is creating.

Consider the financial reserves available to them. We know that, even after the recent Nikkei nosedive and subsequent readjustments, at least eight of the world's 10 largest banks are Japanese. Beyond bank capital, Japanese industry is expected to have raised 200 billion dollars in equity capital during 1989, six or seven times what United States corporations raised that year.

By the first quarter of 1989, the war chests of Japanese firms were staggering. Hanwa steel had 17.2 billion dollars cash in reserve; Mitsubishi 15.2 billion; Toyota 11.8 billion; Sumitomo 11.3 billion; Hitachi 7.0 billion.

The 25 largest Japanese life insurance companies dwarf these figures. Their combined assets are 100 trillion yen, (700 billion dollars). And the money keeps pouring in. Nippon Life receives 12 billion yen, (75 million dollars) per day in premiums. Sumitomo Life, an estimated 8 billion yen (50 million U.S. dollars) each day.

Not content with home markets, Japanese companies have borrowed an additional 113 billion dollars on the international markets at shockingly low rates. In October of 1989, Nissan borrowed 1.5 billion at 3 3/8 percent, a full 5 percent below what the most creditworthy U.S. corporations have to pay.

Japanese interests bought 134 billion dollars in foreign manufacturing, real estate, and securities in 1988. In 1989 that figure is estimated to have grown to $170 billion. At home Japan is devoting a staggering 25 percent of its entire gross national product to capital spending in order to make more and better steel, automobiles, copiers, computers, electronics, and advanced technology aimed to overwhelm the United States.

In automobiles alone, Japanese companies are expected to spend 55 billion dollars during the decade to build 14 ultramodern factories able to produce another 2,800,000 new vehicles each year, most of which will be for export. Their plan is to be unbeatable in every technology before the United States during the 1990s can recover its fiscal senses and its lost marketing edge.

They don't plan to stop at manufacturing and technology. The Japanese now control one third of California's banking assets and within a year plan to expand into at least 45 of the 50 states. Japanese banks have access to virtually unlimited capital at 5.5 percent. They lend to their United States affiliates at 7.5 percent. From that point on, the United States affiliates of Japanese banks can most profitably undercut any bank in the United States in making commercial loans.

This would soon make the Japanese banks the principal lenders to much of American business. America got a taste of what that power

meant when Japanese banks pulled out of the United Airlines leveraged buyout recently. Not only did United's stock crash, but the U.S.
Stock market went for a dizzying fall along with it.

THE 500 YEAR CYCLE

The rise of Japan and of what are called the Asian Tigers comes
as a shock to anyone who served in the Pacific theatre in World War II
or who served, as I did, in post war Japan and Korea during the Korean War in the early 1950s.

In 1945 the Japanese military had been crushed by American
power. Her economy was bombed out and destitute; her emperor
and god had been deposed; and an American Caesar, Douglas
MacArthur, now ruled the nation from the Dai-Ichi Building in
Central Tokyo. Japanese products were invariably shoddy. The label
"Made in Japan" was synonymous with junk.

At war's end, China lay defeated not only by the brutal Japanese
occupation but by the vicious struggle between the Nationalist forces
of Chiang Kai-Shek and the communists under Mao Tse Tung. Taiwan did not exist as a nation. The Malay peninsula and Singapore
had been devastated by war and occupation. Hong Kong was without
economic significance.

Korea was a backward primarily agricultural nation which had
been subjugated by the Japanese for decades and was soon to find
itself ripped apart by another war which raged from the Yalu River
in the North to the port of Pusan in the South.

This was a region of warlords, peasants, coolies, and rice pad-
dies. These were the poverty-stricken Asian hordes. To any observer
in 1950 it was clear that this region was destined to be an economic
and cultural backwater well into the twenty-first century.

But at least one observer saw things differently. Dr. Raymond
Wheeler, a professor and historian at the University of Kansas, after
a monumental twenty years study of cyclical history, forecast that
there would arise by the year 1980—a scant 28 years after the cessa-
tion of hostilities in Korea—a resurgence of Asia and an Asian leader.

Wheeler did not pick Japan but India. Perhaps he felt that India
had suffered least during World War II and therefore was the most

probable candidate. Wheeler's work did not consist, however, of fore-casting the rise of individual nations but regions. He clearly saw a free and resurgent Orient before the end of the century.

Professor Wheeler's calculations encompass three one-thousand-year periods and six five hundred year periods during which the pendulum of world economic power, military power, and cultural influence swings from Europe to Asia and back again. During the beginning of the thousand years one society begins its upward growth for roughly 500 years then begins a slow decline for a similar period.

The chart on pp. 132–133 is a vastly oversimplified but relatively true to fact profile of Wheeler's cyclical views superimposed on what we know of history.

Dr. Wheeler called his work "human ecology," the study of environmental forces such as physical geography, climate, social interaction and economic change. His chief premise, however, was that "nations have risen or fallen on the tides of climatic change."

He determined that every five hundred years climatological factors in the biosphere produced a cold dry period which basically caused dislocation of nations all over the globe. With the cooler climate came political chaos, and a shift in power from East and West, but also increasing democratic freedom for the masses whenever these conditions occurred.

Looking ahead to the coming at the new millennium, and the arrival of the twenty-first century, these massive studies drew Wheeler to the conclusion that European civilization was heading into decline while the Asian nations would come front and center on the world's stage. Events of the past 40 years have proved him remarkably prescient.

Wheeler is not the only thinker who has held a cyclical view of civilization. According to James Dale Davidson and Sir William Rees-Mogg in their book, *Blood in the Streets,* the authors of the American Constitution believed that "the destiny of nations was governed by long term cycles of growth and decay." Not the weather or the stars, but the physical, spiritual, and intellectual softness that comes from too much material prosperity.

Nations and empires do not usually fall by some sudden cataclysm but by a slowly accelerating departure from the individual initiative and moral self-control that laid the basis for their prosperity.

	EAST	WEST
	Rising	Declining
1000 B.C.	Kingdoms of David and Solomon; Assyrian empire; Babylonian Empire; Persian Empire.	Barbaric primitive tribes
	Declining	Rising
500 B.C.	Babylon falls; Persia defeated by Alexander; Alexander takes half of India and Egypt.	Beginning of Greek democracy; Empire of Alexander the Great; The growth and establishment of the Roman empire.
	Rising	Declining
1 A.D.	Birth of Christ; growth of Christianity; Christianity fills Middle East, Europe, and Africa, supplants Roman Empire.	Decline of Roman Empire, through spiritual and financial excess. Rome falls to successive waves of barbarians.
	Declining	Rising
500 A.D.	Islam rises and recedes. No significant Eastern empire on the world stage.	Beginning of European Christian civilization. Christianity spreads to France, Germany, England, Scandinavia, and Russia. Muslims defeated at Battle of Tours. Holy Roman Empire consolidates power.
	Rising	Declining
1000 A.D.	Mongol Empire under Ghengis Khan, Kublai Khan, and later Tamerlane occupies greatest land mass in history. Threatens Western Europe	Europe weakened by continual warfare among nations and within nations, disease, and famine. Church becomes divided and corrupt.

	EAST	**WEST**

	Rising	Declining
	at Danube in Hungary. Flowering of Chinese culture. Ottoman Empire captures Middle East.	One quarter of total European population dies from plague known as "black death."

	Declining	Rising
1500 A.D.	China free from Mongol influence. Successive emperors grow weaker and inward looking. Ottoman Empire declining. India, Southeast Asia, backward, poor, superstitious.	Reformation and Renaissance, Voyages of discovery. Colonization of Western hemisphere. Industrial revolution. Rise of Portuguese, Spanish, French, British, Dutch, Italian, and German Colonial empires in Africa, Middle East, India, and Asia. Christian European nations totally dominate the globe. Rise of constitutional democracy, wealth, and military power of the United States as a Christian nation.

	Rising	Declining
2000 A.D.	Influx of wealth to OPEC nations and Japan. Dramatic rise of Japan and nations of Pacific rim. Rise of fundamentalist Islam and Hinduism. Technological superiority. Military power yet uncertain, but Saddam Hussein of Iraq a fore-runner. Rapid spread of Christianity in Korea, China, the Philippines, and Taiwan.	Enormous debt. Budget instability. Family break-up, crime, drugs, declining educational standards. Losing technological advantage. Declining birthrate. Post-Christian era. Loss of religious faith. Threat of hyper inflation and economic collapse. Ability to maintain military power in grave doubt.

THE GREATEST EASTERN EMPIRE

If history indeed repeats itself, will the next millennium bring forth an oriental empire to rival the last one? In the late 1100s a Mongol Chieftain named Temujin took power. He was bloodthirsty and utterly ruthless. Under the name Genghis Khan he conquered North China in 1215 then turned to other conquests.

He subjugated China, Korea, Mongolia, Persia, Turkestan, and Armenia. His empire included parts of Burma, Vietnam, Thailand, and Russia. In 1241 his son, Ogotai, laid waste Hungary and Poland, and threatened the civilization of Western Europe.

When I was in Budapest, Hungary, this spring, my wife and I were taken at night to the Buda heights above the Danube and shown the statue of the king, St. Stephen, who brought Christianity to his people. From that vantage point we were then proudly told that in the plains beyond the Danube, Christian Hungary had stood fast to save Europe from the Mongol Hordes.

Ogotai's son, Kublai Khan, enlarged the empire, and then gave it the splendor recorded by Marco Polo. Kublai Khan sent a message to the Pope requesting missionaries to come and teach his people Christianity.

The British used to say, "Scratch a Russian and you find a Tartar." History shows us that a vast portion of the Soviet Union is more closely allied with the Middle East and Asia than with Europe. Only Russia, itself, the Ukraine, and Moldavia can truly be considered European.

The province of Georgia is East of Turkey, bordering Iran. For almost 3,000 miles the Soviet Union borders Manchuria, Mongolia, China, India, Afghanistan, and Iran.

In June 1990, leaders of Kazakhstan, Turkmenstan, Kirghizia, Usbekistan, and Tadzhikistan met to protect their interests from Russia. This was the first step toward establishing a large independent state of Turkestan, presumably independent of Moscow.

Will there be a resurgent empire coming from the East? We should expect that a possible break-up of the Soviet Union would bring forth a vast Oriental nation. Would it ally itself with China, Mongolia, and Manchuria to form a power like that of Genghis Khan and Kublai Khan? Would it then subjugate Southeast Asia and control the sea routes?

We may not live to see it happen, but eventually, absent God's intervention in history, such an Asian super power may emerge. If a modern nation of one and one half to two billion people were to come about, and such a thing is entirely possible, the description in the book of Revelation regarding the armies of the "Kings of the East" would be literally possible. Such a power could dominate the entire world.

On a less apocalyptic note, most likely the next several decades will bring about the fall of communism in mainland China and the break-up of the Soviet Union. In all probability, without a strong autocratic government, China will break-up into regions which differ from one another either by the military nature of their government or the economic theory under which they are organized.

When I visited China in 1979, I learned that a skilled artisan was then paid the equivalent of 26 dollars per month, and a foreman of a factory employing 2,000 workers 70 dollars per month.

The Chinese are probably the world's most astute business people. If mainland China moves to the same free market capitalism that has brought such a remarkable standard of living to Taiwan and Hong Kong, and if indeed the Chinese in vast numbers continue to embrace Christianity and the democratic freedoms which invariably accompany Christianity, within forty years the per capita income in China should reach 4,000 dollars and the Chinese economy would have grown to a level in excess of 4.5 trillion dollars per year.

The Central Asian landmass, with its vast population, would create the most extraordinary internal market in the world. Imagine what it would take to supply such a population with housing, transportation, clothing, furniture, electronic products, electricity, telecommunications, and services. **If the future of capitalism depends on markets, a free resurgent Central Asia could guarantee a booming internal market and a virtually limitless market for the surplus output of the world's farms and factories.**

As I see it, the key will be to teach the people now the truths of Christianity, the principles of democratic self-government, and free market economics. This is why Regent University, of which I am Founder and Chancellor, jumped at the invitation of the present government of China to establish a branch of our Graduate School of Business Administration at Yellow River University in Central China.

OIL POWER

In 1973, suddenly and without warning, the East reached from the sands of the Persian Gulf and began to choke the lifeblood of Europe and America. All modern industrial life was built upon petroleum—cheap petroleum. Our automobiles, our airplanes, our trucks, our farm tractors, our plastics, our fertilizers, our light, our heat, our machine lubricants and our defense establishment all required oil. Oil was so essential to our life that its price was a multiplying lever on the cost of every single product in our entire economy.

To our shock and amazement the Arabs and their OPEC partners raised the price of oil from $2.80 a barrel to $13.00 a barrel. Europe and America were totally unprepared for such a happening and watched in horror as some 80 billion dollars of their wealth poured into the coffers of the Arab sheiks each year.

The Western economies went into a serious recession. Bankruptcies by the thousands littered the economic landscape.

During the 1970s, Western economies alternated between virulent inflation and recession. When a religious fanatic, the Ayatollah Khomeini, took power in Iran, the price of oil tripled to $39 a barrel. The Western nations were gripped by inflation and no growth stagnation at the same time.

A new term, "stagflation," was introduced to describe what was happening. The American hostage crisis was merely a symbol that the Western nations were being held hostage and bled white by Eastern leaders around the Persian Gulf.

American inflation hit 13.3 percent and interest rates soared to an undreamed of 21.5 percent. Millions of Americans were put out of work. The powerful industrial heartland of America began to be known as the "Rust Belt." A crisis of major magnitude gripped America's farmbelt. The suffering and heartbreak of steelworkers, auto workers, and farmers was overwhelming.

The poorer, non-oil nations of the world, particularly those in South America and Africa, were forced to borrow tens of billions of dollars to pay for the increased price of oil in order to survive. These Third World debts now exceed one trillion dollars and still exist as a threat to the long-range future of major United States banks as well as the political and economic health of hundreds of millions of desperate people who live at or below a level of misery unthinkable in America.

In his book, *The Kingdom,* published in 1981, Robert Lacey tells of the rise of Saudi Arabia as a nation. In 1930 the founding monarch of Saudi Arabia, Abdul Aziz Ibn Saud, survived on a 200,000-dollar annual stipend from Great Britain. When King Ibn Saud in the 1920s began an expedition against Kuwait, he was stopped by British planes, British armed cars, and British ships. In Lacey's words, "It was his Majesty's Government who determined for Abdul Aziz the frontiers of the possible."

In 1990, the entire world shuddered when the Dictator of Iraq, Saddam Hussein, seized tiny Kuwait and thereby controlled an estimated twenty percent of the oil supply of the entire world. Hussein, with an army of 1,000,000 men, some 5,200 tanks, plus rockets and poison gas, suddenly became a world figure.

It is virtually impossible for Americans, accustomed to Middle East power, to realize that in March of 1921 Winston Churchill, as his Brittanic Majesty's Secretary of State for the Colonies, convened a conference in Cairo for the purpose of disposing of Hussein, the Sharif of Mecca, a rival to Abdul Aziz in Saudi Arabia.

Churchill's plan was simple. A map was drawn. Mesopotamia was called Iraq and given to Feisal, the son of Sharif Hussein, but under British tutelage. The Sharif's other son, Abdullah, Feisal's brother, (and grandfather of the present King of Jordan), was given a new territory adjoining Iraq called Transjordan.

Palestine was made a British mandate. The French kept Lebanon and Syria. Kuwait was a British protectorate. The Sharif was acknowledged as King of Hijaz in Saudi Arabia.

That is the way the Middle East worked just seventy years ago. Over a cup of tea the British divided territories, set up kings, and deposed kings. No one questioned their authority. They were a European power and the Middle East was their sphere of influence.

In 1973 the cycle of change from West to East began to work. By 1980 it was clearly set in place. By 1990 America is once again importing over fifty percent of her oil requirements. America's known reserves are steadily dwindling. The only known major pool of oil in the world exists in the Middle East.

Whatever the United States and Europe do to bolster their economies, the fact remains that from now on the economies of the once powerful Western nations are in some measure hostage to the nations of the Middle East who will continue to build up enormous wealth as it is being steadily drained from the rest of the world.

To be sure much of this oil wealth will be recycled back into Europe and America. The Japanese are doing the same thing with their wealth. But every dollar that is recycled makes the Arabs and the Japanese owners of that much more Western real estate, banks, stock, bonds, and factories.

With loss of ownership goes loss of control. With loss of control goes the power to make the decisions which we deem good for our nation, our businesses, and our own lives. It is the long range loss of control over our own destinies which will be the price we pay when power flows from the West to the East.

THE ASIAN TIGERS

During the 1980s, the economic story did not focus on the Middle East or on the Asian landmass where the long range future lies, but on the extraordinary economic growth around what is called the Pacific Rim.

Japan is not the only booming economy in the East. China, Hong Kong, Taiwan, Singapore, Malaysia, and Korea, and others have been growing their business interests in the West and multiplying their export markets exponentially over the past dozen years.

Robert Hormats, of Goldman Sachs in New York, believes that Japanese investment in the area has been the greatest single factor in the creation of a sort of Asian Common Market. What Hormats calls the "integrated production zone" actually involves more than a dozen separate nations, some who are suppliers and others who are primarily developers and entrepreneurs.

If we look at the dynamic growth among the six member nations of the Association of Southeast Asian Nations, which includes Thailand, Malaysia, Indonesia, Singapore, Brunei and the Philippines, we can see just how broadly that economic power has spread.

The *Wall Street Journal* reported that in the five years, from 1984 to 1989, Japanese companies tripled their investments in these Asian nations to 5.57 billion dollars. The Japanese investment in

Thailand alone in 1988 topped 705 million dollars—ten times the United States investment that year in that country.

The network of trading and bartering between Southeast Asian nations has created a bonanza in the East. Japan's GNP, now topping 2.9 trillion dollars, has more than doubled since 1980 and has outstripped its 1965 level of 84.6 billion dollars by a factor of 35. Over the same period, the per capita income increased from an annual 8,638 dollars to over 23,600 dollars in 1988.

South Korea's GNP jumped from a mere 2.9 billion dollars in 1965 to 125 billion in 1988. Per capita income rose from a poverty level of 103 dollars per annum to almost 3,000 dollars. Singapore, now at 24.7 billion dollars, has experienced a 24-fold increase in GNP since 1965; and Hong Kong jumped from just over 3 billion dollars to nearly 45 billion in the same 23-year period. In 1965 Hong Kong had a per capita income of barely 900 dollars. Today the figure is 10 times larger, topping 9,200 dollars per person.

When you total these various International Monetary Fund, World Bank, and United Nations figures, you begin to get the picture that something is indeed happening in the East. Suddenly, we see a major player in the world marketplace with a current combined GNP exceeding 4 trillion dollars, clearly on a par with Europe's 4.3 trillion and the United States' 5.2 trillion.

If the Japanese economy grows at 6 percent per year, then slows to 4 percent, by the year 2000 their economy would total 4.75 trillion dollars, roughly the size of the present U.S. economy. If Japan maintains its white hot 1980-88 growth rate, it will reach a staggering 7.98 trillion dollars by the year 2000.

Using the conservative growth calculation, in the 1990s South Korea's economy would grow in ten years to a 205 billion-dollar GNP; Hong Kong would be at 73 billion; and Singapore would likely top 40 billion.

THE ASIAN SECRET

At the end of World War II, a key group of Japanese business leaders invited a middle level manufacturing engineer from Westinghouse Electric to teach them techniques of manufacturing.

The principles set forth by their American teacher, W. Edwards Deming, were actually very simple. They were accepted by his Japanese pupils as holy writ and assiduously put into practice. Basically this extraordinarily humble man told the Japanese to insist on quality, to respect the dignity of their workers, and to organize their enterprises for maximum flexibility through the participation of workers in key manufacturing decisions.

In fact, Deming taught the Japanese two key tenets of Christianity. The first: "Let him who is great among you be the servant of all." Managers were to be servants of the workers, listening to them and providing them an environment in which they, in turn, could produce excellent products. The second principle was equally important: "A house divided against itself cannot stand." Management and labor should not be adversaries but co-workers in a shared enterprise.

As a people, the Japanese began saving money at a rate of about 17 percent a year. At that pace money doubles every four years. By saving, they applied another key tenet of Jesus, related in what is called the parable of the talents: "Unto him who has more will more be given." Their savings mounted, soon doubled, and then doubled again and again, to provide an enormous pool of capital to finance their industry expansions.

In Japan, as in the other fast growing Asian nations, the government has sponsored and promoted a pro-business environment. The Asians rejected European and American-style political liberalism and government-sponsored redistributive economics where a huge, wasteful bureaucracy set out to move vast sums of wealth from the producing segment of society to the non-producing segment.

It is also instructive to note that in Japan there are roughly 33,000 lawyers. In the United States there are 700,000 lawyers. Asian enterprise has been spared the internal warfare and economic drain which our litigious society has placed upon us.

In the Asian nations, a permissive attitude toward illegal narcotics and crime is just not tolerated. In Japan drug dealers are swiftly given life imprisonment. In Singapore they are summarily executed.

Finally the Asians have strong family ties and a strong, disciplined work ethic. Each family member is expected to work hard and support one another. When prosperity comes they have been known to spend very lavishly, but they are willing to sacrifice and defer spending until they succeed.

According to the conservative newspaper, *Human Events,* in 1985 the crude divorce rate in the United States was three and a half times as high as that found in Japan. Illegitimacy accounted for 21 percent of all American births in 1984, only 1 percent of all Japanese babies were born out of wedlock in the same year.

In the United States 50 to 65 percent of all 17-year-olds report sexual activity. Japanese officials express concern when just 10 percent of their high school students engaged in pre-marital sex.

Divorce and illegitimacy have helped drive up the cost of American welfare programs. American families are increasingly unwilling to care for their aging parents while Japanese families typically honor and care for their elderly.

Small wonder first generation Koreans, Chinese, and Vietnamese in the United States have been so successful. Despite language and cultural barriers these people have repeatedly risen within a few years of their arrival in this country to an income level equal to or exceeding our norms. And time after time their children take top honors in American schools and Universities.

The East is rising because the people there have embraced hard work, a disciplined life, individual initiative, family values, and in most cases strong religious faith.

Europe and America are declining because we have become self indulgent, dependent on large governments, and are permissive in our behavior. We have turned our backs on faith in God, individual self reliance, and strong family values.

The United States borders two oceans, one facing Europe, the other facing Asia. California, Oregon, Washington, Alaska, and Hawaii are all part of the Pacific Rim and even now are participating in the Asian boom. Our nation has a choice of following the sterile decline of post-Christian Europe or the long-range future of a booming Asia.

During the coming decades we should expect the Asian boom to act like a magnet to shift population and wealth from the East Coast toward the West and Southwest. The existing population growth trends in the Southern and Western portions of the United States will only increase in the years to come, and along with it the continued shift in economic and political power away from the Northeast and upper Midwest.

These trends will affect housing prices, jobs, and investment opportunities. Right now property prices are plunging in the Northeast and the infrastructure, crime and welfare problems of cities like New York are virtually insoluble. It is highly unlikely that the downward trend will reverse itself but will grow progressively worse in the Northeast over the next decades. The fall of Donald Trump's empire in 1990 may become a highly publicized symbol of the irreversible decline of the urban Northeast.

DANGER SIGNS IN JAPAN

After World War II, our brilliant commanding General Douglas MacArthur, flashed an urgent message to the churches of America, "Send me Bibles and 10,000 missionaries." The post-war American Christians had other things on their minds. There were families to be formed, jobs to begin, houses to build, children to educate, and churches to plant and build.

We had the opportunity to turn Japan from a nation of emperor worshipers to a nation of Christians. But the American Christians failed this unparalleled opportunity.

The Japanese are ready students, and they copied everything about America. They copied our law and government, our cars, our clothes, our communications, our motion pictures, our advertising, our music, our hamburgers, our baseball, our golf. Many of the women even had plastic surgery done to copy actress Raquel Welch's belly button. They copied our Christmas celebration without reference to Jesus Christ. Most of all they copied our materialistic preoccupations and love of money.

Everything they copied they improved on. As one person told me, "The Japanese make everything smaller, cheaper, and better." The one thing that they did not copy was our soul: our faith in God, in Jesus Christ, and the Holy Bible.

The Japanese preoccupation and skill in making money has led to absurd anomalies. The United States Dow Jones stock average and the Japanese Nikkei average in the late sixties both stood at 1000. The so-called price earnings ratio of Dow stocks has traditionally been twelve or thirteen to one. The U.S. Stock market averages trended as high as 3000, but the Nikkei went to 39,000 and their stocks were selling at a wildly speculative price ratio of 60 to 1.

Their land values are reminiscent of the tulip bulb craze in Holland when one tulip bulb sold for 17,000 dollars. The *Wall Street Journal* quoted a foreign banker in Tokyo as saying, "The property market here reminds me of a boulder perched at the top of a pinnacle of ice. A little heat and it could all come crashing down."

The total property market in Japan is listed at 15 trillion dollars, and the most choice land in Tokyo is selling for 200,000 dollars a square meter which translates to 978 million dollars per acre.

If the Japanese land market crashes, the defaults could cripple some banks and dwarf America's savings and loan debacle. With cross ownership of stock among major Japanese corporations, and with the use of land for collateral to support stock purchases and stock for collateral to support land purchases, the possibility of a world-engulfing economic collapse taking place in Japan is very high.

Japan has a population of only 123 million on a relatively tiny landmass. They have incredible manufacturing capability at home and overseas, and astounding financial reserves, but more and more the Japanese people and their economy are beginning to show alarming signs of speculative hangover and premature aging.

If they could match their incredible material success with a deeply held religious faith, I would say that the Japanese economy will correct for its current excesses and sail ahead.

However, as things stand now, my money would be on Japan as the forerunner of the Asian renaissance, but on a spiritually renewed China after communism as the long-term Asian super power of the new millennium.

GROWING THE BUSINESS

The best management book that I have read, other than the Bible, is *Thriving On Chaos* by Tom Peters. Peters' basic theme is that rapid change and chaos will be the norm in business from now on. He proposes that decentralization, service, innovation, and creative problem solving will be the trademarks of business in the coming era.

American people and American business can no longer comfort themselves by crowing over our superiority. All of us from now on are on a course of continuous gut wrenching change and fierce competition from East and West. We will no longer be insulated from any development in our world whether it takes place in Brussels or Berlin, Moscow or the Persian Gulf, Tokyo or Beijing.

Seeing the role of business in such global terms offers a striking new vista. Imagine tracking the business news as it follows the rising sun. The stock market opens up in Japan, and as the day continues it opens in the Middle East and in Europe and across to the United States.

Satellites are beaming trading information as it happens to terminals connected by fiber-optic cables, and computers are standing by to assess and interpret trends in mere microseconds. Suddenly the world has become a gigantic trading bazaar.

People can no longer say, well that happened in Hong Kong, so it doesn't affect us. Everything is interconnected because the transfer of funds takes place so rapidly. The investments of United States capital in the Orient and in Europe, and the investment of Asian and European capital in the United States, is dynamic and absolutely volatile.

This kind of cross-cultural activity going on around the world will mean that national boundaries cannot stop the flow of information.

Of course, this trend started with the multinational corporations several years ago. At one point, Citibank was taking 74 percent of its profits from overseas loans. Once that happens, then a corporation isn't just concerned about its home country anymore.

In an international trading environment, the multinational corporation cares about its holding and investments in foreign capitals just as much as its operations at home. So if General Motors has a bigger operation in West Germany than it does in Detroit, then the health of West Germany will be just as important to General Motors management as the health of Detroit. They can no longer be concerned solely with the well-being of American workers.

This will also mean that the worker in America cannot be protected in the American environment. He or she is now in competition with workers in Taiwan, Japan, Singapore, and Hong Kong, as well workers in Europe and the Middle East. Consequently, those workers are in competition with America.

Because of the ease of the shipment of goods—although there might be a time when politicians do the wrong thing and raise tariff barriers—the trend now and from now on will be toward global markets or global trading blocks.

The developing American Free Trade Zone between Canada, America and Mexico—and very possibly including both North and South America—will have great importance in the emerging global marketplace.

For now, there will be three major players on the scene. The American contingent, the Japan-Asia contingent (along with the Pacific Rim), and of course the European Community contingent. So we are rapidly coming to the point where the three major trade blocks will be in direct competition with each other.

Some forecasts for the future are both mind-boggling and encouraging. Because they do not factor in recession or decline, I do not necessarily endorse these figures. Nevertheless, the Mitsui Research Institute has projected worldwide output to reach 39.2 trillion dollars by the year 2000.

Of that total, the United States is forecast to have a 10.4 trillion-dollar economy, Asia 10.2 trillion, and Western Europe 12.7 trillion.

Of course, these blocks may also complement each other. The rational way of encouraging fair trade on a global basis would be to lower barriers as fast as possible and encourage the free flow of goods. That seems to be the real mandate for the tri-lateral perspective.

INNOVATION AND EFFICIENCY

In certain industries that might mean that the standard of living would go down for American workers; but it could be a boon for American workers if the efficiency of American industry goes up as it should and if our historic level of innovation continues.

Despite the claims of people like Shintaro Ishihara—the Japanese author who claims Japan holds the definitive balance of power in world trade and is a formidable innovator—the Japanese do not originate technologies. They are shrewd marketers and superior in the lateral integration of ideas, but they have not invented things as a rule.

North American scientists invented the transistor, the television, superconductors, robotics, mainframe computing, and most of the other modern technological innovations of our time. These things come from American research and development. What Americans have not been able to do is to exploit the commercial applications of the technology the way the Japanese have done.

Japanese engineers are very good at studying and analyzing these devices, learning how and why they work, and then through a process of incremental improvement on an ongoing basis, they manufacture and mass produce an even better product. They never stop improving.

They are constantly asking for information from their customers and their workers about ways to improve their products. Clearly, this is a better way, and today the Japanese are reaping the benefits of that system.

American business is going to be forced—in fact, is already being forced—to adopt some of these Japanese management techniques. Industries will die which cannot serve markets quickly with quality products. Industries will also die where autocratic bosses refuse to empower workers to make decisions.

THE QUALITY DIVIDEND

The worker who only wants a nine-to-five job and who has no interest in or commitment to the business he or she is in will sink to the bottom of the system.

If the strength of the system is worker participation, then workers will have to care about their jobs; however, that is not a threat if the company fosters an environment where a worker's concern is rewarded and where workers and managers, together, take genuine pride in the jobs they do. There has to be an ongoing dedication on a daily, almost hourly, basis to upgrade products and services. There has to be an obsession with quality and innovation.

I don't think we can assume that a demand for quality and innovation on this level will necessarily bring instant peace and prosperity; in fact, in some ways this new system will make it much more difficult for managers and workers alike, since their creative and innovative skills will be taxed to the limit. There may ultimately be a high rate of burnout, increased stress, and even higher incidence of psychological damage. We have certainly seen that happen in Japan.

Nevertheless, I believe there is no way around the dilemma except through the power of faith and belief in God. There may be turmoil around us, but men and women who commit their lives and work to God will discover the real rewards of their labors.

They will have peace in their lives, and because they will have a clearer vision of who they are and what they believe, they will work better. I pray we will have the vision as a nation to have that kind of commitment.

INTERNATIONAL PERSPECTIVES

Even though America's role in world affairs has grown consistently larger over the past 300 years, it was not actually until the end of the Second World War that most Americans began to recognize the significance of the world beyond their own doorstep.

Tens of thousands of young men and women left the farms for the first time in the 1940s in order to help wage war in Europe, North Africa, and the Pacific. At the same time, the demands of war forced government and industry to pour millions of dollars into the development of new technologies, including new systems of communications and transportation. Those achievements not only helped win the war, but opened up new perspectives on the world.

Today, we have become a global community, or as Marshall McLuhan phrased it, a "global village." What happens in America affects the entire world; conversely, what happens in Europe or Africa or Asia now affects America. And one of the implications of seeing the world in those terms is the continual broadening of our horizons.

Once we establish links with the world around us, we can no longer see ourselves as a single group of people in a particular city or nation, but we must see ourselves as citizens of the world.

Looking beyond our shores today we observe that we are now over five billion people on this planet, some 220 nations, and 22,000 distinct groups of people. It has been estimated that 75 percent of the world's population speaks or understands one of the 25 major languages, but researchers believe there may actually be as many as 5,445 distinct language groups.

At the end of World War II, as mentioned earlier, Western nations comprised about 30 percent of the world's population; by 1990 that figure dropped to roughly 15 percent. By the year 2030, some say it will be down as low as seven and a half percent, which means that the influence of Western thought and culture on world affairs will be greatly reduced over the next 50 years, one day perhaps to irrelevance.

THE CHURCH WORLDWIDE

In China, we have now discovered, the church blossomed after the American and European missionaries were expelled in a way it had never done until that time. In Africa, where there is an exploding birth rate, we can see that there is also an incredible explosion of Christianity. Some researchers now estimate that by the year 2000, Africa will be predominantly Christian.

It is estimated that over half of Korea will be Christian by the end of the century. Dr. Paul Cho's church in Seoul is home church to nearly a million evangelical Christians.

According to some reports, there may be as many as 100 million Christians in Mainland China today, and their numbers will continue to grow dramatically over the next ten years. With the exception of India, which is still very much in the grasp of Hinduism and other idolatrous religions, there is a dramatic turning to Jesus Christ throughout the Far East, and around the world.

There is really no explanation for this surge of religious vitality, except that it is the hand of God. The wind of God is stirring around the world, and hearts are desperately yearning for truth. That should give every Christian a personal mandate to get back into a close personal relationship with his God.

Even if traditional Western civilization based on Christianity should be diminished during the coming decade, we can take consolation in the knowledge that Christianity, itself, will not be diminished. There is a unique vitality and vibrancy in the world revival going on now, and God is reclaiming His kingdom.

Reportedly, over 1,800,000,000 people now profess faith in Christ. The Episcopal church, which is the American form of the Anglican church, has more members overseas by far than it does in its home country of England. Liberal teaching in that church has been pernicious until very recently. For every Bible-believing evangelical leader, like Bishop Michael Baughan in Chester, there are six liberals, in Durham and in Canterbury and around the world, fighting to secularize the Anglican creed.

While the problem is still far from over, there are signs of revival. Anglicans who would have been horrified to be labeled evangelical a decade ago are now proud of the term; and some of the most vibrant churches in America, in Africa, and in Asia are charismatic Episcopal churches.

The Anglican church has fallen on very hard time in England, and attendance there has dwindled down to less than three percent of the population. Great cathedrals designed for congregations of five hundred to a thousand people frequently minister to no more than five to ten worshipers on a typical Sunday; and in many cases those few are only there for the sake of form or lost traditions and not, by any means, in hopes of encountering the actual Word of God.

In Africa and Asia, on the other hand, the Anglican church is growing dramatically. Mainline Lutheran, Presbyterian, and Methodist churches, along with evangelical and family-centered Catholic congregations, are rising from the ashes of burned-out theology and misplaced allegiances.

These have become some of the most vibrant churches, with some of the most dynamic Christians, in the world. I have met men of God in Korea, Singapore, Hong Kong, and mainland China whose faith and dedication and knowledge of the Word put all of us in the West to shame.

GROWING THE CHURCH

The Bible has now been translated in its entirety into more than 300 languages, and there are portions of it in another 1,900. As James Combs reports in the *Bible Baptist Tribune,* that means that 90 percent of the world now has some availability to the teachings of Christianity; but lest we feel the job of missions is done, a half-billion people (equivalent to the combined populations of the United States and the Soviet Union) have yet to hear the gospel message for the first time.

Charismatic congregations are helping to transform and reinvigorate tired old churches, and in some cases they are simply supplanting ministries that have been unable to do the job.

In Chile, for example, I understand that the Presbyterian mission gave over its evangelistic activity to the Pentecostals since more than 24 percent of the total population of that country is already Pentecostal and charismatic in their faith expression.

In terms of trends, as we look ahead to the year 2000, I believe that shifting of forms of expression is going to continue. **The gospel is going to have tremendous acceptance among all these other nations, but it isn't necessarily going to be in the context of Western Christendom or Western civilization as we know it. It is going to be in a totally different cultural environment.**

THE ONE-WORLD CULTURE

A trend we see growing rapidly around the world (which does have the Western stamp) is the homogenization of culture. English is now the accepted language of commerce everywhere in the world and, more and more, it is being sought after as *the* language to be taught in the schools.

In January 1990 Vaclav Havel asked for 12,000 teachers of English in the schools of Czechoslovakia. The same trend is evident in Hungary, Romania, Poland, and all of Eastern Europe. There is an earnest desire to move away from any other language.

English has even become the language of trade in Japan and the Far East, so in Tokyo you might well see a Japanese businessman speaking to a German or Russian businessman in English. They have no other common language, and the only way they can communicate with each other is through English.

English has become a *lingua franca* for the nations of the world as no other language has ever been. No other language has had such wide currency. I am told that in every commercial airport in the world there has to be at least one person who speaks English.

Another thing that tends to bring homogeneity to the world is the spread of American films and television.

Even though the things portrayed in Hollywood movies, and more and more on TV situation comedies, may not be true reflections of America nor the image of our culture by which we would want the world to judge us, the world is learning about us by watching TV.

Because we have such a long tradition of quality television production, and because of the sheer size of the market this country has created, we are a major supplier of programming to the world.

The quality of our motion pictures and television right now, from a purely technical standpoint, is so much better than any other nation's that we have a firm hold on the world market. The technology and the production quality of American film and video is so very high, no one, not even the Japanese, is likely to surpass that standard for years to come.

The consequences of this domination of the "entertainment" marketplace are many and varied. Some are good, some bad, and some are just funny. I remember Malcolm Muggeridge saying that on the fortieth anniversary of television the BBC wanted to determine which of all the shows they program around the world the people were actually watching. It turned out their favorite programs were "I Love Lucy" and "Wagon Train"! Not "elevating," perhaps, but at least the values were wholesome.

Another consequence of the almost universal exposure to American programming, even in nations we would consider very remote and very different, is a desire to emulate American styles, dress, language and customs. Unfortunately, what that means is that they are copying many of those things in our society that are very superficial. They are not at all what we would like to see emulated, but nevertheless the people of the world are doing it.

THE UNIVERSAL TONGUE

From the standpoint of television and radio missionary work, we are suddenly in a position very much like the early church, with a universal language. In the days of Rome, when there was the *Pax Romana,* and the one common language all over the Roman Empire presented a unique window of opportunity for the early missionaries.

Wherever they went, they could converse. Rome had prepared the way—first with Greek and then, from the third century on, with

Latin. When the Empire began to disintegrate after the year 500, the usefulness of either Greek or Latin as a *lingua franca* was greatly diminished.

But when the saints traveled from Asia Minor to Malta and to Rome, and on to Spain and France and Germany and England, the gospel could spread very rapidly because everybody understood the words that were being spoken by the apostles. There was a ready basis of communication.

Today we have much the same situation. We have a language that is becoming increasingly universal, which will enable us to speak to people in a broad number of contexts in an idiom they generally understand. It is not as difficult now to go across cultural barriers because the cultural barriers have already been breached by television, film, radio, and by audio and video cassettes which have proliferated around the world.

I remember my shock in visiting ancient Ephesus where the early church had been born under the teaching of Paul. Standing there in a shop one morning, I was listening to a broadcast coming out of Izmir, Turkey, playing a record of Cat Stevens singing "Morning Has Broken."

It was an odd sensation, and so out of context. But I experienced the same thing again later, on the Island of Rhodes, where American blue jeans and American-style portable radios were the rage. I remember how strange it seemed going into a shop there and seeing a Phillips tape recorder playing a song by a Dutch rock group singing in English, with a Southern accent! But this is the way it is. The blue jeans, the rock music, and the "modern" idiom have pretty much circled the globe.

When Elvis Presley did his international satellite telecast, it was reportedly viewed by a billion people. It may have been the most watched program in history up to that time, and all the people were tuned in to what Elvis was saying and how he was saying it. Although we might not like that type of acculturation, it is nevertheless there for us to use if we will just have sense enough to use it.

Given that platform, it is very foolish for the church to structure its appeal to the nations of the world in a methodology that is out of date, in the garb of the missionaries of fifty years ago, and in the typical idiom of the nineteenth century missionary mentality. All the important communications barriers have been broken down. All that is necessary is for Christians to use the channels and the idiom that have been opened up for us.

The transfer of vast wealth from the West to the East will mean the loss of decision-making power.

The United States is both a Pacific and an Atlantic nation.

Economic and political power will continue to flow out of the Northeast toward the South and West.

Christianity is not a Western religion. Christianity will flourish worldwide in the new millennium.

7

The Undermining
of America

For 70 years America has experienced a relentless attack from its own elites.

If dramatic change does not occur in this decade the process of decay will be irreversible.

From its declaration of independence as a nation in 1776 until 1980, a period of 204 years, the United States of America accumulated a total unpaid national debt of one trillion dollars. During that time we fought the War of Independence, the War of 1812, the Civil War, the Spanish-American War, two World Wars, the Korean War, and the Vietnam War.

During the next six years, from 1980 to 1986, confronted only by a "Cold War" and a "War on Poverty," the United States Government spent so much more money than it received that the unpaid national debt escalated to two trillion dollars.

In six peacetime years we doubled the debt that had taken 204 years to accumulate. That is almost beyond imagination. And if that weren't enough, in the next four years, from 1986 to 1990, the Government did it again and loaded another trillion dollars onto the growing pyramid of unpaid debt.

155

President John F. Kennedy, who took office in 1961, said that he did not want to be the first president to preside over a 100-billion-dollar federal budget. In 1990 the interest alone on the federal debt, at some 176 billion dollars, was almost twice the total United States budget when Kennedy took office.

In 1980, the claims of the citizens and businesses of the United States against other nations were so large that this nation was considered the world's largest creditor. By 1987, the credit balances accumulated by our nation against the world since 1918 had been brought to zero. By 1990, the United States of America was the world's largest debtor nation, with net foreign claims against our assets standing at somewhere between 600 and 650 billion dollars.

Our foreign debt dwarfs that of the "debtor" nations of Mexico, Brazil, and Argentina. America is number one in the world in the category of debt owed.

We excel in other categories as well. We have the highest rate of illiteracy of any developed nation; the highest rate of violent crime and juvenile delinquency; the highest rate of teen pregnancy—six times that of Denmark and three times that of Sweden. We have the highest rate of illegal drug use in the world; and, next only to France and the Soviet Union, the highest rate of alcohol consumption and alcoholism.

The worldwide statistics on venereal disease are somewhat imprecise, but we may be edging up to first or second in these categories as well.

Americans have always considered their nation the world's greatest, and their people the best and brightest. We think of ourselves as winners, but do we really want to win in all these categories?

Isn't it time as a nation we ask how we got this way, and then how we can change?

THE POST WAR YEARS

America in 1945 was the greatest, most powerful nation the world had ever known. It had fought and won simultaneously in Europe and Asia the most terrible war the world has ever seen.

The strategic and tactical skills of our generals and admirals were remarkable by any standard. The bravery of our combat forces was legendary. But it was the ever-increasing output of American industry which enabled America and her allies to grind down the Axis powers. Tens of thousands of tanks, planes, trucks, artillery pieces, and vessels of all shapes and sizes poured out from the industrial might of America.

By the end of 1942, the outcome was no longer in doubt as what Winston Churchill called the "encircling ring" began to squeeze tighter and tighter around Nazi Germany, Fascist Italy, and militaristic Japan.

At war's end, Europe was war torn and prostrate. The Soviet Union had been left crippled and bleeding by the ruthless Nazi invasion. Japan and the rest of Asia were stunned and destitute. Only the United States of America remained—its industry intact, its farms brimming with surpluses, its cities untouched by war and ready to begin the post-war boom.

America was unselfish with its wealth. Through the Marshall Plan we helped rebuild Europe. Through direct aid we strengthened Soviet Russia. Through enlightened military occupation we introduced democratic government to Germany and Japan, then we gave generous aid to help them rebuild their ravaged economies.

The United States Navy ruled the seas, the United States nuclear shield controlled the skies. American automobiles, tractors, machine tools, computers, television sets, appliances, and hundreds of products dominated world commerce.

In 1944, the finance leaders of the major allied powers met at the Mount Washington Hotel in tiny Bretton Woods, New Hampshire, and agreed that the United States dollar would become the strong reserve currency of the world, backed by gold. As one participant gushed, "Gold is the sun, the dollar is the earth, and all other currencies are the moon."

Money was pouring into America, and the American dollar was "as good as gold." This was a different world than that of 1979 when presidential candidate Ronald Reagan quipped, "Yesterday my doctor checked my heart. He said it was sound as a dollar, and I almost passed out."

SEEDS OF DESTRUCTION

In the 1930s, while America endured a severe depression, we experienced 25 percent unemployment, bread lines, soup kitchens, a stock market collapse, and tragic business and bank failures.

Sensitive intellectuals saw the Great Depression as the failure of capitalism. They were easy prey to the hard core Marxists who had been organizing the United States since 1918.

In 1930, a powerful atheist and communist sympathizer, John Dewey, began his work in education at Columbia Teachers College. Undoubtedly the despair of the Depression era provided fertile soil for the rapid growth of Dewey's anti-Christian thinking.

During the height of the war effort, when Soviet Russia was our comrade in arms, it was easy enough for pro-Soviet Marxists to find a ready home in the State Department, the Treasury Department, and in those departments conducting crucial top secret research.

At war's end, a dying Franklin Roosevelt and his advisors held back our victorious forces from taking Berlin and East Germany. Then, in a misguided attempt to secure lasting world peace by what he called "*noblesse oblige,*" Roosevelt gave over to the crazed butcher, Joseph Stalin, control of Poland, East Germany, Estonia, Latvia, Lithuania and, ultimately, Hungary, Czechoslovakia, Romania, Bulgaria, and Albania.

In the East, the Russians did not join the war effort against Japan until after the United States dropped atomic bombs on Hiroshima and Nagasaki. Then when it was obvious Japan was finished, Soviet Russia declared war. With United States acquiescence, the Russian troops looted Manchuria. It is reported that they stole everything—rail cars and locomotives, iron rails, whole factories, even metal doors.

Then under the constant barrage of left-wing press reports decrying the "stench of corruption" in China, the United States abandoned its wartime comrade in arms, Chiang Kai Shek, and turned the nation of China over to Mao Tse Tung and the communists.

In America, in the academic circles and the liberal press, they were described as "agrarian reformers" seeking a better life for their people by freeing them from the greed and corruption of their former leaders.

THE POLITICAL NATION

With a few notable exceptions, the foreign policy record of the United States from 1945 to 1980 is one of defeat, betrayal, and shame. Under the pounding of the liberal press and the powerful urging of what the London *Economist* termed the "Political Nation," America repeatedly undercut pro-Western and pro-Christian leaders of Third World countries in favor of Marxist or communist regimes.

The pattern was the same. Batista was corrupt, but Castro and Che Guevara were revolutionary heroes. Somoza was greedy and corrupt; the Sandinistas represented freedom. The Army of El Salvador is full of right wing bullies; the rebels represent justice. Haile Selassie in Ethiopia is old and corrupt; the communist Mengistu should take power. Ian Smith in Rhodesia is a racist oppressor; the Marxist Robert Mugabe represents his people and deserves our support. The communist Allende is the new savior of reactionary Chile.

The real stench was not the corruption of the pro-Western Third World governments but the incredible leftist, anti-Christian bias of leading American journalists covering the foreign desks of their respective news organizations.

I have been privileged to take my own cameras and news producers into some of the world's hot spots. I often have extensive briefing papers. I usually am able to interview key leaders in the places I visit.

My staff can talk to people in their own native languages. My only conclusion after years of experience is that with few exceptions the American overseas press has been biased in favor of Marxism and communism and opposed to pro-Western governments. They in turn order the facts to fit their own biases and attempt to tilt American public opinion against our friends and in favor of our enemies.

If, as Marx once claimed, religion is the opiate of the people, then for the past 40 years Marxism has been the opiate of the media.

THE NEW WAR POLICY

In World War II, the United States and her allies were fighting a fascist country which had invaded the communist homeland. Therefore, the American left and the American right were joined together.

We mobilized our entire industrial might with one objective—crush the Axis powers and bring about unconditional surrender.

We gave no quarter. There were no "privileged sanctuaries." There were no complex "rules of engagement" tying the hands of our military forces.

Four years after the war, the then Secretary of State, Dean Acheson, with the advice of suspected leftist, Owen Lattimore, sent a signal that the Korean peninsula was not a vital part of the American defense perimeter. In June of 1950, the communist government of North Korea took him at his word and invaded South Korea.

President Harry Truman, taking advantage of a time when the Soviet delegate was absent from the United Nations Security Council, was able to secure declarations from the United Nations which condemned North Korea's action and authorized a United Nations force to resist it.

American troops entered the fray but were quickly pushed back to a tiny defense perimeter around the southern port city of Pusan. Then General Douglas MacArthur in a brilliant but risky move, launched an amphibious strike near Seoul at the port of Inchon on the West Coast of South Korea.

Our forces outflanked the North Koreans, then cut their supply lines and began a race into North Korea. As they neared the border of China, at the Yalu River, large numbers of Chinese soldiers entered the conflict about the time that the bitter cold of winter swept in from Manchuria. Our troops were forced to withdraw but were able to regroup and begin a second advance further south.

MacArthur realized that if we could bomb the Yalu River bridges and then attack by air the troop emplacements on the Chinese side of the river, our forces could catch the North Koreans and Chinese troops in a relatively simple pincer movement and could utterly destroy them.

By these operations, our troops could have sealed Korea at the Yalu and instituted a free democratic government in a unified Korea. But this war had one very significant difference from World War II: now we were fighting a communist country, and the prevailing doctrine in Washington was that we could *fight* a communist country but we could not *defeat* a communist country.

KOREA AND VIETNAM

MacArthur, who knew that in war there is no substitute for victory, insisted on winning. Truman and his advisers insisted on giving the Chinese a privileged sanctuary even though they had been killing American troops with men and supplies from China.

So MacArthur was removed from command and we settled for a "peace line" on the 38th Parallel. North Korea stayed communist. South Korea stayed democratic. America had lost its first war.

I served in Korea with the First Marine Division. I felt we had made a mistake, a policy error to protect American lives. I thought it could never happen again.

But we repeated the same mistake in Vietnam. Only, this time I knew it was not a policy error but part of a deliberate calculated plan. The new policy put in place by those holding the ultimate power in our society, and supported unwittingly by a leftist press, was obvious.

For full employment, rising prices, and financial growth, the experts determined that the United States needed some mechanism by which roughly 10 percent of our output could be wasted each year.

A shooting war would accomplish full employment, but its results were unpredictable and messy. The ideal solution was a "cold war" during which the United States would maintain a semi-war footing against an enemy which we, in turn, propped up with loans and aid.

If communism were defeated, then there would be no more troops to pay, ships to build, airplanes to become obsolete, advanced weapons to develop, or government debt to finance. Either this is the underlying policy or our government had been seriously infiltrated by pro-Marxist liberals. No other explanation accounts for the continuous, ongoing foreign policy "blunders" of the United States for 30 years.

If a shooting war developed, as it did in Vietnam, it was acceptable for our servicemen to die and our treasure to be squandered, but no communist power was to be defeated by America.

The Vietnam War took the heart and resolve out of America. It drained our economy and debased our currency. It was the second war America lost. It was planned that way. American military power would never be the same again.

THE ACADEMIC FIFTH COLUMN

What we see in economics and foreign policy springs from attitudinal roots that are fashioned in the classroom, in academia, in the think tanks, and only then in the newsrooms.

Charles Sykes has caused a panic on the campus of Dartmouth College. Sykes, whose book, *ProfScam,* helped shake up faculties all over America in 1988, is now looking into the practices of the faculty, examining curricula, and exploring evidence of the continuing "politicization" of teaching philosophy at Dartmouth.

An article in the *Washington Times* reports that blood pressures are soaring on the New Hampshire campus. Sykes' research comes at a time when Americans are already beginning to question the things their sons and daughters are being taught. Faculty liberals are clearly nervous.

Like most American campuses, Dartmouth has been invaded by professors trained in the liberal, secular, socialist biases of the academy. Unfortunately, they have tried to inflict their beliefs upon students on a traditionally conservative campus, and at a time when the lie of Marxism is suddenly visible to the entire world.

With an Ivy League education costing upwards of $20,000 a year, parents are wondering why they should be paying that kind of money for college professors to train their children to be angry, rebellious, self-centered, and close-minded when the kids can stay home and be all those things for free. Sykes' forthcoming book on the Dartmouth affair should make interesting reading.

How long will it be until the radicals on America's campuses are finally exposed and deposed? Washington columnist and scholar Arnold Beichman recently wrote, "The Marxist academics are today's power elite in the universities, and by the magic of the tenure system they have become self-perpetuating." Instead of "a search for objective truth," he says, the academy has "successfully substituted Marxist social change as the goal of learning."

Columnist Georgie Anne Geyer has suggested that, despite the apparent collapse of East European and Soviet communism, Marxism continues to thrive in the universities because American academics are utopians, intellectual idealists who compare culture not to history or tradition but to some visionary dream.

CIVILIZATION'S DEATH WISH

Malcolm Muggeridge once said that Western civilization's flirtation with liberalism is evidence of its "death wish." The liberals in society seem to be hell bent on the ultimate destruction of Western culture.

In his Harvard lectures, Aleksandr Solzhenitsyn traced this flirtation back to the Enlightenment, but added that "liberalism" assumed its most somber and most sinister aspect in America. For in America, like nowhere else, a subculture of liberal intellectuals has attempted to undermine and to disassemble the entire fabric of Western society.

This plundering of traditional morality and Christian values was never accidental. It has been a deliberate and methodical assault on the tenets of society—what Muggeridge calls Christendom—and has proliferated from the classrooms to the courtrooms, and from the newsrooms to the living rooms of America. More and more, it even comes from the pulpits of America.

The end has not just been to supplant Christian values with humanism, but to weaken American sovereignty and supplant it with a one world socialist government.

In the book, *The End of Christendom,* which is a collection of classic lectures, Muggeridge offers a stunning insight. He says,

> Previous civilizations have been overthrown from without by the incursion of barbarian hordes. Christendom has dreamed up its own dissolution in the minds of its own intellectual elite. Our barbarians are home products, indoctrinated at the public expense, urged on by the media systematically, stage by stage, dismantling Christendom, depreciating and deprecating all its values. The whole social structure is now tumbling down, dethroning its God, undermining all its certainties. All this, woefully enough, is being done in the name of the health, wealth, and happiness of all mankind.

The great irony of this situation is that the very men and women we have entrusted to educate and challenge our children have been the corrupters. While few students have become communists or Marxists, per se, their trust has been shattered. Many no longer have faith in their nation; they no longer believe in God; they no longer believe justice and public service and patient labor within the framework of a Christian society will bring about progress and social change. They have been programmed either to drop out or to dissent. They no longer belong to the team.

Suddenly we are being challenged by new and powerful forces from many corners. At the international level we are feeling the pressure from the East which, as we have seen, will crescendo during the coming decade.

We are enduring the assault on faith and values in the courts as the ACLU and other liberal organizations wage their violent and relentless war. We are, of course, in a profound conflict with the false cults of the New Age.

Considering the death of our Western values, Muggeridge says,

> Christendom has played a tremendous role in the art and literature, in the mores and jurisprudence, in the architecture, values, institutions, and whole way of life of Western man during the centuries of his dominance in the world. But now as Western man's power and influence recede, so Christendom itself comes to have an evermore ghostly air about it, to the point that it seems to belong to history already, rather than to present day actuality.

Over the past three decades we have seen a gradual chipping away of America's deepest and longest-held values. The family is under attack from feminists denying the legitimacy of motherhood and guardianship of the home; homosexuals and lesbians are waging a violent campaign against their natural gender; abortion activists are on the attack seeking the right to destroy the unborn; and secular humanists are bringing their overt God-hatred into the public forum and laying siege to the church.

FOUNDATIONS OF AMERICAN LIBERTY

When the founding fathers of America, who had been meeting at Independence Hall in Philadelphia completed on September 17, 1787, the drafting of a constitution for the newly formed United States of America, John Adams, who was to become our second president, remarked, "This constitution was made only for a moral and a religious people. It is wholly inadequate for the government of any other."

Washington, Adams, Jefferson, Madison, Franklin, and Patrick Henry—in fact all our founding fathers—recognized that constitutional government was only possible when the people being governed were ruled by inner moral restraint and self-control.

At the signing of the Constitution, the 13 colonies comprising the new nation contained an estimated 3,000,000 Protestants, 300,000 Roman Catholics, and 5,000 Jews. America was predominantly a Protestant Christian nation, united by a moral consensus based upon biblical values. When George Washington signed our constitution, he dated it "In the year of our Lord, 1787."

There was only one Lord whose birthday dated back 1787 years: Jesus Christ. The founding document of the United States of America acknowledges the Lordship of Jesus Christ, because we were a Christian nation.

Constitutions in effect at the time of the Declaration of Independence give the tenor of our national beliefs. The Delaware Constitution of 1776 proclaims, "Everyone appointed to public office must say, 'I do profess faith in God the Father, and in the Lord Jesus Christ His only Son, and in the Holy Ghost . . . and I do acknowledge the Holy Scriptures of the Old and New Testaments to be given by divine inspiration.'"

North Carolina's constitution of the same year states, "No person who should deny the being of a God, or the truth of the [Christian] religion or the divine authority . . . . should be capable of holding any office or place of trust in the civil government of this state."

These laws and others like them were in effect in most of the states during the better part of the nineteenth century. In 1892 in the Supreme Court case titled, *Church of the Holy Trinity v. United States,* the court stated explicitly:

> Every constitution of every one of the forty-four states contains language which either directly or by clear implication recognizes a profound reverence for religion and an assumption that its influence in human affairs is essential to the well being of the community . . . . These and many other matters which might be noticed, add a volume of unofficial declarations to the mass of organic utterances that this is a Christian nation.

In 1931 in *United States v. Macintosh,* Justice Sutherland reiterated that part of the *Trinity Trustees* case when he wrote in the majority decision, "We are a Christian people."

A CHANGE OF VENUE

Only by destroying the Christian consensus could this nation be undermined and its power destroyed. The assault against America has taken the following avenues.

First, the liberal left realized that no elected body in the United States would adopt its radical agenda. Therefore, a deliberate plan was put in motion to claim for non-elected judges power that they had never been given under the United States Constitution. Lawyers and judges would then, under the guise of "constitutional rights," dismantle systematically the Judeo-Christian majority consensus that had guided this nation since its founding.

Second, and concurrently, the educational system would first be taken from its Christian roots and used as a psycho-political indoctrination ground to move the young toward the agenda of the left.

Third, the left would infiltrate wealthy and powerful tax-free foundations and government agencies where taxpayers' funds would begin to pour out to support the left at home and abroad.

Fourth, organizations such as Planned Parenthood, the National Education Association, and more recently the National Organization for Women, People for the American Way, the Gay-Lesbian Caucus, and their ilk would arise to champion unrestrained sex, homosexual rights, abortion on demand, while they attacked Christian beliefs, conservative organizations, and all the traditional family structures of America.

Fifth, the nation's once conservative Christian press would be virtually overwhelmed by those dedicated to undermining Christian America in favor of this brave new world of humanism and socialism.

In 1990 we see family disintegration, unrestrained sex, a holocaust of abortion, an epidemic of drugs and alcohol, deteriorating educational standards, growing poverty amidst unrestrained opulence, business greed and fraud, and a runaway federal budget.

We have these things because we have allowed Christian and biblical standards to be removed from our national life. It has taken

the left some 70 years to reduce us to this level. As we enter the decade of the nineties and the coming new millennium, we must ask ourselves whether we have enough spiritual strength left to throw off the parasites that have been wasting our national strength, or whether there are now so many parasites leeching onto us that our nation has passed the point of no return.

REWRITING THE CONSTITUTION

Some years ago Supreme Court Justice Felix Frankfurter is said to have passed a note to Justice William O. Douglas which read, "If we can keep old bushy [Justice Charles Evans Hughes] on our side, there's no amount of rewriting the constitution that we can't do."

Here was a former Harvard law professor communicating with a former Yale law professor, candidly laying out his agenda, the judicial rewriting of the governing laws of America.

Equally cynical was the arrogant assertion of Justice Hughes, "The Constitution is whatever the court says it is." America no longer had a government elected by the people under a timeless constitution to be interpreted according to the clear intention of the framers. America no longer had judicial interpretation but legislative rule by five out of nine non-elected judges who had taken unto themselves the power to change the constitution of the United States to suit their own philosophical biases.

Thomas Jefferson had warned so forcefully that if on matters of constitutional interpretation the judges were the sole arbiters, "we will find ourselves under the tyranny of an oligarchy."

And tyrants they have become. They have virtually destroyed neighborhood schools; they have permitted a district judge to force Kansas City to levy 500 million dollars in taxes for social programs they support but the people do not; they have forced an irreligious value-neutral educational system down America's throat; they have dramatically hindered law enforcement; they have trampled on the prerogatives of the United States Congress and the legislatures of the fifty states; they have opened the doors for a bewildering array of high-damage plaintiff's tort rights; and most heinous of all, they have participated in legalizing the murder of 25 million unborn babies in America.

THE WRATH OF GOD

In 1958, in a case entitled *Cooper v. Aaron,* the Supreme Court announced that its decisions were the "supreme law of the land." Even though in my opinion this is an unconstitutional usurpation of power, since *Cooper v. Aaron* the Supreme Court itself, the lower court judges, and attorneys practicing before federal courts all act as if each decision of the Supreme Court is the supreme law. Therefore, under the evolutionary theory of the constitution, the court sits as a continuing constitutional convention making up new constitutions as it goes along. Therefore, since it controls the constitution, it has made itself the supreme branch of government. When it speaks, it speaks for all the people of America, and if it errs all the people must suffer.

On June 25, 1962, the Supreme Court ruled in a case titled *Engle v. Vitale* that state-sponsored prayer could not be said in public school rooms. On June 17, 1963, the court ruled in the case of *Abington v. Schempp* that the Holy Bible could not be read to students in classrooms.

On November 17, 1980, in *Stone v. Graham* the court ruled that the Ten Commandments could not be posted in the classrooms of America's schools. On June 4, 1984, in *Wallace v. Jaffrey* the court ruled that a moment of silence prior to a class was unconstitutional if that silence was called prayer. And more recently, they ruled that a state could not mandate the teaching of a course acknowledging that the origins of life began with a creator.

Acting on behalf of all the citizens of the United States, our government has officially insulted Almighty God and has effectively taken away from all public school children any opportunity for even the slightest acknowledgment of God's existence. By rejecting Him, we have made the Protector and Champion of the United States its enemy.

The events that followed are not coincidence. On November 22, 1963, less than six months after the Bible-reading decision, President John F. Kennedy was assassinated. Within two years after that decision, America was massively embroiled in its second most painful war, which decimated our treasure, our servicemen, and our national resolve.

By 1966 the real standard of living of the average American worker stopped growing. By 1969 the stock market took a dizzying plunge, and by 1971 because of inflation we took our currency off the gold standard. By 1973 the OPEC nations quadrupled the price of oil, and the United States economy went into the worst recession since 1930.

In 1974, for the first time in American history, a president resigned in disgrace and a vice president pleaded *nolo contendre* (no contest) to a charge of extortion. All of this took place against a backdrop of violent student demonstrations which had set the nation's campuses aflame.

By 1978 our trade deficit was at an all-time high. Iranian students assaulted our embassy in Teheran, took our diplomatic officers and staff hostage, and we were seemingly impotent to help them.

By 1979 inflation was out of control and interest rates were pushed to an unbelievable 21 percent to stop it. Our president was the laughing stock of our allies and our country was termed "ungovernable."

LOSING CONTROL

Ten years later, when the 1980s ended, the United States had seen an assassination attempt against its very popular president who, in his second term, was discredited because of an arms for hostages transaction with Iran. And in a long list of media scandals, both the Speaker of the House of Representatives and the Majority Whip resigned in disgrace—one amid charges of profiteering, the other amid ethics charges.

By 1990, Michael Milken, the leader of the 200-billion-dollar junk bond industry, pled guilty to securities violations even as billions of dollars in junk bond values were collapsing along with the bankruptcies of over-leveraged major airlines and some of the nation's best-known department stores.

The savings and loan industry has collapsed and the price tag to clean it up may well top a trillion dollars. Real estate values have also collapsed, or are collapsing, and with them may go a sizable part of the banking and insurance industries.

Going into the 1990s, the United States Government has direct debt of three trillion dollars and contingent liabilities of some six and one-half trillion dollars. At some point government debt may become worthless; and we are faced with the very real prospect of a stock market collapse coupled with a collapse of the dollar and the government bond market. The prospect is for depression followed by runaway inflation.

Since 1962, intertwined with budget deficits, high interest rates, and business failures is the rapid breakup of the social fabric of America.

Since 1962 the number of divorces in America has increased 250 percent; the number of single family households headed by women increased 250 percent; the suicide rate in the 15 to 19 age group and the 20 to 24 age group has increased 253 percent.

From 1962 to 1981 the reported cases of sexually transmitted diseases climbed from 400,000 cases to 1,100,000 per year. By 1986, when diseases such as genital herpes and chlamydia were added, the annual number of new cases of sexually transmitted diseases soared to 12,000,000.

In 1962, 4 percent of high school seniors indicated they had tried marijuana. By 1982 that number was approaching 60 percent. Since 1962 the incidence of violent crime, alcohol and drug abuse, child abuse, teenage runaways, adultery, and "living together" outside of marriage has skyrocketed.

In short, over the last 28 years the moral and social fabric of the United States has been progressively torn apart. Has a watchful God given us up? These words from Benjamin Franklin spoken at the Constitutional Convention should be instructive:

> Have we forgotten this powerful Friend? Or do we imagine we no longer need His assistance? . . . without His concurring aid, we shall succeed in this political building no better than the builders of Babel; we shall be divided by our little, partisan local interests; our projects will be confounded; and we ourselves shall become a reproach and a byword down to future ages.

THE DUMBING OF AMERICA

On March 17, 1984, New Jersey Senator Bill Bradley reported on the Senate floor the results of a survey taken two months earlier of 5,000 high school seniors.

Forty-five percent of those tested in Baltimore could not shade an area on a map where the United States was supposed to be. Nearly half the students in Hartford could not name even three countries in Africa. Thirty-nine percent of the students in Boston could not name the six states in the region where they lived, New England. Twenty-five percent of the students in Dallas could not name the country that bordered Texas on the south.

In two parallel tests of college students, 84 percent of students tested in 1950 identified Manila as the capital of the Philippines. By 1984, only 27 percent of the students tested gave the correct response. In 1984, 70 percent of the college students could not name one country in Africa between the Sahara and South Africa.

We sent our CBN news crews to the University of Maryland to ask a few college freshmen and sophomores there some random questions. None could name the three states bordering California. None that we spoke to could name the U.S. presidents between Truman and Reagan. Only one could correctly identify the method of determining the area of a triangle.

I learned firsthand—and my wife confirmed the report on a subsequent visit—that 85 percent of the graduates of the high school in a city near Philadelphia had graduated as functional illiterates.

Is it any wonder that American business cannot find employees for high tech jobs? Is it any wonder the armed forces have had to "dumb down" their manuals to a minimal level for the new generation of recruits?

A program we started at CBN, called "Heads Up," has trained over 300,000 people to read and write during the past five years. I have personally brought literacy programs to Watts in Los Angeles, the South Side of Chicago, Bedford-Stuyvesant in Brooklyn, and the inner cities of Philadelphia, Detroit, Atlanta, Houston, Birmingham, and Memphis.

I have participated in literacy programs in the prisons and in communities in the Mississippi Delta. In all of these places, I have found learning of reading skills to be a breeze for people of all ages and social backgrounds. A breeze, that is, if reading is taught the way God made us to talk—by syllables, by what is called phonics, not by the "look say" method forced on the schools by the behaviorist models.

But the tragedy of humanist education is that the educators

do not believe that reading, math, history, and geography skills are important. The important thing is the sociological and behavioral indoctrination of the children.

THE BURDEN OF PROOF

So now, 60 years after John Dewey, we have 73 million Americans educated at less than a fifth grade level, 28 million functional illiterates, a school dropout rate of one million pupils per year, and an annual burden of 225 billion dollars on the American economy because of illiteracy.

The scores of American high school students on the Scholastic Aptitude Test (SAT) have dropped every single year from 1962 until 1980. There were 18 years of unbroken decline. In 1980 there was a slight increase in the average, but this was caused in whole or in part by the fact that some 32,000 Christian schools had come into being during this period and, together with private schools, accounted for 12.4 percent of the nation's student population: a total of some 5,580,000 pupils.

Depending on whose numbers you read, there are in addition between 300,000 and 600,000 students being educated at home, through home schooling programs, almost all of whom test superior to the products of the public schools.

When I served on President Ronald Reagan's Task Force on Victims of Crime, I learned that the public schools are the most dangerous places in America. More than 250,000 crimes are reported each month in the public schools. I am not referring to fist fights and scuffles, but to assault with a deadly weapon, rape, robbery, dealing narcotics, possession of narcotics, and other crimes of that nature.

I learned from our "Heads Up" sources that up to 70 percent of all students in the New York City public schools system read at or below the third grade level. This means that virtually all instruction from the third grade on is incomprehensible to them.

Boredom, coupled with crime and narcotics in the schools, has obviously created a hostile and dangerous environment. It should come as no great surprise that up to 45 percent of the students in that school system drop out before finishing high school.

THE WISDOM OF FOOLS

It has been stated that all that is necessary to succeed financially in this rich and free land is to graduate from high school, get married and stay married, and take an entry level job and keep it.

To see the hopelessness and despair of young people in our inner cities and to realize that the only future ahead for many (perhaps most) of them is a short and unhappy life of stealing, selling narcotics, prostitution, or welfare is to bring forth a cry of rage against an education establishment run by wise fools.

Despite spending hikes on education in American in excess of 600 percent from 1951 to 1988, and over 320 billion dollars annually, the 1989 SAT scores were described as "grim" and "especially disheartening" by Education Secretary, Lauro F. Cavazos.

America has heard appeals for more money for teachers, the need for lower teacher to pupil ratios, better staff to pupil ratios, on and on. The facts are plain. In 1949 there were 27 pupils per teacher, now there are about 17 pupils per teacher. Despite enormous increases in spending per pupil (from $900 per pupil in 1949 to over $4,800 per pupil today), the total portion of school expenditures devoted to teachers' salaries has fallen from 55 percent to 40.4 percent. In 1949-50, teachers represented 70 percent of the total adult employees in the school system. Now they represent only 53 percent.

According to *Forbes* magazine, only Switzerland spends more money on education per pupil than the United States, yet the United States ranks last among the industrialized nations in the relative performance of its students.

THE EDUCATION POWER

The National Education Association (NEA) is without question the most powerful labor union in America. Formed in 1857 as a follow-up to the anti-Christian revisionist education movement started by Horace Mann, it now has two million dues-paying members in all fifty states.

The NEA operates from a national headquarters through state chapters (known as the Michigan Education Association, the Virginia Education Association, the Texas Education Association, etc.).

Because of the power of these state affiliates, the NEA has a virtual stranglehold on education in America.

The NEA is highly political and undeniably partisan. It was estimated that one third of all the delegates to the 1980 Presidential Convention of the Democratic Party were NEA members. Critics alleged at its creation by then President Jimmy Carter that the Department of Education was the only cabinet level department ever formed as a payoff to one labor union.

Since membership in the NEA is compulsory—or virtually compulsory for most teachers—it is obvious that there must be many fine teachers who are members of the NEA by force and who deplore the current state of American education. But that grass roots sentiment never influences the national leadership of the NEA.

At its top, the NEA is a radical, leftist organization which seems totally committed to the present course of education in America. One of its officials recently stated on my television program that the NEA was completely opposed to teaching any form of moral values in the schools of America.

He then gave the usual justification that the teaching of moral values would "be an unconstitutional establishment of religion."

The extremes that this NEA position can be taken to is illustrated by a television interview I conducted with a Christian teacher who had been using a "value neutral" teachers manual in a Mobile, Alabama, public high school. The teacher was told that if a discussion began about morality and a student should ask, "Is shoplifting right or wrong?" the answer from the teacher should be, "I can't tell you if it is right or wrong. You must find out for yourself."

If this was the answer about the potential commission of a crime punishable by prison, just consider the confusion of students in interpersonal relations, sexual relations, and marriage.

By its literature, seminars, and public utterances, it is clear that the number one goal of the NEA is to maintain power over schools to the clear exclusion of parents and taxpayers. Parents are the natural enemy of the NEA. Jim Mattox, former attorney general of the State of Texas, summed up the position of the NEA when he said, "The state owns your children."

It is equally clear that the NEA is committed to a radical socialist, one world agenda. The prime thrust of the NEA curricula is to wean children away from loyalty to "the outdated religious superstitions," loyalty to the family, loyalty to the United States, and belief in free market economics, and then to introduce them to socialism and world citizenship.

The actual education of the young is a totally secondary issue.

The NEA plays on the respect we accord education and educators in America, and it wraps itself in a mantle of the high and lofty goals of education. It tells us that it stands for the strength and independence of our public education. Since the press favors the NEA positions, and since most legislators don't dare come out against "public education" or the local teachers, it has been virtually impossible to dislodge the NEA from power.

In this decade I believe that the scandal of public education will have gotten so bad that the people will finally be willing to overthrow this radical power bloc in favor of a free market system that works.

EDUCATION IN THE FUTURE

Imagine a time in America when in late August the parents of school age children would be mailed a voucher worth $2,500 for each child in their family.

All summer long the parents and their children would have been poring over the brightly colored brochures advertising the available schools in their community. Some schools would be specializing in physics or computer science. Others would emphasize the study of Latin, romance languages, and the classics.

Some would stress religious teaching and Bible study. Some might advertise regulated dress codes and strict discipline. Some might stress a less structured environment and education based on field trips and laboratories. Some might claim a fast track for college entrance; others might emphasize vocational training. Each school would be accredited by a public or private agency and would be required to provide a basic core curriculum for each student.

Some schools would be in existing school buildings. Others might be located in newer facilities. All the schools would have transportation available to serve the citizens of their community.

There would be no more education monopoly where parents had one choice: the gray mediocrity of present-day public schools.

If any of the schools in question did not deliver a product which satisfied their customers, these customers would take their vouchers and buy elsewhere.

Obviously if some schools wanted to offer a premium curriculum instead of the standard fare, they could charge more and apply the voucher toward the increased price. If parents could afford pricey extras, that would be their private decision.

All students would be guaranteed a basic quality education. Those who wanted more would not be forced to pay the full price of private education and the full tax burden of public education at the same time.

True parental choice is clearly an idea whose time has come, and it has been put in place in Milwaukee, Wisconsin, over the vehement protest of the education establishment and some civil rights groups. The plan was developed and implemented by an unlikely partnership between State Representative Polly Williams, the former Wisconsin chairman of liberal Jesse Jackson's presidential campaign, and conservative Republican Governor Tommy Thompson.

The plan, which has already cleared a court challenge, will allow parents of 1,000 low income public school students to receive a $2,500 voucher to pay for tuition at the private school of their choice. If the Milwaukee Plan (which does not currently include sectarian schools) is successful it will be expanded throughout Wisconsin.

Other programs like the Milwaukee Plan, and modifications of it, will be repeated over and over again all over America. By the year 2000 America will have firmly in place a free market educational system well on the way to returning quality to our classrooms. If 40 percent of our school systems move into the free market, I predict that the remainder will follow quickly.

The fight to establish the initial beachheads of quality education will be acrimonious and bloody. The old system cannot be reformed. Like communism, it must be replaced.

THE SUPREME COURT IN THE NINETIES

On July 20, 1990, 84-year-old Justice William Brennan resigned from the Supreme Court. This man was not just one more justice, but the intellectual leader of the Supreme Court liberal bloc which had pushed the judicial revision of the Constitution to its ultimate power.

Going into the 1990s, the court will be led by Chief Justice William Rehnquist, a strong conservative. It will also be influenced by two brilliant Roman Catholic conservatives, Justices Scalia and Kennedy. On most issues, Justice Sandra Day O'Connor can be counted in the conservative camp. If the strongly conservative Appeals Court Judge David Souter is confirmed by the Senate, there will exist a five vote conservative Supreme Court majority, to be frequently joined by Justice Byron White.

Both Justices Marshall and Blackmun are advanced in years and either could resign during the presidency of George Bush. If one or two younger conservatives were appointed to the court, there would be an overwhelming conservative presence on the court well into the twenty-first century.

With David Souter on board, in my opinion the court will, at its first opportunity, overturn the *Roe v. Wade* decision which in 1973 made abortion a constitutional right. Without a doubt, if the appropriate case is brought before them, the court may well reverse the tortured view of the establishment of religion clause of the First Amendment and lift the ban on prayer, Bible reading, and other expressions of religious belief in our public life.

This means that in the 1990s, the left will have lost its stronghold: the courts of America. And the power that has been accumulated for the left will more and more begin to serve conservative moral and social values.

However, courts customarily decide cases that have been brought to them by opposing parties. **During the 1990s, Christian pro-family, pro-life litigants have an increasingly positive opportunity to win lawsuits.** However, like the ACLU for the past 70 years, Christians must adopt a legal strategy which combines scholarly research with a strategic plan and powerful courtroom tactics.

The first major victory for the rights of students to observe their religious beliefs in the schools was decided by the Supreme Court on June 4, 1990, in a case titled *Mergens v. Westside Community School.* That case was funded by CBN through a legal foundation.

The case was argued and won at the Supreme Court by Jay Sekulow of CASE. Simply stated, in this landmark case the court ruled that the private expression of Bible study and prayer by a student club in an Omaha, Nebraska, high school did not constitute an impermissible establishment of religion under the First Amendment. The high court acknowledged the right of "equal access" for the religious interests of students by the same standards that sports or other extra-curricular activities are recognized.

This case will become a powerful weapon to stop the anti-Christian vendetta that has been waged incessantly in the schools of America. But a case or a law is no better than its enforcement; therefore, Christian people must be prepared to wage an ongoing and relentless battle against the educational establishment in every jurisdiction in America in support of the rights of Christian values in our schools.

Then there must be the preparation of the new cases to bring before the post-Brennan court to restore once again the legal foundation of the Judeo-Christian moral structure that this nation was built upon.

To this end, and in association with the Regent University Law School, CASE, and the Christian Coalition, CBN has established the American Center for Law and Justice to spearhead the exciting legal fight of the nineties.

TRIUMPH OF THE KINGDOM

The ten years from 1990 until the year 2000 will determine the destiny of America.

Despite our flaws, we are still the richest, most powerful nation on earth. We have more innovation, broader markets, a better standard of living, and greater opportunity than any place else on the globe. So far, the ships are still bringing the poor, huddled masses to our shores. They are not carrying them to other shores.

Beyond material things, America still has a vast tradition of faith, and the most vibrant and active church life of any developed country on earth. We may fail in literacy, but we rank number one among Western nations in spiritual faith and values.

It is ironic that these very Christians who are so despised by the secularists may be the only thing standing between them and the complete destruction of their way of life. Indeed, it can be said that the Christians and the Christian gospel are the early warning mechanism in any society, warning of the perils of rejecting God's standards, and urging moral self-control.

America can return to faith in God, individual initiative, and moral living. We can throw off the bondage of humanism, rid our institutions of the parasites which have been sapping our vitality, curb the excesses of big government, and turn the powerful engine of America's free enterprise system loose to pull us out of the current economic doldrums and into a new millennium filled with undreamed of technological and spiritual progress.

On the other hand, America can intensify its attacks on the Christian faith and spiritual values and, slowly and inexorably, watch its standard of living and its economic and political freedom be taken away and given to those who display the discipline and spiritual vision secular America so despises.

Christian people who have so loudly proclaimed that they are not interested in "politics" must realize that the decline in economic standards in America is not just going to affect the "heathen." The "dumbing of America" is not just going to affect the children of non-Christians. The rise in teen pregnancies and abortions in America is not merely for the unchurched. And the hand of some future conqueror of America will not rest only on those who have forsaken God.

Yet at the same time, we must be aware that the future of God's kingdom is not tied to Europe, America, the Middle East, Asia, or Africa. God's kingdom will triumph in the hearts of people. For Jesus said, "My kingdom is not of this world."

KNOWING THE DIFFERENCE

Although every one of the issues facing us—whether pornography, abortion, prayer in the schools, excessive government spending, or self-destructive foreign policy—may be very important for the moment, we must be careful that we do not identify the cause of Jesus Christ with passing, temporal concerns.

God's kingdom will stand whether or not people abort babies, read pornography, or desecrate the flag. God's kingdom will stand whether or not homosexuals proliferate in our society. We know that if abortion continues it will be hurtful to society and will ultimately bring God's wrath and judgment. We have a moral duty to speak out against evil, but we must make sure that our hope in Christ is at least as visible as our condemnation of sin.

Whatever we do as Christians in taking a stand against evil and abuse must reflect our faith in God and His right to judge evildoers. Even as we point out the evil, we must point out the kingdom of God. We must say the way of the world is death, but there is a better way!

The biblical way is against abortion. If children are unwanted, the solution is not abortion but adoption. Too often abortion has been a cheap, handy way of getting rid of the evidence of sin, or of killing off the child whose birth might force us to face up to adult responsibilities.

God's way is life. It is loving, caring families. It is a husband who loves his wife, and a wife who loves her husband; it is children brought up in the nurture and admonition of the Lord.

In the early Christian era, the Romans said of the Christians, look how they love one another! Coming from a pagan background and a violent and bloodthirsty culture, the Romans had never encountered such genuine love. They also said, they have such extraordinary women.

There was something about those Christians. The women weren't like the ordinary heathen women. They had a poise and a dignity, and a stability and radiance about them that was different.

That visible expression of Christianity from within was evidence of the light which would transform the world. It made Rome a Christian empire, and it allowed the Christian faith to span the globe. Christians today must live in that way. We have to proclaim the kingdom, and we have to point people to Jesus as the answer to the world's problems; then we must demonstrate our own faith in Him through exemplary living.

THE WAGES OF SIN

If the non-Christians, the ungodly, and the people who don't know Jesus continue in their sin, they will pay the price of that sin. If homosexuals continue in their homosexuality, they will commit genocide. Even without the implications of the AIDS epidemic, homosexuality is nothing short of self-extinction and suicide.

If the people who share that philosophy continue their self-destructive lifestyle, sooner or later their share of the population will die out. The same thing is true of abortion. Those who support the murder of the unborn will continue to kill off their own young, and sooner or later their share of the population will diminish and die out.

This is true of many other activities as well. Pornography is self-defeating. People who indulge in pornography desire more and more extremes of filth. Before long their perversion debases and destroys all their human relationships. It destroys their families, and it will destroy their lives.

Alcoholism, drug addiction, gambling, all these things will inevitably destroy the people who participate in them. In the depth of their self-destruction, such people will either realize that they must find a better way, or they will die. And, ultimately, they as a class of people will diminish because other people can see their self-destruction and will not want to participate in it.

There has to be a reaction sooner or later to homosexuality, adultery, abortion, alcoholism, drug addiction, the use of tobacco, and all the things the church has been saying are sin. It takes a few years sometimes; it may not happen overnight, but we are seeing signs of change.

Any time a society moves into blatant sexuality, especially into homosexuality and any type of sexuality in which the marriage vows are violated and there is widespread adultery, that nation can expect the judgment of God and the full weight of God's wrath against them.

From the beginning of time, any nation which has allowed itself to fall away from God and to fall into carnality and vice, and to continue willfully in that sin without national cleansing and repentance, that nation has suffered the scourge of degradation and disease and eventual destruction.

In the book of Leviticus, Chapter 18, there is a catalog of offenses so heinous they will not only cause a society to fall but will cause the land itself to "vomit out" its inhabitants. The list includes homosexuality, adultery, incest, bestiality, and the sacrifice of children. Every one of these offenses, with the exception of bestiality, is now rampant in America.

Either there will be a major national revival or there will be a national purging.

Have we gone so far that we cannot come back? No. Is there enough spiritual and moral strength in America to bring it back? Absolutely. Could there be a purging short of destruction and then a national restoration? It has happened before and can happen again.

Only God knows what the future holds for America, but this is certain. The decade of the 1990s will determine the future of America.

If God's people do not exert maximum effort in prayer, in evangelism, in education, in the courts, in the media, and in politics during this decade, America will have reached a point from which it cannot recover until after the massive judgment of God is visited upon it.

8

The Assault
on the Family

**Assaults on the traditional family by government and
radical feminists have weakened the family.**

**In 1990 the traditional American family is neither in the
majority or normative for others.**

"Marriage has existed for the benefit of man; and has been
a legally sanctioned method of control over women . . . we must
work to destroy it. The end of the institution of marriage is a necessary condition for the liberation of women. Therefore, it is important
for us to encourage women to leave their husbands. . . . All of history must be written in terms of the oppression of women. We must
go back to ancient female religions like witchcraft."

So said the "Declaration of Feminism" drafted in Houston,
Texas, in November 1971.

"In order to raise children with equality, we must take them
away from families and communally raise them." So wrote D. Mary
Jo Bane, assistant professor of education, Wellesley College and editor
of *The Wellesley*.

"Overthrowing capitalism is too small for us. We must overthrow the whole f_____ patriarchy." So stated feminist activist
Gloria Steinem, the editor of *Ms* magazine.

183

When asked what she thought of China's policy of compulsory abortion, Molly Yard, president of the National Organization of Women, was quoted in the October 10, 1989, issue of the *Washington Times* as saying, "I consider the Chinese government's policy among the most intelligent in the world."

Margaret Sanger, the founder of Planned Parenthood, which has received hundreds of millions of taxpayer dollars, wrote decades earlier, in her book, *Women and the New Race,* "The most merciful thing a large family can do to one of its infant members is to kill it."

To complete the anti-family, pro-feminist agenda, the appeal to women was not only to renounce marriage, murder children, overthrow capitalism, and seek spiritual insight from witchcraft. Sexual relations were to be transferred from heterosexual to homosexual.

In the January 1988 issue of the *National N.O.W. Times* were these words: "The simple fact is that every woman must be willing to be identified as a lesbian to be fully feminist."

THE MILITANTS

When I viewed films showing the uncontrollable rage of the National Organization of Women members against pro-life picketers at abortion clinics, I wondered what difference it should make to them whether women had babies or not. Frankly, I could not understand the pathological hatred of these militant feminists against unborn children.

Then one day I realized the answer: giving birth is the most feminine thing a woman can do. Motherhood is the most fulfilling activity a woman can ever enjoy. The radical feminists, especially the lesbians, realize instinctively that women who bear children have enormous emotional, psychological, and physical superiority over their radical counterparts. The real reason they oppose the birth of children is their agonizing desire to deny traditional women their clear advantage.

We have often heard that misery loves company. At our CBN phone centers we lovingly counsel some 2,000 gay and lesbian people every month. I can assure you that no homosexual is "gay." They and their lesbian sisters are among the most driven, confused, guilt-ridden, and miserable people on earth. To entertain their anti-family rhetoric and to give their lifestyle a legally protected place in our society is nothing short of lunacy.

NO MORE BEAVER CLEAVER

The typical American family of a wage-earner father, stay-at-home mother, and wholesome, mischievous, drug-free children was humorously portrayed in the very popular situation comedy, "Leave It to Beaver." What we now know as the "Beaver Cleaver" family is no longer in the majority in America, nor is it any longer normative for all our families.

When President Jimmy Carter called for a "Conference on Families," many of us raised strenuous objections. To us there was only one family, that ordained by the Bible, with husband, wife, and children. But the White House was bowing to the realities of the day—homosexuals living together; couples living together outside of marriage; divorced men or women with children—all the non-traditional combinations now called families. So the government sponsored a conference on "families" not on "the family."

During the early part of this century, with one or two notable exceptions, every state had laws governing divorce that were based on biblical principles. The only biblical grounds for divorce and remarriage are adultery and desertion. It is obvious that physical cruelty is "constructive" desertion, and so were some types of mind destroying mental cruelty.

Each state recognized that stable families were the building blocks of society; therefore, state law protected marriages and made divorce difficult. To obtain a divorce it was necessary for the aggrieved spouse to prove legal "fault" on the part of the partner.

Beginning in 1970 in California, the first "no fault divorce" law was passed. A divorce could be granted on the petition of either party without proof of adultery, desertion, cruelty, or any fault. By the 1980s every state except South Dakota had some type of no-fault divorce laws.

According to the May 1990 issue of *The Family in America,* the divorce rate soared from 9.2 per thousand in 1960 to 20.3 per thousand in 1975.

With the *Roe v. Wade* decision in 1973, the number of legal abortions jumped from 100,000 in 1960 to 586,800 in 1972 and then to 1,409,650 in 1978. The number of illegitimate births climbed from 245,000 in 1962 to 400,000 in 1970, and to 448,000 in 1975. By 1988, one out of every four births in America was to an unwed mother, and 1,000,000 births were recorded to unmarried women.

THE FAMILY WAGE EARNER

In the traditional family, the father was the wage earner. Since he had the responsibility to support not only himself but a wife and several children, it was expected that his pay would exceed that of a single man or woman.

Of course, a man with a secure home and a wife caring for the children had a distinct advantage over a working woman, especially a working mother.

The feminists protested this supposed "discrimination" and in 1963 the Congress passed the Equal Pay Act and Title VII of the Civil Rights Act of 1964 which made payment of a "family wage" to male heads-of-household illegal.

Coupled with the anti-family rhetoric of the feminists and the release in 1969 of Paul Ehrlich's *The Population Bomb*, social planners in Washington, to quote Dr. Allan C. Carlson, ". . . opened a campaign against the fertility of the American people." As Dr. Carlson points out so cogently, "We get more of what we pay for and less of what we tax."

From the Vietnam War and President Lyndon Johnson's "Great Society" to the 1980s, the inflation burden on America's families rose rapidly, the tax burden on families with children went up about 225 percent, and male heads of families were placed at a competitive disadvantage.

Yet government welfare was now being generously extended to unmarried mothers with children. So the government got what it paid for—1,000,000 illegitimate children. It also succeeded in making motherhood so costly that couples began to have fewer children and many more women were forced to go to work.

The feminists also got what they asked for—a rapid breakup of families and along with it the pain and anguish of divorced women with children reduced to poverty, with no male family head or bread-winner.

As one woman put it, "A woman voting for divorce is like a turkey voting for Christmas."

THE DEATH OF A CULTURE

A report on the mounting dangers to the family in America prepared by the Washington, D.C.-based Family Research Council concludes that the negative trends which began in this country in the 1960s have not yet run their course. Citing the evidence of three decades of consistent decline, the report states that the outlook for the family for the rest of the 1990s is bleak.

The conclusions of the study show that the number of families headed by single women has increased 150 percent since 1960. Today, one in four families with children is headed by a single parent, and if the trend continues there will be 13 million single-parent households in this country by the end of the decade.

Perhaps even more disturbing, the number of illegitimate births has increased more than 300 percent since 1960. Yet that fact doesn't even reveal the true horror of the problem since unmarried women also have four out of five of the 1.6 million abortions in America each year.

The trend indicates that fully half of all births in America will be illegitimate by the end of this decade.

Today we are witnessing the disintegration of all the values we once considered "American virtues." The traditional family is in shambles; our culture is in a nosedive of moral decline; government is raping the American taxpayer through its own arrogant and self-absorbed greed; and the courts have legislated Judeo-Christian values out of American public life and, in effect, turned the nation over to the godless.

After a period of head-scratching and regrouping, conservative and religious Americans are beginning to realize that they are under assault. What is happening in America is not a debate, it is not a friendly disagreement between enlightened people. It is a vicious one-sided attack on our most cherished institutions.

Suddenly the confrontation is growing hotter and it just may become all out civil war. It is a war against the family and against conservative and Christian values.

Even as we are witnessing an ongoing crisis in the Middle East, we are engaged in a war in our midst of profound spiritual dimensions, and as stated so well by Gary Bauer, "To the victor goes the next generation of young Americans."

THE BREAKUP OF THE FAMILY

In his public addresses and writings, Gary Bauer, who is the president of the Family Research Council, has warned that the goal of the secular welfare state is to render the family obsolete and to usher in an age of "rule by experts." That is not surprising, but we have already seen that the consequences of secular rule without spiritual values can be disastrous.

Bauer says that modern history has shown us, over and over again, that "neither a free economy nor a strong national defense can be sustained without the Judeo-Christian bedrock. A nation of hedonists, incapable of postponing gratification, cannot resist the siren-song of big government; and a nation that smiles at the slaughter of its young, and leers at the degradation of the human person on the video screen, is probably doomed, in the long run, to go the way of Carthage."

It is truly shocking, by any standard, to see how the values of this nation have crumbled in such a short period of time. In 1950 the so-called nuclear family was based on the traditional model of one husband as the bread-winner, one wife at home, and a couple of children. At that time approximately 55 percent of all American families fit this model.

A couple of years ago, Bureau of Labor Statistics reports suggested that perhaps as few as 10 percent of all American families could be considered traditional. However, newer research from the Family Research Council suggests that about 39 percent of American families are traditional, in which the mother is the primary caregiver to her children; 18 percent are semi-traditional, where the children are continually cared for by at least one parent; 19 percent are careerist, meaning the children are regularly in day care; and 24 percent are single-parent families.

But regardless which standard you choose, the number of women working is continuously escalating. There is growing social pressure on mothers to work outside the home as well as a greater financial burden on the family which forces mothers into the workplace.

I fear that if this trend continues, it will take us to the point that as high as 90 percent of all married women will be working outside the home by the end of this century. What will that do to the family? What will it mean for the next generation of children?

The mere prospect offers a shocking vision of the future and has already had some far-reaching consequences. It does means that the work force is expanded; it means that there are more skilled people in the work force, and that the pre-tax incomes of families will go up.

The median income of families in 1987 was just over 30,000 dollars. If the trend continues, the median family income could conceivably increase to as much as 50,000 dollars by the end of the decade. But there is another side to that promise. There will clearly be a direct impact on the structure of the family, and that will bring with it other far-reaching consequences.

THE UNCALCULATED COSTS

When you consider the relatively low pay most women receive, subtract taxes and the cost of transportation, extra clothing, cosmetics, meals at work, child care, and other related expenses, you discover that the actual take-home pay of the average working mother is insignificant.

Financial advisers Ron Blue and Russ Crosson have documented this fact in their research reports and books on the subject, suggesting that the actual net pay after expenses of the working mother is frequently no more than 1,900 to 2,000 dollars a year!

Even if most families haven't stopped to calculate such things, they know it's true when they discover that their two incomes have not actually improved the quality of their lives. Families who once thought the solution to their money problems would be for mom to work have discovered that suddenly they're deeper in debt than ever, they're no happier, and their kids are growing up with no mother, no father, and absolutely no sense of family.

Black Americans are at greatest risk. The Family Research Council report shows that 61 percent of all Black children are born out of wedlock, and 44 percent of all Black families are headed by a single woman. Those unfortunate trends suggest that by the end of the decade less than half of all Black families will be built on the traditional model of a married couple and children.

Since the first federally funded government welfare programs were introduced in the 1960s, teenage pregnancy, out-of-wedlock child birth, and abortions have skyrocketed. Value-free counseling and sex education has escalated the disintegration of the nuclear family at an astronomical rate.

It is as if the federal welfare system has set out to put government in the place of father and mother in the home. At the current frightening pace, Bauer states, "The family may soon be void of any significant role in society."

Even more compelling, we should be horrified that what we have created, instead of more security or greater affluence, is a day-care system which, without question, is harmful to children.

Every sociological test that has been taken for years has indicated that prolonged absence of either parent is damaging to children. Prolonged absence of the father or of the mother leads to dependency, lack of assertiveness, submission to peer pressure, susceptibility to drugs, inferior performance in school.

In addition, the increase of women in the work force has put ever greater strain on marriages. At this point, the financial and career ambitions of women equals that of men.

Just like the competitiveness and the stress and strain of the workplace, competition also develops in the home over which partner makes the greater contribution, which job takes precedence, and which roles various partners should take with regard to child care, housework, and all the various responsibilities of mothers and fathers in the home.

It is obvious that even greater strain is placed on women who feel a responsibility to be not only good employees but good mothers: the so-called "Super Mom" complex. In order for a woman to work, to maintain a home, and to look after her children, she has to have incredible endurance and resolve. All those demands can get to be nerve-wracking, and in many homes it leads to broken marriages and ruined lives.

If you look at the leading causes of divorce in this country you will discover that "lack of communication" is often listed as the number one reason. People just don't talk to each other. But it should be obvious that if they're not home at the same time, and especially if they're working shifts where they don't even get to see each other, then lack of communication is inevitable.

BECOMING STRANGERS

The nature of the work environment means that both husband and wife are now receiving most of their emotional and intellectual stimulation outside the home, in the workplace, and from different groups of people who never meet or interact with each other.

Given that situation, it's not hard at all to understand how a husband and wife can quickly become estranged from each other and from each other's friends, and how their conversations (which seem to grow fewer and fewer) reflect that differing input, different circle of friends, and different frames of reference.

When they do focus on the things they have in common, it is often only to solve problems with their children, the home, or their mounting debts. It's not the kind of loving interaction and kinship that brought them together in the first place.

The second leading cause of divorce is financial. Strains in relations due to bills and mounting debts and disputes over the allocation of funds are a genuine problem. And they become more and more problematical as the partners each have their own income, and as they squabble over who gets what.

Today the divorce rate has skyrocketed. For every two marriages formed in America, one marriage ends in divorce. There are more and more people these days who are chronic divorce victims, who may go through four or five marriages. The divorce rate is up 700 percent since the turn of the century.

The strain this puts on people's lives is unbelievable. Next to the death of a spouse, divorce is one of the most traumatic experiences anyone can have. The feelings of inadequacy, of failure, and of guilt can go on eating at both these individuals for years. But perhaps even worse, the damage to the children is beyond calculation.

I think everybody recognizes this fact, and we want the best for our children, but couples grow so embittered toward each other they willingly jeopardize the future welfare of their own children. In one survey I saw recently, even though the warring parents recognized, and freely admitted, that a divorce would damage their kids, 75 percent of them said they would go ahead and get the divorce, which shows again the selfishness and lack of commitment that can develop in a damaged marriage.

The awful trends these statistics are setting in motion are a shame and a scandal. The epidemic of shattered families and broken homes in this nation is producing a generation of emotionally and psychologically impaired young people who will, in turn, grow up to be adults who will be getting married with less and less commitment to marriage, which in turn will produce future generations even more impaired, and without a healthy sense of love or bonding. We can only wonder where it will end.

THE PATHOLOGY OF DAY CARE

I can't help but think of the seminal studies of Professor Harry Harlow and his team of behavioral researchers at the University of Wisconsin in the 1950s. Harlow discovered that little baby monkeys, when deprived of their birth mothers, would frantically cling for comfort and protection to stuffed mother substitutes. He learned that, even though the baby monkey could be fed from a wire mannikin, the infant would cling, when frightened, to the comforting, padded surrogate mother.

We know that infants deprived of the affection of a mother—and it is equally true for monkeys and humans alike—will become sick and die. The lesson is quite simple: we cannot live without love.

Any child who does not have a mother with it, especially in the early days, is deprived. In a research project at Regent University, we found that day care doesn't work, whether it's institutional day care, church-run day care, skilled franchised day care, or company-provided day care. It is absolutely certain that government-run day care will be devastating to little children.

It doesn't work because institutional day care does not provide the same support and psychological nurturing that a mother can give.

A few years ago we came up with an alternative child care program at CBN called Mother's Touch, in which a woman would take as many as six or seven children into her home during the day. The woman is very much like a loving aunt or grandmother to the children in an environment psychologists call *in loco parentis;* that is, "in the place of" parents.

We found that, unlike institutional day care, those situations worked very nicely. We believe it was successful because the element of nurturing and one-on-one affection and reinforcement was diligently provided for each child.

For years we have known that children need natural, one-on-one reinforcement. Each child must know that, to someone, and hopefully to his mother, he is the most special person in the world. The child needs warm, loving attention. When he says, "Mommy, look at me!" he is begging for that nod of approval, for that look that says, "Yes, my precious child, you are special to me." But group day care does not provide that.

After a remarkably short period of time, even little children grow cold and withdrawn. In some cases they grow shy, their personalities become stunted. Still others react in the opposite extreme by becoming loud and assertive and demanding.

As if they have given up on love and affection, many children confined in day care institutions for years become angry and antisocial. There's not enough bad things I can say about what day care does to children.

A new survey co-sponsored by the American Academy of Pediatrics and *Working Mother* magazine recently reported that medical professionals recognize that day care is especially harmful to children age three and under. Of the 1,100 pediatricians polled in the survey, more than two-thirds said they believe day care is harmful for children under six months; 61 percent said it may be harmful for children six months to one year old; and more than half, 52 percent, believe it is still harmful for children aged one to three.

That is strong evidence from a purely secular source. But sadly, the typical response of working mothers is to say they will simply demand better day care instead of saying they will give their children what the child wants—and needs—most in the world: its own mother.

Toward the end of its lengthy focus on the day care issue, *Newsweek* magazine actually confessed that infants in day care for

20 or more hours a week are at risk. The researchers said that the high turnover rate of paid caregivers and the high disease rate among institutionalized children make day care a very uncertain and unhappy place for children.

"Despite the compelling evidence about the dark side of day care," the magazine reported, "many experts say there's a great reluctance to discuss these problems publicly." Why? "Because they're afraid the right wing will use this to say that only mothers can care for babies, so women should stay home."

As so aptly expressed by Phyllis Schlafly in her April 1990 newsletter, "What the liberals and the feminists are really afraid of is not the right wing but the eternal truth that the traditional family is still the best way to live, and that babies still need mothers in the home."

The long range effects of the neglect and mistreatment of our young people is going to be the creation of a whole generation of people who will be lacking in commitment, shallow in their personalities, and unable to form lasting bonds and attachments. That may translate into an inability to form bonds with their business associates, their fellow employees, and with their community; or with their nation.

How will that affect our long-range ability to defend a country, to make sacrifices in terms of taxes, or to give the time and energy it takes to run a complex society? The prospect is frightening.

How sad to think that it comes down to the fact that we have become a consumer-oriented, greed-driven society whose motivations and morals are based on the acquisition of things, and the inevitable accumulation of enormous amounts of debt. And the commonly accepted belief, even among Christians, is that the way to accumulate the things that pay off the debts is for the wife to go to work.

THE HIGH PRICE OF FULFILLMENT

This is, in part, the legacy of the feminist movement which says, "Do your own thing, Baby. You are the New Woman. Fulfill yourself!" They are not willing to recognize that a commitment to the next generation is more important than fulfilling your own desires right now. For what does it profit a man or a woman if they gain the whole world but lose their own soul, and destroy the souls of their innocent children on the way down?

I readily acknowledge that some women do have to work. I also recognize that women without children and women whose children are grown may want to get involved in a career for many reasons.

However, let's be sure we understand that the problem we will have to face in the '90s is not that some women work, but that women who should be home nurturing and building the next generation are worshiping, instead, at the shrine of materialism: the lust for bigger and better and more, and lots more of it.

Indeed, as I illustrated above, many women have to work. They have no choice. But many do not have to work. These women must recognize that the nurture and training of the next generation is *the most important career any human being can have.*

Having so many mothers in the workplace now means that there is inadequate day care for the children of working mothers. So the government's new solution is to spend 23 billion dollars more of taxpayer money to provide for the children in day care. This in turn will bring on more inflation and force more women into the workplace.

Long range, children without commitment, latchkey children, children who are pregnant out of wedlock, children who begin sexual activity at age 12 or 13, children who are drinking alcohol at 11 or 12, teenage alcoholics and drug addicts, and other problems too outrageous to mention, can be traced directly to family breakup, poor home life, and the absence of both parents during the crucial formative years.

An article in the *Los Angeles Times* in September 1989—citing research in the journal, *Pediatrics*—reported that "latchkey" children, whether from rich or poor families, are twice as likely to use cigarettes, alcohol, and marijuana as youngsters cared for by adults after school. Yet 40 percent of children under 13—somewhere between 2 million and 6 million—go home to an empty house after school.

These reports may be low because parents are reluctant to admit that their young children have no adult supervision. Because of the growing problem of divorce, which has left an estimated 14.6 million children with single parents, there will be an ever increasing number of at risk, unsupervised young children.

GATEWAY TO DESPAIR

The impact of drugs and drug abuse on the American family does not seem to be going away. The casual attitude of many people toward so-called "recreational drugs" has had terrible consequences.

The 1988 Bureau of Justice Statistics Sourcebook reported that over 60 percent of people between the ages of 18 and 25 say they have used marijuana and 25 percent have used cocaine at least once.

Among Americans aged 26 to 34, 58.5 percent have used marijuana and 24.1 percent have used cocaine. This says that the younger you are, the more likely you are to experiment with marijuana or cocaine at some time. But it also says that getting drugs is easy, and a lot of people are doing it.

Even while many people say they do not consider such statistics a problem, there is a dramatic positive correlation between drugs and crime, and each year the evidence becomes more damning. Between 1974 and 1986 the proportion of state prisoners under the influence of an illegal drug at the time of the offense for which they were incarcerated increased from 25 to 35 percent. The number under the influence of cocaine alone increased from 1 percent to 10.7 percent.

The Bureau reports that typically the first use of drugs among prisoners surveyed was at age 15. The typical "user" first became a steady user at age 18. Ever more distressing is the information gathered from users in juvenile facilities, where 19 percent said they first used drugs before age 10, and 40 percent said they were using before age 12.

The number of people convicted of drug possession in this country more than doubled from 1980 to 1988, while the number convicted for sale or manufacture of drugs went up 180 percent, from just under 103,000 in 1980 to 287,858 in 1988. This bad news affects every city and town in America, and involves every law enforcement agency.

The Federal Government seized 4,175 clandestine drug laboratories between 1975 and 1988. In 1988 alone, 810 labs were seized; 107 million marijuana plants were destroyed in 38,531 plots, leading to 6,062 arrests and the seizure of 2,034 weapons. In that same year, the Drug Enforcement Agency (DEA) confiscated 125,000 pounds of cocaine, 2,000 pounds of heroin, 73 pounds of opium, and 1.2 million pounds of marijuana.

Add to that the U.S. Customs Service seizure of 1.7 million pounds of marijuana, 87,900 pounds of cocaine and close to 4 million dosage units of LSD and other barbiturates; plus the Coast Guard's confiscation of 356,000 pounds of marijuana and 9,000 pounds of cocaine. The total number of suspects prosecuted for drug offenses escalated from 7,003 in 1980 to 17,729 in 1987, an increase of 153 percent.

What will it take for America to wake up to the danger of playing with drugs? A National Institute of Justice survey of 20 cities reports that from one fourth to one third of all males arrested in 1988 tested positive for marijuana.

In New York City, 75 percent of males and 74 percent of females arrested tested positive for cocaine. And of the juveniles incarcerated for violent crimes in 1986, 60 percent reported being regular drug users and 40 percent were under the influence of drugs at the time they committed the crime for which they were incarcerated.

THE WAY OUT

How many times have we heard bureaucrats scream, "We must educate the people to the dangers of drugs"? How many billions of dollars have we poured down the drains of federal bureaucracy? And why do we keep on thinking that education in the hands of federal bureaucrats will ever change the situation? Don't the statistics speak for themselves?

You don't have to be a genius to see that the billions we have thrown at "education" have failed to produce results. It is perfectly clear that drug use is worse now than ever, that alcoholism is on a crazy upward spiral, that drug- and alcohol-related crime show no signs of slowing down.

Every public and private agency in the world has been "educating" the American public to the dangers of tobacco for more than a decade. We have all seen every imaginable kind of media and advertising crusade telling Americans that smoking will cause cancer in long-term habitual users, yet nearly a third of all Americans continue to smoke.

Smokers interviewed about the obvious dangers of their habit say they know it is deadly, they know they are at risk, but they are willing to take the risk. In other words, they have the education, they know the facts, but it hasn't changed their lives.

Alcoholics know the dangers of alcohol abuse. Many of them, in similar interviews, say they know that driving under the influence of alcohol is dangerous and deadly, and they know they are at risk. They even know that alcoholism causes conflict in the home and broken marriages. But they continue to drink and to drive and to put lives in jeopardy because they cannot stop.

Either they believe they are in command when they are not, or they have accepted the fact that the habit owns them, or else they just don't care who they hurt.

Education has not changed them. So why is government telling us, "We need more education"? The answer to all these questions is the same. The federal bureaucracy doesn't have a clue. They have no idea what to do, because the answer does not lie in education or training or demonstration of the facts. Fundamental changes in the desires of the human heart are God's territory.

Changing lives is ultimately a profound philosophical and theological matter. It is an issue which can only be dealt with through submission of our own wills to the will of God.

PROTECTING OUR FUTURE

Unless there is a dramatic change in our habits and beliefs, there really is not a great deal of hope for the children of America in the next decade. The United States Department of Health and Human Services, which monitors the incidence and prevalence of abuse and neglect of children, has released figures which show that child abuse is increasing at an alarming rate in this country.

In their 1988 study, the figures showed that cases of maltreatment had increased 66 percent since 1980, with an increase of 74 percent in cases of physical and sexual abuse.

Some 63 percent of the cases reported in that study involved neglect, which means that out of every 1,000 children, 15.9 were reported as victims of neglect: 1,003,600 children. Another 43 percent suffered from abuse, which is 10.7 children in 1,000 and a total of 675,000 children reported.

The incidence of the sexual abuse of children has tripled since 1980. The sad fact is, this is only the tip of the iceberg. These are only the cases which are actually reported and which pass the government's screening verification processes. What must the actual numbers be?

When we look at the implication of such studies in the context of the overall cultural and spiritual climate of this nation, we have to recognize that it all comes back to the same foundation: selfish, egotistical self-interest.

Since the early 1970s the trend has been to ever greater levels of selfishness, materialism, addiction to sex, alcohol and drugs, the breakdown of the family, and the destruction of the natural bonding between parents and children.

Responsibility, restraint, concern for the welfare of others, and the kind of maturity that considers the future consequences of our actions seems to be missing in a huge segment of our society.

The type of self-indulgence we are seeing in this country today doesn't even stop at self-destruction; it even seeks to destroy others, and to eliminate the inconveniences created by its own excesses. That is the real sin at the heart of the abortion problem in this country.

MORAL ACTIVISM

The Bible makes it clear that we must lift the yoke of oppression. If we see a wrong being committed, we have a positive obligation to do something about it. In the Old Testament we read that anyone seeing his neighbor's ox in a ditch was supposed to go to the ox and pull it out. Certainly if we see an animal in trouble and have an obligation to help it, how much more do we have an obligation to help protect innocent children, to prevent them from being abused and, in the case of abortion, from being killed?

In the days of slavery, if a slave owner was seen whipping or abusing his slave, any Christian had an obligation to speak out about it. Slavery was a very old custom—as old as civilization—but there came a time when men and women of faith saw that they had to try to do something to change the laws to protect the people who had been enslaved.

Did Christians have an obligation to get involved in the legal processes? Yes. Were they responsible for doing their part to shut down slavery, which was a violation of human dignity? Absolutely.

It should be a symbol of just how far the values of this nation have fallen to see, as readers of the magazine *Christian Century* recently did, the comments of America's first suffragettes and feminists on the issue of abortion. A notice placed by a group called Feminists for Life of America quoted several of those early leaders and their opinions on the issue.

Susan B. Anthony, for example, said, "I deplore the horrible crime of child murder . . . No matter what the motive, love of ease, or a desire to save from suffering the unborn innocent, the woman is awfully guilty who commits the deed. . . ." And Elizabeth Cady Stanton, in a letter to her friend Julia Ward Howe, wrote, "it is degrading to women that we should treat our children as property to be disposed of as we see fit."

The essential morality of that earlier time was not due to the fact that men and women were better. Certainly children were conceived out-of-wedlock and at inconvenient times then as now. The women were not less militant; each of those women pointed out the complicity of the men in the conception and the abortion. But there was a foundation of morality, inherited from a Christian tradition, that set the natural frame of reference.

It is only now, in this modern and increasingly godless age, that women like Molly Yard and Jane Fonda dare claim that women have a "moral right" to murder their young.

THE LOST WILL AND TESTAMENT

As America has observed the birth and growing up of the enormous generation commonly called "The Baby-Boomers," we have witnessed the making of a generation of Americans who, to a large extent, have been unwilling to make the kinds of traditional family commitments society has always been based upon.

Instead of marriage, they have opted for "living together." Instead of child-rearing and the building of families, they have opted for promiscuous pre-marital and a-marital sex. Facing the prospect of conception, they have used birth control devices of every description and, failing that, they have resorted ultimately to abortion.

Many of the men and women of this generation have shunned the traditional male and female roles, refused traditional adult responsibilities, rejected the bearing of children in order to persist in a prolonged emotional adolescence and self-absorption. It is more than just a joke that they have surrounded themselves with every kind of creature comfort and every conceivable luxury that money and a Visa Gold Card can buy on time.

This huge demographic segment of the population, the pig in the python so to speak, is working its way through our system and is going to come to retirement age during the first and second decades of the new millennium; that is, from 2010 to 2020.

However, some rather mundane and practical issues have to be examined before that prospect can become reality. The only guarantee of a man or woman's retirement is the existence of a large, active work force: that is, their own children and grandchildren, who will be paying into the Social Security system (and various other retirement programs) in order to make their retirement possible.

Wouldn't it be one of those tragic ironies of life if those people who have opted for pleasure now, who have failed to make commitment or to invest in a family, to raise and nurture children, or to spend the time it takes to bring them up with love, will have no one to care for them in their old age?

Wouldn't it be ironic if those same people discovered their need of a family to help provide for their future, but there just wasn't anyone around to take care of them? They may well be the first generation to come to the point where the working young will say, "Enough! We refuse to support you." And those old hedonists who have sunk their life savings into their personal fulfillment and self-gratification may be reduced to abject poverty.

A May 1990 report in *Newsweek* indicated that the Social Security system is already under incredible strain as the numbers of contributing workers in America declines and the number of recipients continues to grow. In 1950 the ratio of workers to retirees was 120 to 1. At the current rate, the ratio will fall to only 2 workers per retiree by the year 2030.

And since they have been such vocal advocates of abortion and euthanasia, wouldn't it be ironic if some kind of government-sponsored euthanasia program is signed into law just in time to make sure they won't have to hang around too long in their lonely and miserable retirement years? We don't have to summon up the fable of the grasshopper and the ant to realize that this predicament is one of the results of hedonism.

The unwillingness to make commitments because they are afraid of what might happen, along with the desire to "fulfill" themselves, may well condemn an entire generation to a cold and lonely demise.

Their unwillingness to invest in the future is the very vehicle that will bring them into a pathetic and helpless old age. The joy and the light of men and women in their later years has always been their children and grandchildren: the family unit. These people will not have a family unit. I'm afraid there will be a great many elderly who will reap this whirlwind.

RETURNING HOME

But perhaps there is yet hope. Already I am seeing a definite trend among some of our young people to experience the rewards of a loving home, to give of themselves instead of always taking from others, and to discover the joys of traditional family life before it's too late.

Today we are seeing women in their thirties, young women reaching the other end of their child-bearing years, suddenly opting to take off from work to start a family. Motherhood is coming back "in." The maternity wards are beginning to get crowded; and fashions seem to be more feminine.

A recent study by the Population Reference Bureau in Washington reported that America has entered a new baby boom. Demographer Carl Haub was quoted in a syndicated news release as saying, "It does appear to be a real upswing in U.S. fertility."

The highest fertility rate in recent history was recorded in 1957, when the average was 3.77 births per woman of childbearing age. That rate dropped to its lowest point in 1976, at 1.76 births per woman. Unexpectedly, it moved up to 2 births per woman in 1989 and it looks as if it may well exceed that average for the next several years.

Gregory Spencer, of the United States Census Bureau, told reporters his department was caught off guard by the sudden increase in births in this country. "The last couple of years have surprised everybody," he said. Now, the demographers believe we are seeing a genuine trend. "People are really saying they don't want to be childless," said Spencer.

Women are having more children, and women in the Christian community are leading the way. As of this year, I am the grandfather of nine gorgeous children, and every one of them is beautiful and bright! If my sons and daughters are in any way representative of their peers and the other Christian moms and dads around the country, maybe some of our young couples are recognizing the importance of the family.

On the other hand, it is still a tragedy that so many women deferred child-bearing too long. In some cases, they may have had an abortion and since discovered that the abortion rendered them unable to bear children. There are many women who are incapable of having children because of abortions.

For years we have seen that it is more difficult to have children, and that the dangers of birth defects are increased substantially for women over 40. However, a new study by Dr. Henry Klapholtz of Boston's Beth Israel hospital suggests that women who keep fit, who are free of addictions, and who have good physical and emotional health may continue to conceive and bear healthy children even after 40.

Thanks to the fitness trend, more women in their 30s and 40s are staying trim and eating healthy food, but it is still a struggle to keep fit after 40. Having a first child after 30 can be difficult and, however you look at it, after 40 the risks are increased.

A CHRISTIAN MONOPOLY

Bill Gothard, who heads a number of excellent family-centered ministries in this country, has been teaching pastors the importance of communicating to their congregations the blessedness of having children. The whole concept of fruitfulness in the Bible context is that the family is a blessing from God.

The psalmist wrote, "Sons are a heritage from the Lord, children a reward from him. Like arrows in the hands of a warrior are sons born in one's youth." Everything about the Bible indicates that fruitfulness is God's blessing.

It seems abundantly clear to me that those who are political liberals—those who are left of center, and those who are atheists—are intent on destroying themselves. The pro-abortion crowd is essentially committing suicide.

The statistics show that it takes 2.1 live births per woman in a country such as the United States to maintain a population at a steady pace. We are now at about 1.9 per thousand in America, so the rate of growth is actually declining. We have already seen that it is equally low in industrialized Europe.

Allan Carlson told me that his studies for the Rockford Institute showed that the only people who want to have children are those who have a strong religious faith. Muslims, Christians, and certain other groups fit this description because they have confidence in the future. Because they believe in a Supreme Being, they are willing to take a chance on the future by bringing children into the world; they have the conviction that there really is a future and a hope. There is something better.

Those who have no religious faith say, this life is all there is. Why should I invest in the future if the future doesn't matter? I had better grab all the gusto I can get, because I only go around once. I might as well have fun and take care of number one. I deserve a break today.

Ever notice how the advertising is all focused on that very self-indulgent, self-gratifying hedonism? But the hedonism is a function of atheism, which says that I am the center of my universe. Looking out for myself and giving myself pleasure is, after all, the ultimate aim of life. So if I can find pleasure for myself and achieve self-actualization, then I will have achieved the goal of my life!

What a sad, disappointing way of life. What an unfortunate legacy to have given an entire generation on this planet. You only have to look at nature to realize that the goal of any biological species is to reproduce itself. Any plant or flower that is sterile is a biological failure.

It's an irony that the greatest sex symbol of the '50s and '60s, Marilyn Monroe, couldn't even bear children. She was a "sex goddess," but she couldn't do what sex was about: namely, reproduce.

But among all these ironies, there is one other which should not escape our notice. If Christians continue having large families and do not have abortions, our percentage of the population is going to rise dramatically, just on the basis of birth-rate alone.

Those who are our philosophical adversaries are deliberately committing genocide. They are doing away with their young, they are not reproducing themselves, and it is only a matter of time until their kind dies out completely. Certainly homosexuality should die out since the homosexuals are unable to reproduce themselves.

Christians and all those who believe in God, in the blessings of life and in the wonder of God's creation, along with all those who love children and want to share their lives with their families, will continue to prosper and their philosophies will grow stronger as their numbers increase. The future is on our side.

I am not in favor of self-inflicted genocide even for the adversaries of Christianity. But nevertheless, as their numbers decrease, our numbers will increase, and our influence will continue to grow.

SOME PRACTICAL SOLUTIONS

Several years ago two young teenagers in a suburb of Los Angeles brutally murdered a young man and his girlfriend who were attending a public sports event at an outdoor stadium. The murderers then sauntered nonchalantly to a MacDonald's restaurant where they ate a "cheeseburger, french fries, and a coke."

There was no guilt. No remorse. Two promising young lives were extinguished in a pool of blood, and these young killers calmly ate cheeseburgers.

Such unfeeling brutality is not unusual in our land any more. I once ministered to a professional killer on death row at the maximum security prison in Raeford, Florida. This young man, under age thirty, had murdered twenty people and not once had he ever cried. Not once, that is, until he experienced the love and forgiveness of Jesus Christ and was born again.

These young people have grown up without hugs, without kisses, without attention, without care. Often the only contact they receive with adults is through physical or mental abuse. They are emotional zombies, lacking human feelings. What they can do to other human beings is horrible to contemplate.

The children of divorce and those who grow up in day care institutions are not that bad, but they are clearly stunted, short of their full potential.

Something has to be done to restore the traditional families in America. Unless drastic changes are made now, by the year 2000 a generation will be lost.

Here are a few proposals that merit consideration:

First, we should do away with no-fault divorce and, again, make it difficult for couples to sever the bonds of marriage.

Second, we must reward stable families with financial incentives. I believe that tax deductions of up to $5,000 per child and tax sheltered educational Individual Retirement Accounts (IRA) will be an enormous incentive for familes with children.

Third, there should be tax credits to reward women who wish to be homemakers. If we can give tax deductions for child care expense for working mothers, we can certainly afford tax benefits for women who want to stay home and care for their children.

Fourth, welfare laws that deny benefits when there is a "man in the house" should be revoked. We cannot allow welfare to become a disincentive for family formation.

Fifth, there should be no welfare benefits for unwed mothers. Those teenage girls who receive welfare should not be able to use welfare to leave their parents home and establish their own residence. Welfare checks should no longer be viewed as a benefit for illegitimacy.

There should be reward, not punishment, if a girl who has a baby out of wedlock decides to marry the child's father.

Sixth, men who father children should be forced to support their own children. The burden should be theirs, not society's.

Finally, this society must be taught that sex before marriage, adultery, and abortion are sinful and wrong. People must be taught that God hates divorce. They must learn that only through stable, loving marriages where children are raised in the "nurture and admonition of the Lord" can this nation rise to its potential and be spared anarchy and heartbreak.

An entire generation of children are now clearly at risk in America.

PART THREE

2000 and Beyond

We have in our power the ability to conquer disease, to extend life, to remove genetic abnormalities, to supply a reasonably abundant standard of living to every human being on this planet, to bring forth an ever increasing cornucopia of technological products to make each of our lives more pleasant, to have at our disposal increased learning, culture, and leisure.

Today we are citizens of a new and different world. As we cast our eyes from East to West we see new allies and new adversaries on every horizon. Furthermore, we are no longer an island, for the world has come to our shores to buy and sell, to proselyte, and to live.

9

Technology and the Environment

Major technological advances await us in the next millennium. At the forefront will be discoveries to unlock the potential of the human mind and spirit.

The primacy of environmental concerns may hinder technology and prove a front for massive new governmental spending and intrusion into our lives.

When Canadian scholar Marshall McLuhan coined the phrase "the global village" in 1964, he had no idea just how soon or how relentlessly the new media technology would circle the globe.

Along with the newest rage for fax machines, cellular phones, answering machines, compact disc players, VCRs, Nintendo and Atari games, and wide-screen TV, we now have sophisticated cable systems, and backyard satellite dishes bringing entertainment into family rooms all over the world.

In more and more American homes you now see personal computers connected to modems connected to libraries, consumer bulletin boards, information services, shopping services, stock brokers, and news retrieval sources nationwide. People are banking with automatic teller machines, by telephone and computer, and suddenly McLuhan's prophecy has come true in the most unbelievable way.

209

In March 1990, *Scientific American* reported on the broad range of information technologies already in our grasp. From "minitel" computerized telephone systems, like those being used in France, to the high-tech online funds transfer networks—such as the SWIFT system, which is engaged in the exchange of hundreds of billions of dollars every single day—the range of technology we're already using is mind-boggling.

Not only does the presence of all this sophisticated technology change the way we communicate with each other, but it changes the way we work. Today thousands of people are working from their homes, using technology to link up with their employers, customers, and suppliers.

The new technology has also allowed American business to focus heavily on information and service-based activities. Today nearly 75 percent of the entire labor force in America is employed in the service sector, compared to only 55 percent in the years right after the Second World War.

Communications and related systems for information delivery are the biggest things on the industrial horizon; and the biggest thing on the communications horizon is fiber optics. Those tiny filaments of dense fiber are incredibly efficient conductors of light, and therefore, they can also transmit all kinds of data in a highly efficient way.

Over a period of time, as it is mechanically and economically feasible, telephone companies will replace traditional cable with fiber optic cable as their primary delivery system for information, and at that point I believe we are going to see a whole new era of communications technology.

In combination with the power of fiber optic transmission of information, satellite links will become more and more sophisticated. Soon we will be leap-frogging voice, data, and image transmission from huge satellites around the world. We're just on the threshold of having access to the types of satellites that can do this.

There will soon be antennae no larger than a couple of panes of glass, which means that every home will have access to satellite. Satellite transmission will leap across national boundaries and physical barriers so that there will be increasingly broader global communication.

We can do it now of course—three satellites can cover the

world—but the new satellite-to-home transmitters are going to be much more powerful than anything we have seen before.

FASTER, MORE AFFORDABLE

The information-bearing capacity of optical fibers is skyrocketing with each new stratum of research. We have read that the newest cable can transmit one trillion bits of information per second; at the same time, the cost of manufacturing and installing the cable continues to fall.

One of the marvelous curiosities of the technology boom is that as the technology becomes more powerful it also becomes more affordable. Successful innovations attract a consumer base almost instantaneously in today's economic climate, which allows industry, in turn, to continue development and to reduce costs.

From a broadcaster's perspective, the programming opportunities are really exciting. Very soon it will be possible to send out several thousand programs simultaneously, which will give viewers a tremendous diversity of programming to choose from. People will be able to access motion pictures, educational programs, or whatever they want, around the clock.

This means, in turn, that the three major networks in America will continue to lose audience and power. Combined, they're already down to maybe 60 percent of the audience, and I predict that figure will drop very soon below 50 percent.

Not only will cable take more of the audience, but the satellite in the sky and the Baby Bells, the telephone companies with their fiber optic delivery systems, will all be major players.

At present we have the capacity to put one picture in the sky and sideband a number of audio tracks so that one message—one motion picture or one program—can be seen by multitudes and heard in their own language.

This also means that there will be a huge demand for software. I think there will be a broad proliferation of film companies in the years just ahead. The public demand for programming on these high quality delivery systems will be an absolute monster, devouring everything we can produce.

GLOBALIZING THE MEDIA

From a Christian standpoint, the opportunities are just enormous to produce movie and video programming. In the coming decade we will see the formation of new production companies creating very sophisticated motion picture materials. This is why we have such a strong film department at Regent University. We are training people to do films. Many of our graduates are already producing films, and we are in the process of establishing a fairly large motion picture company to do this kind of work.

Through our International Family Entertainment group, we are in partnership now with producers in France, Canada, and Australia. We have produced a major series in Japan. In the coming years there will be a globalization of this kind of activity.

We have seen the Japanese coming into America to buy up companies like Columbia so they can have access to their libraries of motion pictures. But I also see creative talent coming out of the East Bloc nations as well, and out of Europe and other parts of the world, beginning to challenge U.S. filmmakers on costs and quality.

Again, from a Christian standpoint, there is a hunger now for high quality programs that have family values. The emerging nations do not want the sex, crime, and violence that is so typical of American television. They want high quality shows, but they don't have them available.

So much of today's European fare is extraordinarily dull. They haven't had the production budgets necessary to move into the type of massive motion pictures that the United States is familiar with. The new Europe will become a huge market for quality films in the coming decade.

RETIRING THE GATEKEEPERS

Until now, about 200 writers, producers, and directors in Hollywood have determined what people around the world get to see and believe. They have been the gatekeepers and, by and large, not very good ones. That will have to change.

Global competition will diminish the role of the old gatekeepers

and bring in new ones with fresh ideas and better character. In the future there will be much more diversity.

With the emergence of the new technologies there will also be many more gatekeepers to help ensure quality programming. The new writers, producers, and directors, must have a clearer vision of their message. Ultimately they will provide many more opportunities for the kinds of productions the world wants to see.

If the Christian church will take advantage of the technology, it can have at its disposal delivery systems for high-quality programming that have been virtually undreamed of in the past.

IMPROVING THE VISION

It is clear that we will be moving into high definition television that will be crystal clear, much more beautiful than anything we have imagined, and much more realistic. Consumers will have not only compact disc audio, but compact disc video, which means that soon people will be able to record on disc at home. That means program producers can, in turn, dramatically simplify the distribution of programs to the world.

Compact disc technology provides incredible quality. In recorded music, in digital imagery, in compact data storage, and in speed of access, the compact disc has opened up entirely new horizons. That trend will continue in the decade ahead.

Right now the proliferation of video recorders is very high. In the Middle East, in Africa, in Eastern Europe, everywhere you go, people have video recorders because the state television has been so bad that the people have come up with their own alternative sources.

PIRATING THE GOSPEL

There is already a fabulous market in the Third World for any kind of videos. We produce a series of programs for the Japanese market called *SuperBook* and *Flying House*. These are animated Bible stories for children that were produced in Japan for CBN. We have heard that today they are the best-selling videos in Turkey, a Muslim country.

Basically, local entrepreneurs have pirated our programs! They are reproducing them without any kind of copyright license fees and they are selling them in video stores and kiosks all over the country. Consequently, hundreds of thousands of people are watching Bible stories and hearing the gospel in their homes because we have entered into the channels of commerce in that country.

It would be impossible to get a Christian program on the air in Turkey on their government television, but the people are hearing the gospel because people want to make money, and they can do that by fulfilling the voracious demand of the audiences for high-quality, Western-style television.

In terms of evangelism, this is the opportunity of a lifetime. It will break down any type of control. It will mean that speech, thought, and religious values can be disseminated much more rapidly. This will be a great opportunity for missionaries and other Christian workers if they will take advantage of it, but the benefits of the technology flow to everybody else as well.

It means that anybody with a thought he wants to disseminate can have some channels available to him—many, many of them. Whether it is Shirley MacLaine with her occult fantasies, or some sort of self-help motivational program, there will be channels for every conceivable interest. These will range from aerobics to geriatrics, and from aviation to zoology. All of these things will now have worldwide distribution potential.

The importance of this kind of information explosion is that now we can get the ideas to the people. The bad news is that it will also be possible for some dangerous charlatan to have global distribution capability which is literally awesome in its scope. Because of that threat, we must always be on the alert that the technology is used for good and not for evil.

WORLDWIDE NEWS

Already, the Cable News Network (CNN) is global. It is all over Europe, in parts of Asia. It is certainly in the hotels wherever you go. This network provides worldwide, up-to-the-minute news. The markets of the world are integrated. This is now a very small globe we live on.

News-gathering services such as Reuters, Worldwide, CNN and others are now doing something that has never been done before: bringing instant news and pictures of everything that happens, as it happens. The sophistication of information that is being beamed out to the world is extraordinary. There is nothing any longer that is done in a corner.

We have access to a global information system, which allows us to focus in on places like Washington and Moscow, and soon possibly Brussels or Strasbourg with the European Community coming into being. As these things happen we will all be much more involved in the global community, and the names and faces of public figures in these countries will be as well known to us as the leaders in our own country.

Because of datalinks and satellite transmission of information, we will have instant access to business and financial information and commercial transactions with unprecedented quality and speed. I understand that the SWIFT system—the Society of Worldwide Interfund Transfers which runs out of a great big computer in Brussels—handles over one hundred billion dollars a day in bank transfers. The amounts involved with currency transactions—the actual buying and selling of currencies—are reportedly vastly larger than that.

TECHNOLOGY IN REVOLUTION

Absent some war or other catastrophe, the consumer able to afford the product is going to be getting much better quality, in almost everything. Appliances, automobiles, consumer electronics, all these products will be much better. Also, they will become more affordable as the markets expand.

I expect to see explosive new developments in these and many other areas during the coming decade. This will happen not so much through dynamic breakthroughs in technology, not just through new products and discoveries, but incremental increases and improvements in the products we already rely on. During the coming decade we will see product *improvements* that will amount to dramatic breakthroughs.

This will be "the age of the supers." Superconductor technology is racing ahead at breakneck speed. Powerful new super-fast chips being produced both in the United States and Japan are capable of out-performing today's standards by factors as high as 10,000 to 1.

Some of the newest silicon products coming from the laboratories into the marketplace are nothing short of revolutionary. In mid-1990 the Japanese announced that they are developing neural networks on silicon wafers that duplicate the functions of the human brain. They say one five-inch microchip can contain the equivalent of 19 million transistors and operates 100,000 times faster than existing supercomputers.

One of the most fascinating insights I have seen concerning the proliferation of computers in our society comes from George Gilder, author of many important works including *The Spirit of Enterprise.* In an essay for the volume, *An American Vision,* published by the Cato Institute in Washington, Gilder suggests that micro-computers have also helped to prove the futility of socialism.

In the beginning, IBM thought the small "personal computer" (PC) would be a simple tool to help them sell more mainframe computers; however, what they actually discovered was that PC networks were out-performing their mainframes and, in millions of instructions per second per dollar, were 90 times more cost efficient than supercomputers.

Gilder's conclusion is that "computers make socialism totally futile and obsolete. By their very nature, computers distribute power rather than centralize it. . . . The evolution of the industry therefore constantly increases the power of the individual workstation. . . ." The very architecture of the technology decentralizes and gives immense value to the distribution of power.

The "economies of microscale," as Gilder calls it, dictates that "power continually devolves into the hands and onto the laps of individuals." Having demonstrated some of the fallacies of Marshall McLuhan's predictions of the 1970s, I have to agree with Gilder that "What is important is not the medium but the message."

HARD REALITIES

We will have to face many problematical issues in the decade ahead concerning biotechnology, gene splicing, and the like. The use of fetal tissue for medical experimentation, the modification of the fetus in the womb to alter the genetic code or the physical and mental traits of the unborn child, along with experiments in cloning human beings—these and other very questionable issues are being debated even now.

We will have to address the practice of euthanasia, issues such as Dr. Jack Kervorkian's suicide device, as well as use of the RU-486 abortion pill from France which not only strangles the fetus in the womb but threatens the life of the rejecting mother.

We will also see revolutions in the application of computer technology to certain types of medical experiments—fusing biology and cybernetics. Dr. Louis Sullivan, Secretary of Health and Human Services, recently announced that the government is launching a massive program to study the power of the human brain.

In one experiment cited by Sullivan, researchers implanted a microchip into the brain of a laboratory rat. Not only did the chip transmit signals successfully, but the rat's brain actually accepted and fused with the chip. Will human beings be the next to carry digital programming in their brains?

The new gallium-arsenide (GaAs) microchip technology—or perhaps some hybrid derivative of it—may soon allow scientists to store as much information in a single bank of chips as is contained in all the books in the Library of Congress. They say that's not even a very far-fetched dream; it's practically a reality now.

Super-computers like those being developed by Seymour Cray—along with new discoveries from Alan Huang, engineers at IBM, and others now in the hunt—will continue to blossom. *U.S. News* and *Time* both reported that Huang recently previewed a new optical computer, powered by light, that can run up to 1,000 times faster than today's most powerful super-computers. There seems to be no limits to this type of technology.

In physics, the super-collider will also be very much in the news as the scientists in Texas begin to explore the processes and applications of advanced nuclear dynamics.

In transportation, we will see even more revolutionary advances. We are certainly going to see super high speed bullet trains that ride on air cushions with a potential speed of anywhere from 500 to a thousand miles per hour. We are going to see supersonic airplanes that can go from Washington to Tokyo in two and a half to three hours in a sort of sub-orbital flight.

In the foreseeable future, we will have smart highways where people can lock their cars onto an underground computer system and essentially punch up their destination and sit back and enjoy the ride while the highway conducts them to their point of exit, then lets them off.

Recently General Motors announced it has already designed the prototype of a whole new generation of automobiles that will be powered by high-energy batteries. Subsequently, *Time* reported on research for a new highway system featuring an electrified underground cable that would allow electrically powered cars to recharge their batteries while driving.

COMBINED TECHNOLOGIES

There will also be a continuing trend to merge all these technologies. For example, there will be increasing uses of computers in the automobile industry, not only the computer consoles we now have to monitor operating systems, but also to avoid accidents, cars that can avoid impending collisions and apply the necessary safety precautions to prevent accidents.

Along with the advances in computer technology, improved fiber optic communications, improved transportation, and advances in engineering procedures, there will be changes in the physical workplace. Perhaps most notable, the demand for improved quality of life will accelerate the tendency for many more people to work at home, or in smaller offices close to home.

Airports all over the world are so congested today, there will have to be some new breakthroughs in air transportation. The vertical takeoff and landing method, generally called VTOL, may well be the answer, especially for commuter flights.

The aircraft of the very near future will likely be something that can hover, land in a small area, take off and then fly very rapidly to its destination. On a commercial level, this could be something like the Harrier Jump Jet.

Instead of the long landing patterns we have in our airports today, we will see landing pads no larger than a small parking lot. Instead of being located very far outside the cities, they can be much closer, more convenient, and less noisy.

Ever-increasing congestion in our major cities will add additional impetus to the public's desire to move to smaller towns where the quality of life will be much higher. This will be a major issue for cities like New York, Boston, Chicago, Detroit, and others which will be losing huge numbers of people over a fairly short period of time.

When the trend toward home business was first predicted a decade ago, nobody really believed it would happen; but it is happening, and it's changing the way America does business.

Just look at the way the fax machine has changed business in the last three years. And for many people, especially for those who work outside the office, the cellular phone has become indispensable. We have access to instant communications from anywhere in the world at any time. This is not only the trend for tomorrow, it is the reality of today.

It is a reality in churches as well. A nationwide poll of Protestant churches conducted by the Barna Research Group found that fully half of the churches they contacted currently own or use computers in their ministry. That is a dramatic increase from the 21 percent who reported using computers in their work in a 1985 study.

UNLOCKING RAIN MAN'S SECRET

In what may well have been the finest motion picture of the past decade, *Rain Man,* actor Dustin Hoffman delivered an award-winning performance as the autistic older brother opposite fast talking Tom Cruise. Hoffman's character, Raymond, was what psychologists term an "idiot-savant," someone with the IQ of a moron yet who has a mental ability which seems superhuman. Raymond was unable to care for himself in society, yet had the ability to do complex mathematical calculations in his head almost instantly with absolute accuracy down to three or four decimal points.

Such people are rare, but they do indeed exist. Last year my co-hostess, Sheila Walsh, had the privilege of interviewing such a remarkable individual on the 700 Club television program. He was a young black man named Alonzo Clemons from Denver, Colorado.

We were told that Alonzo's IQ was a sub-moronic 55. Yet he had two extraordinary gifts—artistic expression and total detailed recall. If, for instance, he could look once at an animal, he could then return to his studio and craft a clay statue of the animal, perfect in dimension and accurate in every detail.

Alonzo was shown a large color photograph of my big stallion, Aristocrat. Then without further reference to the photograph, within 15 minutes he had crafted a perfect scale model of the horse—head, ears, neck, shoulder, legs, feet, barrel, flanks—all beautifully symmetrical and true to life. I was frankly overwhelmed.

Some savants are gifted musically. They can play from memory complex musical scores. Others, like the movie character, Raymond, are gifted in math. It is possible, for example, to ask such a person what day of the week Christmas fell on in 1776. Within seconds they can give an absolutely correct answer. Others can perform calculations that would strain the ability of our finest computers.

I learned that savants are windows God has given us into the true ability of the human brain. As best I can determine, the normal human brain functions at about 10 percent of capacity. The truly gifted among us may reach 20 percent. In their compensating specialties, the savants have been allowed to move up to 80 percent or 90 percent of capacity.

Think what would happen if God would somehow enable all people to operate at the level of wisdom and discernment of which we are capable. The discoveries and breakthroughs in science and technology would beggar belief.

More recently some not too scientific experiments have been made in pre-natal teaching with startling results. Pregnant women are playing gospel music or recorded scripture readings to their unborn children along with clear, distinct prayer. I have been told, but I hasten to add without scientific verification, that children so taught before birth later evidence IQs which are off the top of the genius range.

The Bible says, "Your sins have separated you from God." Can it be possible that innocent little children—like the completely innocent idiot-savants—could receive extensions of their abilities that are nothing short of remarkable? I think this is possible and may prove, along with the understanding of the human spirit, one of the great breakthroughs in the decades ahead.

In my opinion the experiments of J. B. Rhine at Duke University and other researchers into ESP and paranormal phenomena are merely conducting kindergarten classes in spiritism. We must understand that there exist in the world God's intelligence revealed by

His Holy Spirit, man's intelligence, angelic intelligence, and demonic intelligence. God's intelligence comes to man through man's spirit. Demonic intelligence comes to man through his soul. The Greek word for soul is *psyche* from which we get our English word psychic.

Those who begin to enter the realm of intelligence beyond ourselves—without the spiritual rebirth that comes from Jesus Christ and a clear understanding of the Holy Bible—will invariably find that they have neither tapped into an extension of man's intelligence or God's intelligence, but demonic intelligence.

I hasten to add—as I have already outlined in detail in chapter 4—that we are entering the age of the supernatural. To quote the apostle Paul, there will be "lying signs and wonders to deceive as it were the very elect." We can expect extraordinary breakthroughs accompanied by extensive media publicity in the field of paranormal activity. Invariably these signs and wonders will beckon us to a brave new world and salvation—*apart from Jesus Christ*.

As the old fades away and new perceptions of reality come quickly into focus, it will be absolutely crucial that Christian people have a thorough understanding of the Bible and that they are trained in spiritual discernment and perception to identify clearly what is true and what is false in the coming new millennium.

COUNTING THE COST

As always, there will be economic and cultural repercussions from the advances in science and technology. As individuals move away from the mega-cities, rental and ownership patterns will begin to change. Real estate values in small and medium-sized cities will go up, and some of the core cities that are so terribly congested now are going to begin breaking down.

Both economy and quality-of-life changes will impact these cities, and we will see some rather substantial out-migration from cities where congestion and pollution and the breakdown of the infrastructure have already become intolerable.

After a long period of intense debate over the importance and the uses of nuclear energy, I think we have finally come to the time when we have to admit that controlled and responsible use of atomic power is essential to our future.

We have learned—not only from Chernobyl but from a long list of films, movies, and books on the potential dangers of mishandling nuclear power—that there are legitimate concerns. But we are also discovering that there are substantial advantages as well, and we simply have to begin to discover how we can use these advantages realistically.

I believe that we will harness the power and the technology for efficient applications of nuclear energy in the very near future. One of the developers of the Chicago Project—an engineer who worked with Enrico Fermi on atomic fission—was a guest on our television program. In the course of our interview, he said that with 20 billion dollars and a dedicated program, America could achieve nuclear fusion. I believe he is right, and I believe we must do it.

We cannot continue to rely on fossil fuel indefinitely. We are consuming our resources at a staggering rate. It is absolutely essential that we have alternate sources of energy, and solar power has proven to be too expensive and too unreliable. So I maintain that the long range hope is nuclear fusion, and it seems to me that America should take the lead in producing and using it.

That is an attainable goal. We can get controlled fusion, but we need to focus our research efforts on it now to maintain our lead. The Japanese are already at work in this area because they also recognize that it is the power for the future. We know the Germans, the Russians, and several Middle Eastern countries have constructed very advanced systems. In 1990, France was receiving fully half of its power from safe nuclear reactors. The French goal is 100 percent nuclear power by 1995.

Nuclear power—especially that from the development of hydrogen fusion—could be created from water. It boggles the mind to conceive of the world we could have if both poorer and richer nations had unlimited cheap power at their disposal with no more dependence on sky-high fossil fuels.

Think what could happen when one day we are able to enter the world of what we now call science fiction and ride on bullet trains powered by nuclear energy and floating on electromagnetic cushions, hurtling across continents at two or three times the speed of sound.

Think of vehicles powered by tiny nuclear reactors, and houses where the power bill was less than $100 each year.

Even more utopian, consider the world that we could have if the nearly one trillion dollar arms budget of the world were turned to innovation, to improving our cities, making the deserts green, lifting the masses from poverty, and sharing the goodness of this earth.

MAINTAINING AN EDGE

If Americans learn from the Japanese and are willing to be humble and listen, we can exceed any other nation in terms of the quality of our products. That has been a dream and goal of mine, that the term "Made in America" can be synonymous with "the Best in the World."

There's no question that we can do it, it's just a question of whether or not we have the will to do it and take the necessary action. If we insist in our factories that nothing goes out unless it is the best, and if we demand the intelligent participation of our workers to the extent the Japanese do, we cannot help but achieve this goal.

Becoming that kind of nation is really an emotional commitment. It is having the attitude and belief that we cannot permit errors. Milliken, a South Carolina textile manufacturer, has shown us that it can happen here. That plant is a leader in involving workers in improving the quality of their products, and as a result there has been a dramatic improvement in quality in their mills, in their techniques, in the worker involvement, and in upgrading their manufacturing systems.

Creative worker involvement sets them in the top rank of textile manufacturers in the whole world. There is no question that this kind of company can compete on a global basis with anybody.

In the marketplace of the next decade, it will be government's responsibility—and consequently our responsibility as citizens—to see that there is a fair and open market for American products. There cannot be discrimination against American products if we are to survive.

From the long view, I believe government will begin to take the initiative in these matters and use America's diplomatic clout to pry open world markets. In the short range, however, I suspect we could see some punitive tariffs that come out as we approach the end of the current business cycle and begin to work out our existing debt.

If American business interests suffer, there will be a cry for protectionism and, in my opinion, that would be the wrong thing to do. Protectionism will not help America. Instead, I fear it would bring on a replay of 1930 all over again, and we could see a devastating depression which could hurt the world very badly. What we need are free and open markets with fair trade among equal partners.

ECONOMIC PRECAUTIONS

This is the thing I fear most when looking at the prospects for the decade ahead. There could be such a major economic dislocation that it would plunge the world into economic chaos which would lead, in turn, to political chaos and possibly even war. That's the dark side of the scenario.

In a sense, we are at a crossroads in our history where we have in our power the ability to move either toward Christian values in our spiritual life and enlightened capitalism in our material life, or toward a much more somber alternative.

We can choose to move toward less government regulation and more openness among nations, which would lead to international prosperity, or we could move toward the tightening of barriers, of tariffs, trying to protect inefficient industries in order to preserve domestic jobs a little bit longer.

One way will help bring us an era of prosperity and peace, the other would very likely plunge the world into a depression which could lead to war and collapse.

The image which then comes to mind is too much like the prophecies of Revelation for comfort; for within the collapse of the peace and order of the world there is the threat of a global dictatorship and the end of democracy as we know it. That's a scenario no one looks forward to.

We have in our power the ability to conquer disease, to extend life, to remove genetic abnormalities, to supply a reasonably abundant standard of living to every human being on this planet, to bring forth an ever increasing cornucopia of technological products to make each of our lives more pleasant, to have at our disposal increased learning, culture, and leisure.

We could have all of that but for one thing. We lack the spiritual and ethical standards to stop killing, cheating, and oppressing our fellow human beings. And we lack the wisdom and self-restraint to stop pillaging, raping, and polluting the land, and the sea, and the air, and the other creatures that share this planet with us. In short, we realize that the Millennium cannot come unless God brings it by changing all our hearts.

WHO OWNS THE ENVIRONMENT?

Along with the mushrooming of technology, the environment is suddenly on everybody's mind. As if someone had turned on the faucet, suddenly we are being flooded with articles and ads and campaigns of every description urging us to save the environment.

Obviously, this will be one of the issues of the '90s, but where does it come from and what does it mean? When we look at any subject that receives as much exposure as this one has had over the past couple of years, it's generally a good idea to see who's involved. Who are the out-front, outspoken leaders of the environmental movement? What is their past record of accomplishment? What have they done to make the quality of life better in America?

When a detective starts to investigate a murder, the first question he asks is, who stands to benefit? When you find out who stands to gain the most you generally find the fatal motive. By the same token, when I see the passion of this new movement, I'm impelled to ask that question. Who stands to benefit?

Those who are interested in getting their hands into the government purse are usually close by when such movements begin. Liberal interests in this country have always pushed for greater government involvement in the lives of people.

For one thing, the government habitually tries to solve problems by throwing money at them. Also, when government takes over, it begins to take control of the lives of everyone involved. It does not take a genius to see that federal programs have failed miserably in this country. So who's pushing for a new one?

It's astonishing how often you see the same people who have always tried to socialize business and run the lives of the American people. They seem to come out of the woodwork for movements like this. Now, as if frustrated by the failure of communism, the activists have all shifted en masse to a new cause. Again, their purpose is to get government involved in controlling our lives.

Their real agenda is not the environment: the movements they cluster around are never more than a cover for their hidden agenda. Their agenda is control, and it is almost always anti-business and anti-growth. In fact, this is the very same bunch of radicals who have been wrong so many times before.

EMBRACING THE MOVEMENT

I believe we have a genuine right and responsibility to be good stewards of our environment. The Bible is very clear that we are to plant and harvest wisely, to use the animals and the other resources wisely. So I agree with many of the scientists and professionals who are pointing out the genuine dangers to the environment. But I think we have to be very cautious before we embrace the agenda of "the Movement." We certainly have to be wary of embracing it as some have done, as a religion.

Former Secretary of the Interior Donald Hodel told me that I would never understand the wilderness movement until I recognized that to these people, the activists, the wilderness is an object of worship. It is something they worship as an ideal.

It is not practical to suggest that we can promote tree growth through forest management, or that we build better roads so people can enjoy the wilderness. The wilderness activists believe they are defending Mother Earth and we cannot touch her, that whatever happens in the wilderness is sacred and holy.

Just prior to Earth Day 1990, a *Wall Street Journal* editorial lampooned the event as one of the rites of a new world religion. The writer pointed out that the environmentalists appear to be seeking "contact with the transcendental" in the universe beyond themselves. "We are coming to see the environment as a religion, rather, in a quest for understanding." The author of that piece writes that the movement defies mere logic,

As the second millennium approaches, the apocalypse must be upon us. The devout search frantically to learn which of the seven ends ensues: The fire of nuclear winter. The ice of nuclear winter. The unseen peril of radiation, or a new plague as a judgment for genetic tampering. The roast of global warming, or the judgment of a new ice age, the climatological fear of only a decade ago. Or merely perhaps terminal boredom in the end of history?

An amusing observation, but perhaps not all that far from the truth. Actually, it should not be surprising to see the passion with which activists have leaped into the battle for the environment.

In an age in which religious faith has been slandered and discredited by secular institutions, many of these people are desperately searching for something to fill the void in their own souls. Like the New Agers, these people have lost touch with God Almighty and they are reaching out to Nature as their God.

What happens in the wilderness may be important to nature and the natural processes of the earth, but it certainly is not holy. It is simply "natural," and as such it is subject to all the laws and processes of nature. We must realize that sometimes those changes are dramatic and destructive.

Trees decay and die; there are forest fires, wind storms, lightning damage, insect infestations, and many other types of destruction that come from natural causes. Animals prey upon one another; deserts and woodlands and wetlands expand and contract with the climatic changes that vary from year to year. Man is also a part of nature, and even when he is irresponsible and destroys some part of the environment, he is still a part of nature and does not necessarily change the laws of nature by his presence or his actions.

CYCLES OF GROWTH

Intelligent management of the forests and woodlands is a very wise and important thing. Trees actually grow better when they are not in too close proximity to each other. Trees have a certain life cycle and when they reach the end of that cycle—whether it's 70 years, 80 years, or longer—they begin to die, so it is wise at that point to harvest them, to enable smaller trees to come up, or to replant with nursery-grown seedlings.

Even such things as forest fires may be good for certain species, because only after the earth has been singed by the heat of a forest fire and certain areas have been cleared of timber can new seedlings germinate and bring life to whole new forests. The redwoods of California and some of the other trees considered sacred to the environmentalists are actually in that category.

The natural thing is to permit a certain amount of clearing of growth. Wildlife management is much the same. Unless the populations of North American deer that run wild in many parts of this country are thinned out by manmade methods, predators or disease will take them.

When their herds grow larger than one deer per acre, deer cannot forage or breed freely, and many times the ravages of nature are more costly than the alternative, which is to permit hunters to thin the herds.

If the reverence we have for the wilderness becomes a kind of religion, and if what we feel for the environment is not just respect but worship, then the environment actually becomes our god and it cannot be touched by anyone. That sort of idolatry is a frontal assault on our concept of stewardship.

The biblical mandate is for man to have dominion over the earth, over all living things, over the animals, over the creeping things and flying things, over the forests and rivers and seas. As intelligent stewards, under the authority of God, we are to tend the garden and cultivate it and look after it.

CYCLES OF DESTRUCTION

We are to care for the environment, but never did God give us a mandate to desecrate it. What has happened in some places is that lumber companies have gone in and clear cut virgin forests for pure greed and with no concept of stewardship. That kind of wanton deforestation is alarming.

In Brazil in 1989 unlicensed lumbermen and poachers were chopping down as high as 18,000 acres of virgin timber a day; that is not only a crime, it is immoral. We know that the rain forests of Brazil, Central Africa, and Southeast Asia are unique biological laboratories. These forests are primary resources for reproducing the world's supply of nitrogen and oxygen, and for maintaining the balance of humidity in the atmosphere.

Many of the forests that are being ravaged, especially in the Third World, are irreplaceable. But the cycle of devastation only begins with the trees. Once the forests are cut down, seasonal rains come and wash away the topsoil.

The arable soil in which crops are grown has a unique composition which, with very little variance, is the same all over the world. It is approximately half mineral, 3 to 5 percent vegetable, and the remainder about equal proportions of air and water; but the average depth of that soil is only about 8 to 10 inches. When we lose that topsoil, we endanger our ability to survive on this planet.

We must have harmony between man and the environment. The tragedy of North Africa, for example, is the clearing of forests, all the way from the Mediterranean Coast south to Mali, Chad, and Nigeria. As a consequence of indiscriminate clearing, nearly half the continent has been consumed by desert, and the toll on human life has been devastating.

We only need to think of the photographs from Ethiopia and the Sudan to recognize the toll in human life. At one time that whole area was forested, but over the years, through war and through periods of prosperity and famine, men have cleared the forests farther and farther south, and as the trees are cut the wind and rain wash away the topsoil until nothing is left but sand and desert.

Satellite photos reveal the consequences, with the desert creeping southward across Africa at a relentless pace of seven to eight miles every year. The nomadic tribes are always running just ahead of the desert, but they cannot outrun the famine. Millions of people have starved to death because there isn't enough food for them and the productive capacity of the land has been utterly destroyed for years, possibly ages, to come.

BRINGING NEW LIFE

I saw that damage when I flew from Khartoum in the Sudan across Egypt and over the Mediterranean. Over Egypt, I noticed little puffs of clouds over the few scattered areas where trees were growing.

I realized then—since I had seen it proven in Israel—that planting trees helps bring about cooling, which brings moisture and rain, which can also help accelerate other climatic changes. And as the trees drop their leaves in the fall, over a period of time there is a gradual building of solus and humus, which form the topsoil.

So I asked a friend, Bob Macauley, who is head of a company with timber interests, why don't we plant a million trees as a demonstration project and let others join with us? Bob jumped at the idea, so CBN formed a partnership to add trees to a project begun by a Danish agronomist active in Kenya. With Bob's help we have now planted close to 3 million trees, and some of them are 12 to 20 feet high!

An area that was once hard, unyielding, near desert, has suddenly begun to flourish. Our agronomist and his team dug a lake, and the weather cycles in the region began to change, it began to rain more and more, and now the lake is full of water. He has now reintroduced the various species of wildlife that disappeared during the drought and famine, and there are even hippopotami in the water. There are birds and literally hundreds of the natural creatures which had virtually disappeared from this natural habitat.

Now, from those first plantings we did, the scientists and the local managers have established a very prolific seedling nursery so they can give plants to other villages who want trees. At this point I am proposing we take what we have learned from that operation and plant a hundred million trees to begin to reclaim Africa from the desert.

President Bush said he would like to see America plant one billion trees a year. That is not an unattainable goal for Africa. It should have been done a long time ago, but it also needs to be done in Southeast Asia, and South America, and in all the areas of the world where the forests are being cut down.

The governments must cooperate not only in reforestation but in conservation. For some reason, in Brazil and other Third World nations, there has not been a responsible effort to preserve the forests. The forests are not only important to recycle the air, to filter out poisons, and to replenish moisture, chlorophyll, oxygen and nitrogen, and other important properties of the air. But the vegetation holds the soil in place and regulates the run-off of water, which in turn helps to prevent devastating floods.

THE BALANCE OF NATURE

The balance of nature is crucial, but we violate it almost casually. We have also violated it in the water. We have dumped toxic wastes into the oceans, lakes, rivers, and streams. We have used increasingly toxic chemicals, and the chemicals run off into the water and kill the wildlife and the aquatic life, and that imperils, in turn, those who live by and from the sea.

Instead of responsibility, we find people whose main concern is with bottom-line profits. They don't stop to think about the air we breathe, so they build factories and mills that belch out fumes, saturating the air with colloidal compounds, such as acid and coal smoke.

Irresponsible managers dump poisonous wastes in areas where it can leach into the water supply. There is no telling how many people die of cancer or how many babies are born with birth defects every year through the irresponsible behavior of managers and supervisors who think that because nobody will see what they have done, nobody will be hurt.

Virginia experienced one of the worst ecological disasters in American history a few years ago because of just such carelessness. It seems that a small, fly-by-night chemical supplier for giant Allied Chemical Company stored some barrels of the deadly chemical, Kepone, in a little storage building the size of a residential two-car garage.

This building was near the banks of the James River at a city called Hopewell, some 40 or 50 miles upstream from the Chesapeake Bay. Some of the barrels containing the Kepone began to leak and the Kepone oozed out of the building and into the James River. As a result, the entire lower Chesapeake Bay was contaminated and the fishing and oyster business in the region was shut down completely.

That single leak destroyed the fishing for several years. It did untold damage to living fish, not to mention the potential danger to humans and animals who ate the fish. It was just a small amount of a deadly chemical, but it was caused by the carelessness of people who didn't understand the incredible potential for harm in today's chemical products.

THE OTHER SIDE OF SCIENCE

When we saw the Bhopal disaster in India and the Chernobyl disaster in Russia, we got just a small glimpse of the horrific consequences of modern technology when the toxic by-products it produces fall into the hands of thoughtless and careless people.

I am for atomic energy, and I think that ultimately the principal energy source of the new millennium will be nuclear power. Hydrogen power is an idea whose time has come. I am convinced that someday we will have a cheap form of energy, as cheap as all the oceans of the world. It will give the world a limitless energy supply, and it won't be priced on the basis of scarcity.

This new energy resource will be available to everybody, but it will involve certain risks and it will demand certain precautions. If we cannot accept the risks and take the proper steps to safeguard ourselves from the risks, then we will have to forego the benefits of the technology. We cannot have nuclear reactors if we have no regard for safety.

The accident at Chernobyl has caused incalculable damage over an immeasurable area. As we know now, people all over northern Europe are still being exposed to dangerous levels of radiation from that accident.

The London *Economist* reported recently that Britain's sheep, contaminated by fallout and poisoned rain from Chernobyl, have to be color-coded according to their level of radioactivity. Those marked with green paint are considered safe, while the sheep with apricot markings and still off limits. The comedy of such a system is hardly offset by the real-life horror.

There is not a lot we can physically do to reverse the damage that has been done there, but we must learn from Chernobyl. We must at least gain an immense respect for the power of technology and for the potential it possesses both for good and for evil.

Incidentally, an ominous biblical prophecy says that in the end times a bright star will fall to earth, and this bitter star will poison the waters of the earth. The name of the star is wormwood. The passage, in the eighth chapter of Revelation, predicts that a third of the earth will be destroyed because the waters will be made bitter. Curiously, the word for wormwood in Russian is *chernobyl*.

We must be cautious that we do not endanger our populations.

Under communism, all that mattered was the ongoing economic welfare of the state, to the exclusion of any outside concerns about the health of the population. A government trying to squeeze every last ounce of productivity from the people, particularly when the people are already impoverished and the economy is collapsing, will not spend much time worrying about pollution.

But pollution is a legitimate concern. Whether it is from trash and garbage, from radioactive contamination, or from lead or aluminum contamination, we have to care.

Many scientists now believe that Alzheimer's disease may be caused by aluminum poisoning, from cooking with aluminum utensils. We already know that excessive exposure to or ingestion of lead causes mental retardation and birth defects of various kinds, so it is not unreasonable to suspect that aluminum—an alloy—may have a similar effect.

As a matter of fact, historians and scientists have applied some of the new findings to earlier cultures with some startling results. Many believe that the short lifespans of people in the Middle Ages may have been due to the fact that their utensils and tableware were commonly made from pewter: pewter is an alloy of lead and tin.

The same evidence suggests that one reason the Roman Empire began to die out was because they used so much lead, not only in their eating utensils, but in the water pipes and sewage systems. They were dying of lead poisoning and didn't know it.

Carcinogenic materials, poisons, and contaminants which damage the central nervous system or which cause birth defects and other serious impairments are matters of great urgency and we have the right as citizens of a free democratic nation to see that the risks are eliminated.

PREVALENT DANGERS

I think we have to take the dangers of pollution caused by automobile emissions very seriously. We have been told that every car and truck on the highways in this country spews its own weight in carbons back into the atmosphere every year. Multiply that times the number of vehicles you see around you every day and the thought is mind boggling.

There isn't a single country anywhere in the world that doesn't have a serious pollution problem. Poorly developed Third World countries; highly developed industrial nations; they all have serious problems. Mexico City is choking on pollution. Tokyo, Rio, and Sao Paulo are all choking on pollution. Every major city in Europe has a serious problem.

Many of us have seen the grim photos from West Germany showing the almost total destruction of the historic Black Forest. It is heartbreaking to see that stately and historic forest being devastated by acid rain caused by the poisonous coal smoke belching from factories in Poland, Czechoslovakia, and East Germany.

In Italy the trees and ancient statuary along the Appian Way, along with many of the great cathedrals and landmarks of Europe, are being eaten away by the ravages of pollution, coal smoke, and acid rain. Unfortunately, we don't yet know what the acid rain is doing to the lakes of New England or the Great Lakes.

In Athens, the air quality is so bad it is nearly impossible to breathe on a hot day. Shirley Temple Black, our ambassador to Czechoslovakia, has said that living in Prague is like smoking two packs of cigarettes a day.

One thing after another indicates that massive pollution is having disastrous consequences all over the world, degrading the environment, causing lung disease, causing emphysema, birth defects, senile dementia, and a whole host of other ills.

GETTING IT RIGHT

The comprehensive reports of the United States Environmental Protection Agency offer grim evidence of the dangers within our communities and public lands. A quick review of the summary documents of the EPA activities published in early 1990 reveals the massive scope of the problem the agency has begun to attack.

Under the single category of clean air, they are involved in programs for control of acid rain, smog, and toxic pollutants. They deal with the problems caused by benzene emissions and radioactivity from mining operations, along with controlling airborne pollutants from the incineration of municipal waste.

Other programs address oil spills, municipal waste disposal, and domestic pollution, plus asbestos contamination, chlorofluoro-carbons, global warming, hazardous waste, radon contamination, medical waste, ocean dumping, dangerous pesticides, and the banning of agricultural products such as Alar.

The EPA is also involved with the FDA, USDA, and the Department of Justice in policing poisons, hazardous waste, and cleanup activities, and in the prosecution of offenders.

Obviously, righting the wrongs already done to the world about us is going to be a major task. It is going to cost hundreds of billions of dollars. First of all we have to clean up the smokestacks and come up with alternate sources of fuel. We not only have to come up with some sort of scrubbers and air filters on the smokestacks, but we have to clean coal at the mine that is being burned in the smokestacks, and ultimately we have to go to some kind of non-fossil fuels.

We have to do something about the fact that automobiles are filling the air with petrocarbons. Right now automobiles are the principal means of transportation in every industrialized nation in the world and, in such massive quantities, automobile fumes are deadly.

But what about the proven dangers of cigarette smoke surrounding us everywhere we go? They tell us that Americans are cutting back on cigarette smoking. In 1964, approximately 60 percent of Americans smoked; today that figure is reported at just over 29 percent. Apparently some people are beginning to get the message, but cigarette smoking still has a stranglehold on millions and it is killing thousands every day.

The vice of cigarette smoking seems to prey on the weak. Teenagers and young adults trying so hard to be cool, to prove their independence, are ready victims of smoking. Inner-city families, low-income Blacks, Hispanics, and now women are the greatest at-risk categories among smokers.

The women's liberation movement, by making women believe they have to be macho, has induced tens of thousands to smoke as a sign of freedom and rebellion, and it is killing women today at a staggering rate.

To their eternal shame, American tobacco companies are luring children and teens and young singles through pernicious advertising playing on sex and glamour. They are luring them to their deaths.

These same companies are stepping up exports at an alarming rate, and because of the greed and exploitation of the American tobacco companies, people in Third World countries are, literally, smoking themselves to death.

I invite anyone who believes it's okay to smoke to go down to the nearest nursing home and talk to the old men with emphysema and lung disease. Visit the rooms of the young men and women with bronchial diseases; or go to any major hospital in any city in the world and speak to the doctors in the cancer wards.

Look in on the patients dying of lung and bronchial and esophageal cancers. These people will not hesitate to tell you what smoking is all about. They will not hesitate to condemn the evil of smoking. Cigarettes and all other forms of tobacco are a man-made source of pollution that is self-induced and is more common, more deadly and, because it so insidious, is more perceptibly evil than any of the others.

As Christians, we have a duty to be worthy custodians of the environment, but we are also commanded to take care of our bodies, which are the temple of the Lord.

We are to be the stewards and live in harmony with the plants, the animals, the birds, the fish. Yes, we can harvest them for food, but we must protect and cultivate and harvest wisely. Any form of wanton destruction is evil, whether it is destruction of our world or our own bodies.

STANDARDS AND DOUBLE STANDARDS

We must be realistic, and we don't need to be faddish. So many at the forefront of the environmental movement have such a double standard, it's clear that the idea of a movement—any movement—means more to them than the issues themselves.

I find it pathetically ironic that the same environmentalists you see at the protest rallies against air pollution and nuclear contamination can't go more than a few minutes without a cigarette break. It's also telling to see that the people who are such staunch opponents of hunting and the use of furs are all wearing leather shoes. Odd they're not saying anything about that. After all, steers have to die for us to have leather.

We have harvested animals since time immemorial; we have always used animals for our food and clothing. Since the earliest days of Genesis, we have used the meat and skins of animals. Meat is a necessary part of the human diet, and fur coats are no more wrong, in themselves, than leather shoes or handbags.

What is wrong, however, is the wanton slaughter of wildlife for the sake of fashion, or greed, or simple exploitation of nature for personal gain. Think what the early trappers and traders did in their appalling slaughter of the domestic buffalo.

A century ago there was wanton slaughter of the egrets in the Everglades of Florida just so the elegant ladies of New York and Boston could have plumes for their finery. Today there is an ongoing slaughter of the elephants in Africa. Poachers kill the elephants but only take the tusks, which are sold for jewelry, and leave the carcasses to rot.

The African rhino is being threatened with extinction because some people believe the tusks make good aphrodisiacs. The tusk of a single rhino can bring up to 20,000 dollars; consequently, poachers are killing them by the thousands. These are horrible losses and an outrage against nature.

The large-scale netting of fish has also been appalling. It is tragic to see dolphins, which are such beautiful, intelligent creatures, being trapped in tuna nets and thrown away, lifeless, because the commercial fisheries are in such a hurry to catch a few tuna.

When it gets to the point that we are no longer catching food for the good of mankind or harvesting crops according to responsible management practices, we are guilty of wanton slaughter and greed. The kind of exploitation which threatens the extinction of entire species is sinful and wrong.

UNNATURAL ACTS

We cannot condone that kind of exploitation, and it has to be controlled by law. But what we don't need, in the process, are wild-eyed fanatics voting legislation to prohibit hunting, fishing, or the killing of beef cattle, hogs, sheep, and chickens. Unrealistic and unnatural protectionism brings about an imbalance in the opposite direction.

For example, once they became legally protected the alligators in Florida began to multiply at such a high rate they have imperiled the population. Today there are alligators everywhere, and they are growing so fast they have become a threat. There has to be an intelligent harvesting of these creatures or mankind cannot live in relationship to them. Even in a wild state, man was able to protect himself against animals and to use them for his own good, and this should continue.

It is amazing to me that the same people who fulminate against the killing of baby seals and who stand in horror of wearing fur coats and who talk about protecting the bald eagle are at the same time at the forefront of the movement to slaughter human beings in the womb. There is an obvious inconsistency in their thinking. They worship the wild beasts and destroy human life made in the image of God! It is paradoxical, confusing, and hard for a rational person to reconcile.

THE GOD OF NATURE

If Christians will bring the biblical worldview to these issues, we can take the lead in this area, because we have insight as to how these environmental concerns need to be managed.

The liberals and radicals who are getting involved for various personal, political, or social reasons are often fanatics, and they are using the environment for their own hidden agenda. While we support the ideas of responsibility and restraint, we must also be cautious who we support and what we sanction.

There are volumes being written about the environment today, and the political movements to protect and maintain the balance of nature just continue to grow, but there is no question that in the next ten years the issue of the environment is going to take on massive proportions. It is probably going to be the number one public concern.

Environmental clean up, especially in the Soviet Union and Eastern Europe, is a top priority. Preserving our world from ecological harm is a clear priority for us all. But let us all be on our guard against that which is excessive, faddish, fanatical, and is being manipulated by people who want to use this issue as a means of introducing government control back into the lives of people on a massive scale.

The Christian view of ecological stewardship can provide the only satisfactory answer to pollution and desertification.

10

The New Economics

The specter of massive debt overhangs the world economy. American debt ratios are dramatically more threatening in 1990 than in 1929.

The French have a saying, "*Plus ça change, plus la même chose.*" The writer of the book of Ecclesiastes said the same thing differently, "What has been will be again, what has been done will be done again; there is nothing new under the sun." Jesus put it differently, "As long as the earth remains there will be summer and winter, seed time and harvest."

As we seek somewhat frantically in the days ahead amidst what seems violent economic changes to discern the economic course for our families, our businesses, our nation, and our world, we should know that although the pace of change may intensify and the people on this planet are drawn closer together than ever before, the economic cycles and rhythms of history will continue over and over again.

In other words, nothing is going to happen in the 1990s and beyond, absent the return of Jesus Christ to establish His kingdom on earth, that has not happened sometime, somewhere before.

Empires have risen and empires have fallen. There has been good weather and bad weather. Abundant crops and food shortages.

Economic prosperity and depression. Stable currencies and inflated currencies. Peace and happiness, war and misery. The earth always remains. The economic laws always remain. There is nothing new under the sun.

INEXORABLE EXPONENTIAL COMPOUNDING

Baron Rothschild called it the "eighth wonder of the world." The first head of the Bank of England, Sir John Houblon, undoubtedly rubbed his hands in joy at the secret he had learned from William Paterson, the wily Scot who had founded the bank in 1694, "We will charge interest on money which we create out of nothing."

These two secrets, the exponential compounding of interest and what is called "fractional reserve" banking can go a long way toward explaining what is going to happen to the economies of the world in the days ahead.

These two principles can bring untold wealth to those who use them and untold misery to the people and nations trapped in their web. It was no accident that God Almighty forbade His people in Israel to charge usury from one another, nor was it accidental that He then instructed them to proclaim a time of debt release every 50 years.

The mystery of exponential compounding works as follows. Money placed at compound interest begins to multiply slowly then at an accelerating pace which over the course of 20 to 50 years becomes absolutely astounding. To determine how fast money will grow with compound interest or how fast compound inflation will make money worthless, simply divide the number 72 by the rate of interest, or the rate of inflation.

At 10 percent simple interest compounded annually money doubles in 7.2 years. At just 10 percent compounded, 100,000 dollars, invested with no additional investment, no work, or no effort, silently, almost mysteriously would grow in 50 years to 12,800,000 dollars.

At 10 percent inflation, a dormant nest egg of 12,800,000 dollars would virtually disappear over 50 years to a real "inflation adjusted" value of only 100,000 dollars. And even as wealth compounds exponentially, even so debt when allowed to compound will grow inexorably until it overwhelms the debtor's ability ever to repay at which time he either repudiates his debts or becomes a slave of the lender.

In making investment decisions, it is crucial to remember that money invested must earn more than inflation or it is being lost. It is tragic to see someone who has put money aside for retirement fail to realize that the money must be sufficient to pay today's retirement needs plus future retirement needs after compound inflation.

For example, if inflation is 5 percent, then bank accounts which yield only 5 percent are not growing at all. At 5 percent inflation, the price of everything will be double in fifteen years. Consequently if a retired person will need 25,000 dollars for living expenses at age 65, he or she will require 50,000 dollars to continue the same standard of living after age 80.

The potential tragedy that inflation can bring on retirees with fixed incomes is evident. What is not evident is that today's young workers who are planning to retire in 2020 would need four times the 1990 level of benefits just to exist if inflation continues to compound at 5 percent per year for the next 30 years. And for everyone this could mean low priced automobiles selling for 40,000 dollars, average houses selling for 400,000 dollars, and meat at 10 dollars per pound.

This illustration should make it clear that interest or dividends which merely keep up with the rate of inflation are no gain at all. Yet current income taxes fall on interest and dividends with no regard for inflation. Clearly the amount of inflation should be deducted not only from capital gains but from all income derived from interest or dividends.

Bad as the exponential compounding of debt is, consider how much worse it can be when multiplied with so-called fractional reserve banking. Here is how that works. Assume that you are paid $100 and deposit that money in your bank. The bank sets aside a fraction, about 5 percent, and loans out the remaining $95.

Assume that the borrower deposits the $95 in the same bank, which again reserves 5 percent, and loans out $90.25. That money is redeposited and can be reserved, and the balance loaned out again. The first $100 has through fractional reserve banking been transformed into many times again as much in loans, all of which are supported by only 5 percent in reserves.

It becomes obvious that almost all bank assets are actually borrowed into existence. If people stop borrowing and begin to pay off their loans, the total supply of credit and banking assets can shrink in the same dramatic way they were created.

It is equally obvious that bank assets are not "money." They are computer print-outs representing the pledged credit of the businesses and individual people that banks are charging interest on loaned "money" which the banks "created out of nothing." When banks deal with one another, they don't pass cash money or gold back and forth. They trade entry balances on computer print-outs.

Since bank "assets" are based primarily on the credit of people who have borrowed from them, or the real assets which stand behind the paper, it is easy to see how a sizable number of bad credits could act like a loose thread in a knit sweater and unravel the entire fabric of world banking. If a "run" were to develop in which all the depositors wanted their money back from the world's banks, it is clear that no real money exists to pay them.

In case of a run, banks absent government help are out of business. Worldwide banking in the final analysis is a finely tuned, completely legal Ponzi scheme that depends 100 percent on the restraint of depositors, the credit of borrowers, and a generous appeal to the law of averages.

The danger of a rupture of the entire financial system is so perilously great in our over-leveraged world that when one sector of the banking industry, the Savings and Loan (S&L) Banks, began to fall apart, President Bush and Secretary of the Treasury Brady were forced to risk a second term in office for the president and the credit standing of the United States government in order to pay off S&L depositors and keep the game going a little longer.

This rescue effort may cost the United States government a total of one trillion dollars. But worse things may be ahead. The commercial banking industry is much larger than the Savings and Loan industry. There exists at best only 70 cents of federal insurance money for every 100 dollars of bank deposits. In recent years commercial banks have been failing at a higher rate than at any time since the Great Depression, and that rate shows no sign of diminishing.

If the government were forced to step up again with a one trillion dollar banking bailout, I believe that the credit standing of the United States would be severely damaged. The government already has guaranteed farm loans, several types of housing loans, education loans, small business loans, veterans loans, amounting to 2.8 trillion dollars plus a host of other off budget obligations which together total some 6.5 trillion dollars. All this is on top of the direct national debt which now exceeds 3 trillion dollars.

If the credit rating of this nation falls, several things begin to happen. (Some are already happening.) The prices of existing government bonds begin to decline. As they drop in price their interest yield begins to rise. This in turn forces up business rates, home mortgage rates, consumer loan rates, and newly issued government bond rates. Secondly, the value of the dollar declines on world markets which has the further effect of lowering bond prices, raising interest rates, and fueling inflation.

The higher interest rates set off a recession which means less tax revenues for the government and greater federal deficits. Greater deficits mean more federal borrowing, a further lowering of the credit rating, and higher interest rates, which trigger another round of the vicious cycle.

If the central bank tries to lower interest rates, investors will seek some other place for their money and in the process bonds are punished and interest rates do not drop but rise farther.

This sorry scenario has been played out for the past ten years or more in Brazil, Argentina, Mexico, Israel, the Sudan, Nicaragua and a host of other countries. Ultimately inflation gets out of hand, fixed securities become useless, and interest rates rise so high that they are meaningless.

There can then be a repudiation of debt, a new political initiative, and usually a new currency backed by some tangible exterior standard of value such as gold or representative commodities.

We are not there yet, but any thinking person must realize that the excess debt creation in America and the rest of the world must someday come to an end. Many observers feel that this decade may see a fiscal blow-out and a new beginning based on sound money and sound economic practices.

THE DEBT TIME BOMB

John Naisbitt, the author of the much quoted books, *Megatrends* and *Megatrends 2000* was both a charming and fascinating guest on my television program. However, I have to take issue with at least one of his very optimistic assertions in *Megatrends 2000,* that the federal deficit is a false mirror, a false reflection giving an unrealistic and hypothetical image of America's debt crises.

Certainly bureaucrats and political pundits have been cheered by Naisbitt's observations and his unreserved optimism, but, sadly, Naisbitt is wrong. The key indicator to look at is the federal debt in relation to our national output, what is called the debt/GNP ratio.

In the late days of the Carter administration inflation was rising rapidly at over 13 percent a year, and the GNP and federal revenues were rising with inflation. In those days the total federal debt was 34.5 percent of the entire gross national product of the country—a very manageable amount.

Under Ronald Reagan two things happened. Inflation shuddered to a halt, federal revenues slowed, and the federal deficit leaped to some 200 billion dollars a year. Along with it the national debt soared to undreamed of heights. The present 1990 debt to GNP ratio has doubled in the past ten years to 60 percent.

This is a very sobering statistic to any economic analyst. Equally sobering is the fact that total on and off budget debt of the federal government is almost twice the total annual output of this nation. If we add debt of business corporations, private citizens, plus the actual federal debt and its contingent liabilities we find that the total stands at 18 trillion dollars which is 367 percent of the annual output of the nation and only slightly less than the value of all of the public and private assets of the entire country.

These figures are imprecise because of possible double counting of private debt and overlapping contingent debt of the government. However one counts the numbers, it is clear that America is in hock up to its eyeballs, with a public and private debt load standing at a markedly higher level than what we had just prior to the Great Depression of the 1930s.

Overall corporate debt figures are not known precisely but I have seen estimates that the debt of American corporations in 1989 stood at 70 percent of their total assets. In 1929 that number was estimated at 25 percent. In 1929 the federal debt was only 16.9 billion dollars, the GNP was 103.4 billion dollars and the debt to GNP ratio was only 16 percent, not the 60 percent it is in 1990.

The total national debt of this country exceeds the combined

external debts of the other nations of the world. Our balance of payments deficit reflects an inability to live within our means.

We have been consuming foreign products—automobiles, computers, electronic devices, clothing, and household goods, along with jewels, perfumes, and all the luxuries that come to us from other nations—and we have been borrowing to pay for our enormous consumption.

The closest analogy to the impending debt crisis in America is the unfortunate example of Argentina just before World War I. Argentina had one of the top ten standards of living at that time. They were incredibly rich, as anyone could see.

The principal river in Buenos Aires is the Rio Plata, the River of Silver, the very name reflecting the atmosphere and attitude of opulence which existed there. The land is nearly as rich as ours, the climate is very similar to ours, there is an abundance of mineral wealth.

But with a great deal of political and material idealism, and with a seemingly monumental capacity for self-indulgence, the country went on an orgy of spending and borrowing to pay for the wild excesses of their lifestyle.

Today Argentina is not even in the top 50 nations of the world. It is subject to continuous political and economic upheavals, and the people are thoroughly demoralized. Unless there is an intervention of God in that nation, Argentina seems destined for some kind of oblivion.

Their sad example should be only too clear to us at a time like this. Yet, despite all we know about the dangers of debt and reckless spending, the same thing seems to be happening in America at this very moment.

CAN GOVERNMENT MAKE IT BETTER?

As I write this chapter the United States economy is either in a recession or approaching one. The stock market was beginning a decline when Saddam Hussein launched a war against Kuwait. Now the market has lost 15 percent of its total value since it reached a high point of 3000 on the Dow Jones Index, a loss in dollar value of approximately one half a trillion dollars.

The Federal Reserve has been tightening the money supply for six months and the broad level of money known as M-3 when adjusted for inflation has been experiencing a 2.5 percent negative growth for almost three years.

Congress desperately needed to balance the budget and was set to raise taxes and cut spending. Oil price hikes following the Middle East crisis may take 60 billion dollars out of the economy and tax hikes are out of the question. The federal deficit may go above 200 billion dollars in the new fiscal year, and if the recession deepens the total could reach a record 300 billion or more.

Congress cannot raise taxes in a recession. It cannot lower taxes with huge deficits. The Federal Reserve Board cannot lower interest rates because the markets will react to fears of inflation, nor can it raise interest rates for fear of making the recession worse.

People and businesses are afraid so they are not borrowing or buying as they once did. Banks are not loaning because of federal regulators and the fear of loan defaults. The growth of credit is dropping.

The huge overhang of property left over from the Savings and Loan collapse has not been sold, so prices for both private and commercial real estate have continuously edged lower.

Undoubtedly we can work our way out of it, but I believe the scene is set for a major global recession, more likely a depression. Frankly, there is nothing much the government can do now to make things better. They helped put us in this mess, but there is very little they can do now to get us out of it.

THE DEBT COLLAPSE

History does repeat itself, and one of the primary lessons of history from Bible days until now is that a society can only accumulate so much debt before something gives. Historically it is possible for national debt to grow somewhere around 50 or 60 years. That was the conclusion of the Russian economist Nikolai Kondratieff, for whom the Kondratieff long wave debt cycle is named.

Simply put, a capitalistic society will begin a period of growth and debt accumulation until a future time when there is excess unused capacity, obsolescence of technology and products, and insupportable debt. After a period of debt cancellation and closing excess obsolete capacity, new products and fresh capital come forward to begin the next cycle of growth.

Some of this has already happened in America. Our steel plants were obsolete and inefficient. Most of them have been closed. So also obsolete automobile plants have been closed down all over the country.

There has been a vast excess of inner city rental office space, some of which in cities like Dallas, is slowly beginning to be occupied. Other rental office buildings stand lonely and empty in cities across the land. There are hundreds of thousands of excess hotel rooms as a result of speculative over-building, and a shake out in that industry is yet to be dealt with.

The market has been swamped by the excess of debt in high interest leveraged buyouts featuring reset bonds, high interest zero bonds, mezzanine debt, and the better known junk bonds. Sellers of junk bonds like Canadian developer, Robert Campeau, have experienced spectacular and highly publicized bankruptcies. Many lesser known companies have defaulted on their debts and have gone into bankruptcy.

I would estimate that no less than 50 billion dollars has been lost by junk bond investors, and that figure may move much higher.

The major banks have been forced to write off billions of dollars in debt owed them by third world countries, and the present and future defaults among United States real estate investors may dwarf that amount. At present the capital structure of most of the big city money center banks is quite strained and vulnerable to any further debt shocks.

So far our economy has weathered progressively devastating economic events with remarkable resilience. I, like many, fervently hope that we can work our way out of it. But as things stand now, if there is a serious recession which takes under a number of over-leveraged businesses, the strain may be too much for an already weakened financial system and we may see a debt collapse of worldwide proportions followed by a painful and protracted depression.

With these prospects before us people would be well advised to avoid the stock market until the smoke clears, to stay clear of all but the most advantageous and necessary real estate purchases, to get out of debt, and to have available investments of the safest and most liquid sort, such as U.S. Treasury bills.

The government will never default on its current short term

paper, and it must market treasury bills, as it always has, to yield interest at a rate at least 3 percent higher than the then current rate of inflation. For this reason funds placed in treasury bills are safe from default and reasonably safe from all but the most virulent inflation.

FOOLISH GOVERNMENT ACTION

In 1929 when the long wave debt cycle was winding down with a stock market crash, the government tried to help the economy out. As is always the case, our government took action to try to change the past not help the future. Incredibly they raised taxes and raised tariff barriers.

It is still a matter of debate as to who took the third false step, the Federal Reserve Board or the credit creating borrowing public, but we now know that between 1930 and 1932, in a time of desperate need of capital, the United States money supply shrank by an unbelievable 25 percent.

People today say that a 1929 style depression cannot happen because the government has too many mechanisms in place to prevent it. The record clearly shows that it was unwise government action before and after the great depression which helped bring it on and then made it much worse after it had happened.

In our day it was government action which allowed the Savings and Loan debacle to occur. The Congress raised the insurance limit on S&L accounts to 100,000 dollars and then authorized the S&Ls to make whatever loans they wished with the government insured money.

The Congressionally mandated lure to fraud was virtually irresistible. Now, true to form, the government by overreacting to the past abuses is bringing on a credit crunch which is helping push the economy into recession. Congressional action, by dramatically raising reserve requirements, has forced even solvent S&Ls into receivership.

Government auditors are poring over bank records, questioning existing loans and in some cases forcing banks to call fully performing loans. As a result bank officials are fearful of taking even modest risks, and a full blown credit crunch has developed which is giving the economy a major shove into recession.

Government does not produce anything. Government never creates wealth. It is one of the illusions of socialism that government somehow makes wealth. All government does is redistribute wealth, and it does so by extracting an enormous administrative penalty.

Some estimates of government programs indicate that something on the order of 70 percent of the total spending goes for administrative costs and only about 30 percent gets out to the recipients. The idea that higher taxes will improve economic conditions is a false promise of those who support the idea of a welfare state and ever-greater expenditures by government.

Thomas Jefferson's opinion of government was very clear in his oft-quoted statement, "That government governs best that governs least." He warned us at the founding of this nation about intrusive government programs and the resulting tax burden. Americans in the highest tax bracket are already paying close to 40 percent now for state, federal, and Social Security taxes, and the average taxpayer is paying upwards of 25 percent of family income for more bureaucracy.

In addition, the burden of Social Security continues to mount. In 1990, the cost of Social Security and Medicaid will top 345 billion dollars, equal to half of all Federal spending if you discount military spending and interest on the national debt. Where most of us feel the crunch, though, is in our paychecks.

In 1958 the maximum withholding was about 189 dollars for Social Security; by 1977 it was up to about 1,900 dollars. But thanks to seven rate hikes during the 1980s, by 1989 it was up to 7,850 dollars. David Boaz, vice president of the Cato Institute in Washington, D.C., wrote in a commentary in the *New York Times* that today the typical American worker actually gives up more of his income for Social Security than for income taxes.

That cost is not going down. To make Social Security solvent, by the year 2020 the combined Social Security tax will be 22,000 dollars (in 1989 dollars), or 88,000 dollars at 5 percent compounded inflation.

For many years, Congress has used the resources of the Social Security Administration like a checking account. No capital has ever been accumulated, and no interest or other benefits have ever been allowed to accrue to these vital accounts.

It is clear now that government has lost its vision and its ability to manage these programs, and it should come as no surprise that

Boaz and other Cato Institute experts, such as Peter J. Ferrara, have been calling for the privatization of the government retirement and Social Security systems.

TAKING THE HIT

The double whammy of high income taxes and high Social Security withholding has created an incredible burden on the average wage-earner. In March 1989 the United States Census Bureau announced that the median annual family income in 1987 was approximately 30,850 dollars. That was the first real inflation-adjusted gain since the previous high of 1973. But again, the average family in America had to work from January 1st to May 5th to pay their tax debt.

Despite the higher incomes and the so-called "tax reductions" of the past five years, that's the longest period of time Americans have ever had to work for the IRS before earning the first nickel for themselves. Shouldn't it be clear to everybody that we don't need more taxes?

Liberal commentators were applauding the 1990 Tax Summit in Washington, saying it was about time Americans realized that somebody has to pay for government. In fact, John Chancellor said that on an NBC News commentary. But Americans haven't missed the point at all; John Chancellor has missed the point, and the liberal Democrats have missed the point.

Americans don't want more government, or even the same amount of government. We want less, not more. We want a lower tax debt, fewer bureaucrats, less meddling in the lives of Americans, fewer socialist giveaway schemes, and less scalping of American wage-earners.

In his remarkable book, *Losing Ground: American Social Policy, 1950-1980,* Charles Murray described a program which would accomplish many if not all of the goals of the socialist agenda. He said it could turn the hard-core unemployed into steady workers, reduce the birthrate among single girls, reduce the breakup of poor families, and improve morale among the underclass.

Quite simply, his suggestion was to scrap the entire federal welfare system, "including AFDC, Medicaid, Food Stamps, Unemployment Insurance, Worker's Compensation, subsidized housing, disability insurance, and the rest." Murray's logic was that "it would leave the working-aged person with no recourse whatsoever except the job market, family members, friends, and public or private locally funded services."

Now if they could be assured of achieving all these goals, government would gladly spend billions, Murray reasoned, and this program would be absolutely free! But naturally the liberal majority, who feel the solution to every problem is to raise taxes and to increase federal control, scoffed at Murray's proposal. To them it was simply too outrageous.

What we must remember is that government is not ultimately interested in helping the under-privileged; government is interested in building programs that extend the power and control of government.

GROWING THE UNDERCLASS

Boaz cites Murray's research in his essay on "Saving the Inner City," in which he shows how the so-called "underclass" was, in fact, a creation of the welfare system.

While there have always been, and will always be, poor in the land, the hard-core unemployable, and those people who have become entirely dependent on government programs, never existed in this nation until Lyndon Johnson's "Great Society" gave them a place to hang out.

The things the Eastern Europeans are learning fast is that central planning, socialistic economies, and government-owned enterprises are wasteful and inefficient. Everywhere I've gone in Poland, in Hungary, and in Czechoslovakia, there has been talk of privatizing state-owned enterprises because people know they are wasting resources, and they're not contributing to the economy.

As a matter of fact, when I was in Hungary an American appraiser of state enterprises told me that a typical beauty shop operator in the United States or Canada with three women working for her would know more about business accounting and economics after three years than the general manager of a state-owned enterprise with 10,000 employees in Hungary.

The accounting—and the level of business accountability—is horrible because the goals are not set by the markets. The key to successful enterprise is a free market. The market tells business what it wants and what it does not want. The state, on the other hand, tells business what it should make, whether the people want it or not.

Accountants in Hungary, for example, are not concerned by what actually sells but what makes it into the warehouse to fulfill the government-mandated quota. If 3,000 pairs of shoes were made but nobody wanted them, the books still show that they sold 3,000 pairs of shoes because they made them and put them into the warehouse.

When state quotas are met in many of these enterprises, they stop counting because they have met their quota and anything else is not relevant. They have satisfied the demands of the state.

CURBING GOVERNMENT'S CONTROL

The aim of free people everywhere is to limit the power and the scope of the government in any way they can, and the best way to do that is through lower taxes. Unfortunately, the bureaucratic lobby is large and powerful.

Those who seek to wield power and control the people have great skill in manipulating the system, while the average taxpayer isn't organized at all. There are very sophisticated pressure groups to represent those who expect to get money out of the system.

The people who profit from the poor have a vested interest in maintaining poverty programs, so they have an effective lobby because they want to keep the things they are receiving from the government.

There can be a taxpayer's revolt, as there was in California. There is certainly a tendency toward (perhaps even a mandate for) lower taxes in this country—and ultimately that trend will have to continue—but the liberal power block is always on the side of higher taxes, increased government involvement in people's lives, and more of the product of our working people going into the hands of bureaucrats.

In a conference sponsored by the Family Research Council in Washington, D.C., Dr. Allan Carlson, president of the Rockford Institute, said that the financial pressure on the two-parent family has become unbearable. He told the conferees that between 1960 and 1984, the tax burden on a two-parent family with four children increased by 224 percent. During the same period of time, there was a 600 percent increase in the family's Social Security tax.

What these figures show is that there is a deliberate discriminatory bias toward the traditional family in this country. The government's welfare programs reward the disadvantaged family, encourage single-parent homes, and provide substantial benefits to dysfunctional families, while the traditional two-parent home is expected to pay the freight for the government's giveaways.

Under such pressure, is it any wonder that Americans have resorted to credit and compounding debt as a solution to their dilemma? Is there any doubt that over the last two decades Americans have learned to believe that debt is desirable, that credit is always available, and that the desires of their hearts are as near as their handy bank card?

WANTING IT NOW

The moral breakdown we have experienced in this nation and the world over the past 40 years indicates a growing lack of self-control. Someone defined lust as "wanting it now." Wanting *anything* now. We have been trained as consumers over the years in America to "buy now and pay later."

We are taught to desire material goods as the means of gaining satisfaction, and then we have placed in our hands an extremely permissive credit system which makes it possible for us to fulfill our desires for material things with little regard for the consequences.

It all starts with the fact that people cannot live within their means. In most cases they are unwilling to trust God for their material needs, so they bow to the false gods of credit and materialism.

The first commandment says, "Thou shalt have no other gods before me," but people begin to set up materialism as a god and they begin to think if only I could have that car, or this house, that boat, or this set of furniture, or this vacation, or that suit of clothes or some other status symbol, then I would be happy.

So there is an unending cycle of materialism. First there is violation of the first commandment. Then coveting, a violation of the tenth commandment. Finally people begin to steal to satisfy their wants. They either go into credit bondage, where the borrower is the servant of the lender, or they will default on their debts which in essence is a form of theft. The honest man pays back his debt, but the thief borrows and he doesn't pay.

By this credit creation, we have introduced a type of corruption into our whole national life. When you add to that the fact that 51 percent of the people take something from government, we have introduced another factor, getting something for free because it comes out of government.

On top of that, we now have lotteries in state after state to help pay for added government expenses. The states are deliberately training people to gamble instead of to save their money.

We no longer train them that wealth comes from hard work, savings, and compound interest. Instead, we have trained people to be wasteful in their economic affairs then to wait for that great windfall profit that comes about when they hit the lottery.

We are corrupting ourselves by our credit and spending policies. Then our government comes in with a further corrupting influence with legalized gambling. We get a false sense of satisfaction, a false sense of wealth. These false values and the resulting dissatisfaction and high debt are major contributing factors to the tremendous anxiety among so many people.

Our people are very anxious. Look at the number of librium and valium tablets Americans consume: some figures indicate it is as high as ten billion a year. When we consider the increased number of visits to psychiatrists, the breakups of marriages, increased family violence and abuse, we have to recognize that at least a big part of the emotional problems in this country must be attributed to financial mismanagement and the financial bondage which is attributable to our national worship of false gods.

We read in the book of Deuteronomy in the Old Testament that God told Moses that if His people would shun false idols and continue to seek His face, the people would prosper and flourish in the land, through all time and wherever they went. But He also warned them that if they turned away their hearts and were lured by their own pleasures and their wealth and the idols of foreign lands, they would be cut off and their land would be laid waste.

Whether we apply God's covenant to the children of Israel or to the Christian nations of the world which inherited God's promises, it is easy to see that we have failed God's commandments.

We go back to the fact that for most Americans their satisfaction is not in God, is not in spiritual relations, or the inter-personal relations which should give us happiness—the love of our wife, our husband, our children and parents—but it is centered in things and the acquisition of more things.

YUPPIES BEGIN TO SAVE

In the 1980s America and the industrialized world went on a spending spree the apex of which is chronicled by a weekly television show hosted by Robin Leach called, "The Lifestyles of the Rich and Famous."

The young urban professionals, or yuppies, led the way. These were the swinging singles or two income couples where annual family incomes of 90,000 to 100,000 dollars were the norm, and salaries of 250,000 to 1,000,000 dollars and beyond were not uncommon.

They went skiing at Aspen or Vail, dined on nouvelle cuisine on the Riviera, shopped on Rodeo Drive, drove BMWs or Mercedes cars, paid big money for memberships in luncheon and golf clubs, and fitted their homes and apartments with jacuzzis, giant screen televisions, surround stereo sound, and the latest and best video recorders, compact disc players, and symphony quality hi-fidelity music systems.

They spent money faster than they earned it and undoubtedly helped push America's saving rate to what may have been its lowest rate in history, a skimpy 2.8 percent.

In the 1990s, the yuppies are older, their children are growing up, and they have either bought everything they need or else they have grown tired of wasting money. So we are told consumption is out, frugality is in. BMWs and Mercedes are out, Jeeps and Ford Broncos are in. Designer clothes are out, discount specials are in. The wine and brie set may be turning into the lemonade and ritz cracker bunch.

The biggest news though is that consumption is out and savings are in. In the September, 1990 issue of *Money* magazine the lead feature was entitled, "9 Great Savings Moves." One of those featured savers was a certified member of yuppidom. He was a 45-year-old newspaper editor of a metropolitan newspaper whose wife is a writer.

This couple with one 17-year-old daughter have been saving 51 percent of the husband's salary, and in five years of frugal living (driving a 1984 Volkswagen Rabbit without a radio) have been able to pay off the mortgage on their 126,000-dollar-home in Southern Florida and accumulate savings and investments of 200,000 dollars.

Economist Dr. Gary Shilling of the New-York-City-based A. Gary Shilling and Company tells me that the trend in America from consumption to saving will be adequate to fund even larger federal deficits than we have now plus the investment needs of the growing United States industry. Shilling, who by the way feels we are heading into a really nasty worldwide recession, is quite optimistic for the long term prospects later in the decade.

The real secret of the economic rise of Japan since World War II has been the extraordinary 17 percent Japanese saving rate. If the American people would move their personal savings rate from its present level to anywhere near the Japanese level, American industry would have more than enough capital to challenge the world. And along with industrial renaissance we could see a zero rate of inflation, a prime interest rate of 3 percent, and home mortgage rates of 4.5 to 5 percent.

If there is any policy that the government should adopt during the next decade it should be a policy that reduces government spending, lowers taxes, and rewards saving. At present, government policy rewards borrowing and penalizes saving.

Corporations are permitted to deduct interest on bonds held by investors, but not the dividends paid on stock held by investors. People who finance their homes on credit are rewarded. People who pay cash for property are not. Interest and dividends received by savers are taxed without taking into consideration the inflation rate.

Savings placed into various types of pensions are highly restricted and limited in scope. No provision is made to allow the tax free build up of funds so that young couples can purchase a first home or pay for the college education for their children.

When an alcoholic or drug addict stops using drugs and goes "cold turkey" the immediate effect is horrible. He experiences chills, cramps, fever, sweating, delirium, and agonizing craving for a drink or a "fix." After a while the body of the addict or the alcoholic cleanses itself of the poison, and the normal processes begin to work again as wholesome food, rest, and exercise do their work.

The physical addiction is gone. All that remains is a possible physical tendency toward addiction and a steadily declining mental addiction.

The debt binge of the past 25 years is over. The punch bowl and the needle are being taken away. We would like to taper off gradually. A depression might demand that we go "cold turkey." If so, the temporary pain will be intense, but if the problems discussed in chapter 7 are solved we can come through it and return to vibrant health. The issue is not whether there will be debt withdrawal—only how and when.

THE ROLE OF THE CHURCH

The church stands to today's society very much as the church stood to Rome at the collapse of the Roman Empire. It does seem that what has been called Christendom, to use Muggeridge's phrase, is in decline. When the Roman Empire collapsed, it took with it the greatest system of political, economic and military power the world had ever known. And in the very dark days of the Roman Empire, after the collapse, the Church of Rome was the only stable force available to rebuild society.

Out of the collapse of one came the flowering of the other, and that flowering and rebirth were based on Christian tenets and Christian morality.

As the most dominant empire since Roman times, America has helped to bring great wealth and prosperity to the world, but its moral strength and vitality have begun to wane. The strong dose of renewal and vitality so greatly needed by American government and business can best be delivered by an injection of democratic morality.

Richard John Neuhaus recently said, "I believe that democratic morality will be both a means toward its achievement and a product of its achievement." In other words, when we commit ourselves to the aims of moral structures and moral government in a pluralist society, our faith in the process of democracy helps to bring about its existence and continuation.

Our faith in the worth of morality and the fruits of democracy offers America and the world its greatest weapon against defeat and decline.

But many argue today that we are already living in a post-Christian era, as far as the culture, traditions and mores of the people are concerned. And it seems that Western civilization—at least in America—is in a period of decline. It is only too clear that much of the vitality and economic power we once prized so highly is moving to the East.

Today we are seeing an even more striking paradox in Eastern Europe. In an area of the world where Christendom has not been a dominant influence for at least 50 years, suddenly there is moral renewal.

In communist countries where the Christian church has been oppressed, and where the political and economic system has been organized around militant atheism and the trampling of individual values under the iron heel of the collective, there now appears to be a new birth of Christian democracy.

The only unifying force in those countries with any moral authority is the Church, and throughout Eastern Europe—in Hungary and Czechoslovakia and in Poland—the Roman Catholic church and the Evangelical Protestant churches have become the rallying point of moral and democratic renewal.

I believe that the role of the church is to call people back to New Testament faith and New Testament beliefs that put transcendent values ahead of present day materialism. Even if the political and economic system that we currently enjoy goes into decline, Jesus Christ will not decline and His kingdom will endure forever.

This can be the church's finest hour, but I believe that we must rise to the challenge by working for spiritual renewal, giving a whole new ethos to Western culture. The church must be prepared to pick up the pieces of shattered materialism.

What a great tragedy it would be for those emerging Eastern European countries if they were to survive the ravages of communist-style materialism and to overcome the tyranny of atheist philosophies only to fall victim to a capitalist-style materialism devoid of the underlying spiritual values that make capitalism human and bearable.

When I met with Billy Graham at the Brandenburg Gate in 1990, he told me that the East Germans he met were shocked when they came across the wall and saw West Berlin. They thought they would be met by fellow believers who would be singing hymns and praising the Lord and rejoicing at their freedom. But there were no believers to welcome them; instead, all they saw was shops and cars and X-rated movies and all of the decadence that now exists in Western Europe. Plentiful goods to be sure, but a heart-breaking lack of moral and spiritual values.

I remember my own shock in making the journey from Hong Kong to Mainland China and seeing the contrast between those two cultures. There was a simplicity, an honesty and openness, even a kind of purity in the people I met in China that was absolutely appealing and beautiful.

When I came back out to Hong Kong and the unbelievable opulence that exists in that colony, I was jolted by the excesses. It was such an incredible irony to see the greed and decadence of Hong Kong juxtaposed against the austerity of Mainland China. There is no question that spiritual values languish when we have material excess.

As we look about us, we see everywhere the signs of collapse. The rationalistic ideologies have failed, the reign of communist tyranny has failed, and the materialistic systems of American-style wealth-building have failed.

But the source of our renewal remains, and there is hope. For the kingdom of God has not failed, and Jesus Christ has not failed. In that truth alone we have reason to hope that the coming decade can be a promising era for freedom and truth, and for building the future world God has prophetically ordained.

That world will not come through greed or materialism or any of the worn-out values of consumerism, but through a new commitment to biblical morality. The very hand of God is stirring in the land, and those who survive and prosper will be those who humbly seek His face and seek His guidance. I am convinced that only a national renewal can save us. Only a global renewal can save the world.

The 1990s will see a debt blow-out which could trigger a serious worldwide depression.

11

The Rise of Anti-Semitism

Anti-semitism will continue to rise in this decade.

The nations of the earth have united against the nation which occupies the site of the Tower of Babel to form a New World Order.

Early on the morning of August 2, 1990, the forces of Iraq at the command of Iraqi dictator, Saddam Hussein, invaded their tiny neighbor, Kuwait, looted the Kuwaiti banks, seized their gold and currency, raped their women, and then annexed their country.

Suddenly a wily megalomaniac at the helm of a nation with only 17 million people, yet possessing a large army, over 5000 tanks, chemical weapons, and the rudiments of atomic bombs, had taken control of 20 percent of the world's oil and was threatening 30 percent more.

The rest of the world, led by the United States, assembled a vast force of planes, ships, and fighting men to blockade Iraq and then neutralize its leader.

A comment in the August 27, 1990, issue of *U.S. News and World Report* gives a true perspective of what was happening, ". . . the looming conflict in the Persian Gulf is not simply a battle

263

for Kuwait, or even for mastery of the Middle East's oil. It is the latest chapter in a 14-century-old battle between East and West, between Islam and its monotheistic rivals, Christianity and Judaism."

THE TRUE MEANING OF SADDAM HUSSEIN

The world's present civilization began in the Tigris-Euphrates valley first with Sumer, where Ur of Chaldees, the ancestral home of Abraham was located. Slightly north the civilizations of Nineveh and Akkad emerged, then successively in the same territory arose the Assyrian and Babylonian civilizations.

The modern nation of Iraq is located precisely where the civilizations of both the East and the West began, in the land of Nineveh, Assyria, and Babylon.

This region has been known as the center of mystical and occult religions—Nimrod, Astarte, the tower of Babel, the false god, Baal, Baalzebub, the court magicians and Chaldean soothsayers of Nebuchadnezzar, and the Babylonian Mysteries of the Roman era—all originated here. In the book of Revelation the Roman Empire and type of a future anti-Christ is identified as "Mystery Babylon, the mother of harlots."

I would not want to make more out of the current trouble than the facts warrant, but it seems to me that the world should take notice that a major conflict at the end of this millennium is pitting all the nations of the earth against the nation which occupies the place where all of our cultures began in ancient history.

Iraq also happens to be in a place identified by the Bible as the land where successive revolts against God have taken place since the beginning of time.

The Sumerian civilization dates back at least to 3500 B.C., possibly earlier. In a Sumerian city called Ur a boy was born about 2000 B.C. whose name was Abram. After Abram was married, his father took him, his wife Sarai, and his nephew Lot to a place in Canaan north of present Israel called Haran.

Abram, who later became known as Abraham, left Haran at the age of 75 because God had promised him the land we now know as Palestine. Abraham had two sons, one was Isaac, the forefather of the Jewish people. The other was Ishmael, the child of a servant girl, Hagar, and was the forefather of the Arab people.

Abraham was 100 years of age when his wife Sarai conceived Isaac, fulfilling God's promise to make Abraham's seed a blessing to all of the nations of the earth. When God told Abraham to sacrifice the young Isaac at a place called Mount Moriah, Abraham's obedience was being tested. But Abraham proved worthy, and the boy was spared by the intervention of God.

This place of holy dedication and unquestioning obedience to God is thought to be the site of the Temple Mount in the city of Jerusalem. By his act of sacrifice and obedience at Mount Moriah, Abraham made Jerusalem the spiritual center for those who, like Abraham and later Jesus Christ, were willing by faith to give everything to serve God.

Jerusalem is therefore the center of the true worship of God. Babylon, on the other hand, is the spiritual symbol of those who refuse God's grace but insist on building systems and institutions which, like the tower of Babel, were to challenge God's rule and authority.

The Bible tells us that at one time all the people of the earth were united with one purpose and one language. At Babel, however, God confused their languages and separated them to prevent a unified, one-world revolt against Him.

Until very recently, I had always felt that Babylon was merely a symbol. Until the Saddam Hussein affair, I never felt that anything would actually bring the power of the entire world to physical Babylon. But this is the era when we should expect the unexpected!

THE NEW WORLD ORDER

On Saturday, August 25, 1990, the United Nations Security Council voted unanimously, with the participation of both China and the Soviet Union, to permit the joint force gathering in the Middle East to use appropriate power to back up the United Nations blockade against Iraq. That afternoon, Lieutenant General Brent Scowcroft, the protege of Henry Kissinger, and National Security Advisor to President George Bush, was interviewed by Charles Bierbauer for Cable News Network.

General Scowcroft was obviously pleased and in his pleasure let slip a phrase that he had learned over and over as a member of the Council on Foreign Relations, "A New World Order." The action of the United Nations to permit military action against an aggressor nation such as Iraq was, in the words of the highest ranking strategist in the Bush administration, the start of "a new world order."

Obviously to those of us who are weary and disgusted by a world divided into rival squabbling camps, the prospect of unanimous joint action by a world body sounds good. But is it really good? Has the crisis in Babylon actually been used to usher onto the world scene something that is not good at all?

Since its founding in the late 1920s, the Council on Foreign Relations has played a dominant role in the foreign and economic policy of the United States. If there is a true establishment, this is it.

Funded and directed in large measure by the Rockefeller family, the CFR has long held what must seem to them a noble goal, the establishment of a one-world government. To that end the repeated thrust of CFR related literature has been the diminishing of the power and sovereignty of the United States of America and the establishment of a global government with courts and military and currency—and yes, of course, banks—which take precedence over the institutions of the United States.

In a benign world where all men are angels such an arrangement might actually be desirable. But given a world in which dictators, fanatics, revolutionaries, and assassins are as often as not in control of nations, the prospect of being governed by such people is not very appealing.

For Christians, the idea of surrendering sovereignty to Muslims and Hindus who are dedicated to the destruction of what we consider holy is anathema. The nation of Israel most certainly has a very similar attitude.

I am writing now somewhat ahead of events developing in the Middle East but, to my thinking, some of the portents seem very clear. If Saddam Hussein is really smart, he will meet with key Arab leaders, and then permit himself to be talked into withdrawing from Kuwait in exchange for an agreement by his Arab brethren to maintain the price of oil at a level of $22 per barrel or more.

At that point, President Bush will have no choice but to bring U.S. troops, planes, tanks, and ships back home, leaving Saddam free to use his oil wealth to build atomic bombs and a more deadly arsenal.

Saddam can then rail at America, and call for a revolt in Saudi Arabia against the family of Ibn Saud, who will be presented as the lackeys of the imperialist anti-Arab American aggressors. If there is then an internal overthrow of ruling monarchs, there is no way the public opinion of the world can be mobilized to resist it.

Saddam may lack that wisdom, but I doubt it. If he withdraws, President George Bush will be revived in popularity as a cool leader who backed down a 1990s version of Adolf Hitler. In reality, a more sinister scenario may actually be unfolding.

The real long term meaning of the Saddam Hussein affair would be this: at the site of the Tower of Babel where the nations of the world were once dispersed, all the nations of the earth came together and entered into a military alliance which began, according to a high ranking American official, "a new world order."

It would be a new world order with military power to force upon individual nations a standard of conduct that the nations of the world believe is proper. It is this power that may one day be used against Christians. It certainly will be used one day against the nation of Israel.

The real future story of biblical world history is not about all the nations on earth coming against Babylon, the center of false religion, but about all the nations on earth coming against Israel, the site and origin of God's true religion. Jerusalem, not Baghdad, is the capital of the land described by the Bible as the navel of the earth.

WASHINGTON CHANGES COURSE

If what President George Bush said in his February 1990 address represents any sort of shift in American policy toward Israel, we can expect to see a much harder line in this country in the months ahead. And if the level of pressure against Israel from within and from without continues to mount as it has in the past 12 months, by the year 2000 we may well see the nation of Israel standing virtually alone.

In his public and private remarks, President Bush has told Yitzhak Shamir that East Jerusalem and the West Bank are still considered off limits to Jewish settlers. He further warned the Israeli

Prime Minister that he could not continue to take three billion dollars a year in aid from the United States on the pretext he would work for peace and bring about an end to the strife with the Palestinians, then do nothing about peace.

Bush's words were understood as a threat to withdraw aid and support to Israel, and in some ways a statement that our long diplomatic relationship with Israel was being reexamined. As a result, the Likud lost the support of the Parliament. Shamir's government fell in March 1990 and it took two attempts and nearly four months, until June 1990, to rebuild a stable coalition.

The problem for the Likud, the conservative wing of government, is that the hard-liners want to ignore the Arab problem and make it go away. The Labour Party, on the other hand, wants to settle with the Arabs and, like Ben-Gurion and Menachem Begin before them, trade land for peace.

The two major parties cannot even agree to disagree, but to complicate matters dramatically there are 35 dissident and splinter parties in the Parliament, circling like gnats, constantly agitating and rendering the prospects of a peaceful resolution virtually impossible.

President Bush and Secretary of State James Baker have repeatedly told Shamir to get serious. They are saying that America and the world will not be patient with the internal bickering within the Parliament forever. If, in addition to all the external pressure from Saddam Hussein and the militant Arab nations and their own internal squabbles, there is also a concerted effort to pressure the Jews, then I believe matters can only worsen.

However, from all indications, the action of Saddam Hussein has shocked many of the Israeli "doves" to the danger the nation would face from a Palestinian state on the West Bank, connected to Jordan, and then connected to Iraq. Prime Minister Shamir's hardline stance has been clearly vindicated and strengthened.

SHIFTING WORLD OPINION

Whether America's new get-tough policy is motivated by sincere diplomatic concern or by more pragmatic financial reasons—because of Middle East oil, the threats of Arab boycotts, or the expense of a three-billion-dollar aid program—there has been a definite shifting in American foreign policy toward Israel.

In addition to the shift in public policy, there seems also to be a shift of the sympathies of the American people toward Israel. Recent public opinion polls show that most Americans feel that other nations are now better friends of America than Israel.

In the press, and in the public opinion, there is a growing consensus that Israel is not as important to us as it once was, and the support for Israel which has come predominantly out of the evangelical, biblical worldview, has diminished even as that Christian worldview has been diminished in American life.

THE HISTORICAL RECORD

The Holy Land is called the navel of the earth in the Bible. It is the spiritual hub of the world. The ancient city of Jerusalem is considered to be the most holy place for both Jews and Christians and, to a lesser degree, for Muslims as well.

If we believe the Bible, the Messiah will come back to Jerusalem, His feet resting on the Mount of Olives, followed by earthquakes and celestial events of catastrophic proportions. The mountains will split from north to south and a great waterway will form in the valley which runs from Jerusalem down to the Dead Sea. The city of Jerusalem will be leveled by the earthquake and become a large plateau.

The book of Revelation offers many such dramatic images, but whether they are all to be taken literally or whether they should be understood to imply some spiritual truth, I can't say categorically. Bible scholars have excellent reasons in support of each point of view.

However you choose to interpret these passages, the Bible clearly speaks of a literal conflict with the nations surrounding Jerusalem and the deliverance of the Jews coming from the Lord Himself. The Old Testament used the phrase, "The Time of Jacob's Trouble." The New Testament called it "The Tribulation."

I believe there will come a time when the nations of the earth will turn against Israel and isolate her, and that she will only be saved by the direct intervention of God.

THE DREAM OF ZION

As we know, Zionism is a political force. It is not a spiritual force. While its underlying beliefs and goals are as ancient as the nation of Judah itself, Zionism has been the unifying dream of the Jewish people since Theodore Herzl and others came together in the last years of the nineteenth century to formulate plans for the establishment of a homeland for the Jews in Palestine.

If we look back to the history of this region, we discover that King David first took the Citadel of Zion by conquest in about 1000 B.C. As I pointed out, it is believed that what is called "The Temple Mount" is Mount Moriah where Abraham went to sacrifice his son, Isaac. It is part of the land given by God to Abraham, and it was given later by God to Moses and Joshua and the people who came up from captivity in Egypt by conquest around 1400 B.C.

As recorded in Genesis 15, God granted all the land between the River of Egypt (The *Wadi El Arish* near Gaza) north to the Euphrates (which flows through Syria) to the children of Israel. And we know that this grant was not only by divine mandate, but it was also by military conquest, and the Bible tells us that 400 years elapsed from the promise of Abraham until the people returned to the land because what was termed "the iniquity of the Amorites" was not yet complete.

We know, further, that when the northern kingdom of Israel was conquered by the Assyrians in 722 B.C., thousands of Jews were massacred by the invading armies of King Sargon II and as many as 30,000 were carried off into captivity.

In the midst of the slaughter, many of the people of Israel fled north and east and west and eventually covered the earth. Those people, who are known romantically as the "ten lost tribes of Israel," found homes in many nations and have seemingly vanished from history.

THE REMNANT OF JUDAH

Those who remained in the southern kingdom were the tribes of Benjamin and Judah. It was from Judah that the modern word, Jew, is taken. It was these people who preserved the Israelite traditions and culture through the dark years between the Assyrian invasion and the next great tragedy in 586 B.C. when they were conquered, carried off, and enslaved to Nebuchadnezzar, King of Babylon, in the region we now know as Iraq.

In those turbulent years between 734 and 580 B.C., there were six separate depredations against the Israelites, and each attack scattered the people and drove them out of the land. Only a small band escaped the Babylonian invasion and remained in Palestine until the captives returned from Babylon, about 70 years later.

But, the people of Judah, the Jews, occupied Jerusalem under foreign rule through the time of Christ, and they remained there until the Romans finally burned and flattened the city in 70 A.D., "leaving not one stone on top of another."

Rome's final desecration of Jerusalem came in 135 A.D. On the pretext of quashing the civil war between the Greeks and the Jews, the Romans attacked the Jewish Zealots in the hills around Jerusalem, and then Hadrian's legions sacked and destroyed all that remained of that once-great capital, thereby ending the Jewish presence in Israel for the next 1,800 years.

REBUILDING A NATION

By the nature of history and the nature of war, it is humanly impossible that the Jews could ever have returned to Israel after 1,800 years to build a nation. While a small number of Jews managed to remain in the land through each of the successive devastations, the surrounding nations moved in quickly and populated the camps and villages, took over the fields and vineyards, and claimed the land.

Every other people on earth lose their national identity after years of living in another country. Only the Jews refused to assimilate, to give up their separate identity, their faith in God, and their hope of returning to their own land. At the annual Passover they would say, "Next year in Jerusalem."

Only God could have worked such an incredible miracle. He had told the Jews that they were His chosen people. They were to keep alive the true faith in the true God. Despite thousands who fell away, the Jewish remnant kept the faith.

The story is told of a conversation between the mighty monarch,

Queen Victoria of England, and her Prime Minister, Benjamin Disraeli. "Mr. Prime Minister," she asked, "what is the greatest evidence of God's existence?" After brief reflection, Disraeli replied, "The Jew, your majesty."

By the late 1880s, Jews started buying land in Israel, particularly in the Galilee and the valleys north of Jerusalem, with a new dream and vision of Zion. Encouraged by zealous young leaders from the wealthy Jewish families of Germany, Poland, France, and Great Britain, they began reclaiming arid, empty land and swamps, wherever they could get a foothold.

In some of those settlements they bought swampy, mosquito-ridden, malaria-infested lands which had to be reclaimed from the sea. They went out into the marshes and planted eucalyptus trees to soak up the water so they could use the land.

The inhabitants of the land prior to the coming of the Jewish settlers were nomadic, by and large. There were few cities of note. Tel Aviv was a relatively small town. The old city of Jerusalem was still small. There were other isolated Arab villages and settlements in some parts of Palestine, but there was not a lot of activity among either Arabs or Jews in those days.

RECLAIMING THE PROMISE

The movement to reclaim Palestine as a Jewish homeland grew into a major diplomatic issue during the first two decades of this century. By the early 1920s, both sides, Arabs and Jews, were participating in skirmishes and terrorist activities to try and swing the tide of world opinion in their own favor.

It was soon to be a turbulent period of struggle and bloodshed. Men like Chaim Weizmann, a highly educated German Jew with capitalist perspectives, and David Ben-Gurion, who came to Israel in the early 1920s from Poland with strong socialist sympathies, rose as leaders of the Zionists.

Ironically, it was Winston Churchill who, as Colonial Secretary of the British government in March of 1921, took it upon himself to settle the situation by giving a territory called Transjordan to Abdullah, the son of the Sharif of Mecca in Saudi Arabia.

Churchill never quite sorted out his feelings about Palestine, the third territory under his authority, but he acknowledged the Jewish right of return and seemed to believe that Arabs and Jews would somehow co-exist there quite peaceably.

Nevertheless, from the end of World War I until the end of World War II, the land of Palestine remained in nearly constant turmoil. Even though Jews all over the world claimed the dream of Zion, it wasn't until the Holocaust and the slaughter of more than six million European Jews that the immigrations to Palestine became a reality.

Suddenly Jews who a decade earlier had thought of Germany or France or Poland as their native home were forced to face the fact that there could only be one home for the Jews.

In 1917 Lord Balfour wrote a letter to Lord Rothschild—who was the most distinguished Jewish financier, philanthropist, and statesman in the world at that time. Balfour declared his support for the establishment of a "Jewish homeland." The Balfour Declaration didn't make the Jewish state a reality, but it gave focus to the hopes of young men like Weizmann and Ben-Gurion.

It was not until after World War II, in 1948, that the United Nations (at the insistence of Harry Truman and the American people) acknowledged the national statehood of Israel. By a vote of 33 in favor, 13 against, and 10 abstentions, the UN gave the Jews a narrow strip of land which included the area around Tel Aviv and north into the Galilee area, but excluding what is now the West Bank. East Jerusalem and the West Bank were then still a part of Transjordan. The Gaza Strip belonged to Egypt.

But Churchill's surmise had been wrong. There could be no peace. Arabs in Palestine and throughout the Middle East were incensed that this essentially Western, European-style, and seemingly democratic nation was being inserted, like a virus, into their midst.

Suddenly the land of Palestine had become inhospitable to the Arabs living there and many fled to Transjordan, Lebanon, Iraq, Syria, Egypt, Gaza and the West Bank. Altogether, more than 600,000 Arabs took refuge outside Palestine.

PROVOCATIONS TO HOSTILITY

But these refugees were also ready warriors, and bolstered by the promise of support by their Arab brothers, the Palestinians declared war on the new State of Israel with the aim of driving the Jews into the sea.

At the same time, a wave of repression of Jews in the Arab countries—from Morocco in the West to Syria in the East—brought more than a half million Jews into Israel at a time when the Israelis were marshaling their own forces. By late 1948, the Israelis had put together an army of 100,000 men with weapons they had purchased from Czechoslovakia, or which had been provided by supporters of Zion in America and other places.

The difference in the re-settlement practices of the Jews with their refugees versus the refusal of the Arab nations to provide a long term solution for their refugees was to become a major factor in the ongoing struggle.

When the Jews arrived from the Arab countries, or from Europe, North Africa, Scandinavia, or any of the other places they had lived, they were immediately given land and shelter in Israel and made citizens of the nation.

The Arabs, on the other hand, were put into temporary dwellings, tents, and refugee camps. They were not settled permanently since they believed it was only a matter of time until the Jews would be evicted and Arabs would regain their homes in Palestine.

The Arabs were confident they would come back victorious and resume their lives. But the Israelis won that war, as they have won every war since that time, and the territories which had been held by the Arabs in 1947 were now possessed by the Jews.

A sort of troubled peace existed in the region for the next 20 years. While there were clashes and skirmishes between Jewish settlers and the half million Arabs who remained in Palestine throughout those years, the first full-scale war came in 1967 when Gamal Abdel Nasser of Egypt provoked what is now known as the "Six Day War." The *causus belli* was the closing of the Gulf of Aqaba to Israeli shipping, which was interpreted by the Jews, understandably, as an act of war.

Israel responded to the provocation with a lightning strike into the Sinai region, and in six days, with the might of the tank battalions commanded by Moshe Dayan, defeated the forces of Egypt, while another Israeli force captured the West Bank, including East Jerusalem, from Jordan.

For the first time in about 2,500 years, the Jews occupied the eastern sector of Jerusalem, including the Temple Mount and the Wailing Wall. They made Jerusalem the capital of Israel, and within weeks they began settling the captured regions of what they began to call, by their biblical names, Judea and Samaria.

After a restive peace, the Egyptians along with the Syrians struck again in 1973 and launched what is now known as the "Yom Kippur War," on Israel's most holy day. Again they were roundly defeated. Israel had trapped a major Egyptian army corps and could have marched on Cairo but was held back by the United States for the sake of world opinion.

At that time they took back from Syria, and later annexed, the high plateau north of the Sea of Galilee up to the Syrian border called the Golan Heights. For years Syrian gunners had used these heights to rain down mortar and artillery fire on the hapless Jewish settlers in the Galilee valley. The battle for the Golan filled the headlines at that time, and television news reports showing the fire power and the devastation in that area were terrifying.

Christians around the world wondered if this wasn't the start of Armageddon—after all, the plain of Megiddo was barely ten miles to the south. As it became clear that the Israelis had won the battle for the Golan, tensions subsided somewhat. The battle goes down as one of the biggest tank battles in the history of warfare. As many tanks massed in that one small area as had ever been marshaled in any battle in history, giving Israel an enormous victory.

THE DISPOSSESSED

The amazing thing about the Palestinians' apparent loss of their land is the reluctance of other Arab nations to take the Palestinians into their midst. The Palestinians are the most highly educated people in the entire region. They are highly skilled artisans, craftsmen, and engineers. They have a tradition of learning that goes back thousands of years, to the first universities and libraries in the world.

But the Arab emirates and surrounding nations were almost afraid of them—apparently afraid their learning and skill might allow them to become the dominant nationality in the lands where they were working.

Consequently, while the Arab nations have allowed the Palestinians to remain as workers, executives, and administrators, they have not really taken them in. With the single exception of King Hussein, who formerly exercised civil government over Jordanian Palestinians on the West Bank, no Arab nation has tried seriously to re-settle them.

Gaza could have been re-settled at any time, yet it has been kept as a United Nations refugee camp for nearly 25 years, which is virtually unheard of. Today the Gaza Strip is the most densely populated area on earth, with more than 3,800 persons per square mile.

When you think that the average population density of the United States is about 66 persons per square mile and England, which has always been considered one of the most congested nations on earth, is only about 600 per square mile, you realize just what a pressure cooker that area has become.

But one wonders if one reason for the continued homelessness of the Palestinians isn't because their leaders—along with their advisers and friends from Syria, Iraq, and the other Arab nations—believe that it will be of greater political advantage to keep them homeless, congested, and belligerent so they can be used as political pawns in the struggle against Israel.

A MANDATE FOR PEACE

Out of that background came the Camp David Accords in September 1978, at the behest of President Jimmy Carter who paid for, and reportedly stage-managed, the event. I am convinced that all the parties to those accords were sincere and believed they had a mandate for peace.

Representing the Arab interests was Anwar Sadat of Egypt, who was a highly religious man. He felt he had a mission from God and was willing to take the risks. On the other side was Menachem Begin, a long-time activist and militant, a warrior, a leader and twice prime minister, and the son of a distinguished rabbi.

Begin agreed at Camp David to surrender the Sinai to the Arabs—along with its oil fields, settlements, and military installations—in order to gain peace. Not since the administration of

Ben-Gurion had an Israeli leader been willing to make such a bold compromise.

That compromise was costly to Begin at home and he lost the friendship of many long-time political confidants. The greater cost, though, fell upon Sadat.

For a while after Camp David, it began to look as if peace was, in fact, a possibility. Cabinet meetings were being held and negotiations were going on around the clock, seemingly with great success. But within a matter of weeks it was clear that the Egyptians were being excluded from the councils of the Arab leaders, even though Egypt had always been at the center of Islamic culture and theology, and was the biggest of the Arab nations.

Sadat's sincere effort to find a reconciliation with Israel had made Egypt a pariah in the Arab world. The old animosity between the Arabs and the Jews was just too deep, the tragic evidence of that fact being the bloody assassination of Sadat by Muslim fundamentalists at a parade ceremony in 1981.

Many of the West Bank Arabs work in Israel. They go into Jewish areas to work. The bridge over the Jordan is open for the transport of Palestinian citrus and other produce. They go across Jordan to Iraq, Kuwait, or down to Saudi Arabia and the Gulf. There has been very active trade. Without question, the status of Palestinian Arabs improved under Israeli occupation.

A CLOSER LOOK

During my visits to Israel in the late 1970s, there seemed to be a genuine movement toward peace and reconciliation in the area. The leader of the Labour Party, Shimon Peres, told me he wanted to establish a confederation where Israel could have secure borders around the whole territory. He hoped for an agreement in which the Palestinians could have self-government and autonomy within the boundaries of greater Israel.

The West Bank Arabs could form a state within a state. He thought that for its own security Israel would have to maintain a defense perimeter around the area. After all, the neck of land between Tel Aviv and the West Bank is no more than nine miles at its widest, so it would be virtually defenseless in the event of a military strike. Peres has been willing all along to make concessions at that point.

However, Menachem Begin and his successor, Yitzhak Shamir, feel that Judea and Samaria are not Arab lands at all, and that in fact they are an integral and vital part of Israel's historic patrimony. To them trading the heartland of Israel for peace will never work and will only serve to weaken the nation by establishing a militantly hostile entity within Israel's natural defenses—which would be like a dagger aimed at their heart.

There were many who felt Israel should have annexed the West Bank territories after the Six Day War. They annexed the Golan Heights after 1973 with virtually no complaint. Golan is now part of Israel and that's the end of it. But the West Bank was allowed to become a seething cauldron, and the repercussions of that fact are not likely to be settled in the foreseeable future.

IRRECONCILABLE DIFFERENCES

The Palestinians have in their leadership some moderates with a desire to make some kind of accommodation with the Jews in Israel and to live at peace with them. People like Elias Freij, the Mayor of Bethlehem, and leaders of village councils, were beginning to take steps toward reconciliation. The process continued in that direction until more and more hard-liners in both camps began to emerge in the late 1980s.

The conservative wing of the Israeli parliament, the Likud, has become very unyielding in its attitude. Since 1987 the pace of building Israeli high rise towers and pre-fab towns called "settlements" has escalated in the West Bank.

One of the extreme groups made headlines in early 1990 by taking over an apartment building in Arab East Jerusalem, owned by the Greek Orthodox Church. They chose Holy Week to do it. These orthodox Jews declared their right to settle anywhere they pleased. The chosen people of Israel, they refused to concern themselves with Arab rights. And so they achieved worldwide press because of their timing, their militancy, and their seeming insensitivity to the rights of others.

While this is going on, the Arab world recognizes the Palestinian Liberation Organization, the PLO, as the natural representative of the Palestinian people. Tawfik Abu Ghazala, a lawyer and counselor at the Gaza Center for Rights and Law, said, "The Palestinian people are the leaders, and Yasser Arafat is their representative." Before the beginning of the Intifada, such an observation might have seemed like just so much rhetoric, but now we see the truth of that comment.

The Intifada has inflamed to white hot intensity the passions of Palestinians in Gaza, the West Bank, and Jordan. Unfortunately, the PLO has in its midst some very radical people. Men like George Habash continue to prey on innocent victims. Whether or not he is still a member of the PLO, Habash is a Marxist and an extremely violent man.

Extremist Mohammed Abbas led the attempted invasion of Tel Aviv from the sea in May 1990. He is not only a cohort of terrorist Abu Nidal and head of the extremely dangerous Al Fatah phalange group—formerly a wing of the PLO—but he is also a member of the PLO executive committee.

Arafat, himself, is also a dangerous man. Though he wants to be perceived as a peacemaker, he has repeatedly advocated terrorism and violence to achieve the goals of the Palestinians. Is it any wonder the world is leery of his overtures?

Others outside the Palestinian camp also counsel violence against Israel and participate in overt terrorism. Their targets are not only Jews, but the United States and other nations who actively support Israel. Western interests in the Middle East are constantly in jeopardy of terrorism because of our support for the Jews.

FIGURES OF SPEECH

Whether or not our perception of Yasser Arafat is correct, he has been the leader of the PLO since its inception, and he has repeatedly stated his conviction that Israel must not exist as a state.

He has made public declaration that his aim and goal is to drive this foreign influence out of the Middle East. He has said he does not want Israel as a sovereign nation within recognized and defensible borders; he wants Israel eliminated, out of the Middle East, and he has said so repeatedly.

In early 1990 Arafat was pressured by the United States State Department to read a line or two in Geneva which indicated that he has renounced those goals, but that isn't what he says in private, from what we can gather.

One gets the impression that Arafat's meetings with Jimmy Carter and the Pope have been staged for political advantage and do not truly reflect any change in his political stance.

To gain attention for their cause, the Palestinian people started a resistance movement inside Israel, Gaza, and the West Bank, called the uprising, or the "Intifada." While it has disrupted the normal pace of the economy, making day-to-day life harder on Jews and Arabs alike, it has really been a highly successful media campaign to gain sympathy for the Arab cause.

Three years ago I was told that on a slow day the Western media could call up and ask for a demonstration before noon and still have time to get something on the evening news in New York. If a demonstration is already planned for noon, the cameras will be in place at 11:45 to film it.

But the uprising has been very successful. The Israelis presumed that the Intifada would go away, but it hasn't gone away; it has only grown more and more determined, and in the process Israeli troops have grown more and more battle weary. In many instances, the soldiers have resorted to tactics that are nothing short of brutal.

OBJECTIONABLE FORCE

In its efforts to silence the disruptive Palestinians, the Israeli military has not used restraint as it should have. They have repeatedly used excessive force which has gone far beyond any recognized or acceptable norms of crowd control.

There are many cases of the deliberate breaking of bones. People's arms and legs have been stomped or twisted with truncheons so they will break. Soldiers have beaten civilians with gun butts, and many shoot to kill. Even rubber bullets, which are actually heavy metal balls covered with a thin rubber hide, are deadly at moderate range.

I have seen the medical reports analyzing the types of injuries found on demonstrators and detainees. These reports show that they are not accidental, but are deliberate attempts to maim and to punish the Palestinians in the most painful way. The violence has been indiscriminate: women and children have been brutalized as well as boys and men.

However you look at it, this kind of behavior shows a serious breakdown of discipline among the Jewish forces. There are similarities to what happened at the 1968 Democratic National Convention in Chicago when hippies went wild and the police, who couldn't take the abuse any more, began using brutality far beyond anything that could be considered acceptable in civilian restraint or crowd control.

We are seeing the same things being done to pro-life protesters all over America today. Under the pretext of enforcing an unjust law, police are viciously brutalizing decent, God-fearing people who simply want to point out the injustices of the system that permits, and encourages, the murder of the unborn.

SERIOUS CHARGES

The violence which erupted in Israel, in Jordan, and in Egypt in the spring of 1990 after a deranged soldier murdered a half dozen Palestinians and wounded scores more, caused a dreadful blood bath. The event spawned military reprisals with death and injuries to another hundred people. As long as that kind of mayhem continues, there can be no peace.

Among the factors that continue to bring censure upon Israel from the United Nations and other world peace organizations is the seeming contempt of the Jewish bureaucratic system for the Palestinian Arabs. It shows up in many forms, from foot-dragging in judicial and administrative matters to the overt destruction of Arab property.

The Israeli Foreign Ministry labels these the Three-Ds: demolition, detention, and deportation. The fact that some 400 Arab villages inside Israel have been demolished since 1948 has been a historic source of antagonism, but sometimes the covert antagonism and reprisals are an even greater irritation.

Arab homes are routinely bull-dozed for undisclosed reasons, and permits to rebuild are either denied or delayed for years. Palestinians can be held in "administrative detention" for undisclosed reasons and imprisoned for up to a year in virtual concentration camps in the Negev Desert. No charges need be brought; and if a detainee can afford an attorney, neither the prisoner nor his attorney may have access to the actual charges. Arabs can be held on the grounds of "secret evidence."

Arabs may be deported from Israel at the discretion of the government or, as has happened with many Palestinians studying abroad, their passport and right of return can be canceled while they are out of the country, leaving them stranded and effectively deported.

Automobiles and trucks belonging to most West Bank citizens must display blue license plates to distinguish them from people living in the Jewish areas, who use yellow plates. Vehicles with blue tags are routinely stopped, searched, and the drivers are physically and emotionally harassed. This is degrading, but worse in the long run, these kinds of harassment incite the Palestinians to seek revenge. Unfortunately, they already have enough reasons.

Statistics compiled by the United Nations Works and Relief Agency and other sources are equally distressing. They show that more than 75,000 Palestinians have suffered serious injuries in Gaza, the West Bank, and Eretz Israel since the beginning of the Intifada in December 1987.

Reports of the Israeli Information Center for Human Rights in the Occupied Territories, a Jewish organization, show that 637 Palestinians have been killed by Israeli military actions, 604 by shooting (including rubber bullets), and 33 by beatings, burns, and other causes. Of those, 41 were children under age 12; 101 were youths 13 to 16.

Tear gas exposure killed another 77, of whom 30 were infants. The figures also report 29 Palestinians killed by Jewish civilians and 5 apparently killed by Arab collaborators.

According to United Nations figures, there have been 8,000 cases of broken bones since the Intifada began, and more than 60,000 Palestinians have been held in administrative detention.

But lest we think the pressure is all one-sided, during the same period, 10 Israeli soldiers and 9 Jewish civilians were reported as killed by Palestinians, and 46 Israeli soldiers have committed suicide. Clearly there is a level of hostility and violence here that is intolerable to the human spirit.

Eventually, it all comes back to the ancient and bitter strife between these two peoples and the reluctance of either side to accept a peace which does not give them final control. It is hard for us in the West to understand the emotions at work here. In America and Europe we are negotiators and compromisers by nature. The idea of each side giving up some of its rights in order to settle a dispute is an old and trusted concept with us. Not so in the Middle East; not so to the Arabs and the Jews.

ASSESSING ALTERNATIVES

So what are the alternatives? Bible scholars feel that the West Bank belongs to Israel. Certainly the City of Jerusalem is—must be—a Jewish city.

Jesus predicted that Jerusalem would be trodden under foot until the time of the Gentiles was fulfilled. Bible scholars decided that when the Israelis took possession of Jerusalem in 1967, this was the completion of a prophecy that had waited some 2,500 years for fulfillment.

Many felt the return of the Jews to Jerusalem was very possibly the most important event of biblical history to take place in our lifetime. Jerusalem was once again in Jewish hands, for the first time since the Babylonian captivity.

Evangelicals do not want the Jews to lose control of that city any more, and the Jews have sworn to maintain possession with their lives. In 66 to 73 A.D., during the terrible revolt of the Jews against Rome, a small band of survivors gathered at a mountain fortress called Masada in the Judean desert near the Dead Sea. There they fought and died, to the last man. The name of Masada has become a symbol of the will of modern Israel to fight to the last man, woman, or child rather than accept slavery again.

A highly respected Defense Department analyst in Washington, D.C. told me that before they will surrender the Old City of Jerusalem and divide Jerusalem into two cities again, the Jews will use any weapon in their arsenal, including atomic weapons if they have to.

If any nation were to attempt to divide Jerusalem, that nation would run the risk of plunging the world into nuclear holocaust. The issue of East and West Jerusalem under Jewish control is the central issue, and it will not go away because of official pronouncements or press releases from Washington, D.C.

The Palestinians talk about Jerusalem being the capital of their state. But, given the realities of this world, it is not practical to have a landlocked state within a state, or for any other nation to accept in its midst a hostile, independent nation.

An autonomous division within military borders would be one thing, but an autonomous state using Jerusalem as its capital just isn't going to happen, so that is an unrealistic expectation for the Palestinians.

If their leaders continue to hold to that goal, the only possible result will be a devastating war. And however large the numbers weighed against Israel in this particular event, Israel will be prepared to fight. They will fight the Russians, the Western Europeans, or the United States if they have to. And they would be willing to fight to the last man, as their forefathers did at Masada.

The conflict in Israel today has the potential of being a tinderbox for the whole world. If somehow the Arab nations push for control of Jerusalem; if Saddam Hussein pursues his threat to use poisonous gas; or if he were to form some league with the Libyan madman, Mohamar Qadaffi, or the Syrians, I believe we would see a cataclysmic war in the Middle East.

The long range goal of the surrounding Arab nations is to eradicate Israel, not just accommodate her. The Israelis know this, and they know they will be fighting for their very lives. Given that provocation, it is not inconceivable that they could be tempted to launch a pre-emptive strike if they ever felt unduly threatened.

If all attempts at peace fail, and if pushed into a corner beyond which they cannot concede any more, the Jews might just say, what else do we have to lose? Let's use the armed might we have at our disposal to eliminate our enemies before they eliminate us. Not a desirable option for anyone, but still conceivable.

MOUNTING PRESSURES FROM ABROAD

Such an event could then be the flashpoint for a much greater war. I don't really foresee a World War III developing between the superpowers or between any of the European forces, but I could see a collection of nations—yes, including the United States—coming against Israel.

The rising tide of anti-Semitism in the Soviet Union and the East Bloc nations may also have far-reaching biblical significance.

No one could have dreamed that the horrors of the holocaust would not have buried the European hatred of Jews forever. Outside the Soviet Union, Jews do not form significant populations in Eastern Europe. There are now estimated to be only 4,000 Jews in Poland, 8,000 in Czechoslovakia, 500 in East Germany, and 60,000 in Hungary. The largest population of Jews in Europe lives in the Soviet Union. Population estimates vary between 1.5 and 2.5 million Soviet Jews, but these figures represent only a meager 1 percent or less of the Soviet population.

Yet my sources tell me that in the Soviet Union a fanatical anti-Jewish group, called Pamyat, is actually searching 400 years back in Russian genealogical tables in an attempt to harass anyone with Jewish blood.

On my recent visit to Eastern Europe I was astounded to encounter virulent anti-Semitic sentiment in Romania, where there are only 22,000 Jews, but where the current Prime Minister, Petre Roman, is of Jewish descent.

Regrettably, after World War II, some Jews, grateful to be liberated from Adolf Hitler, allied themselves with Stalin and were reported to be members of the KGB and some communist politburos which suppressed the captive peoples of Eastern Europe. However, the actions of a few can hardly be used to justify making scapegoats of an entire race.

In Nazi Germany it was easy for an eloquent demagogue such as Adolf Hitler to blame the economic collapse of post-World War I Germany on a conspiracy led by "International Zionist Bankers." This was a lie, but desperate people need someone to blame for their problems. They willingly believe lies, especially when those lies originate from the government leaders they are expected to trust.

Now in the Soviet Union and the East Bloc nations a new lie is emerging, that communism and the collapse of communism was engineered by a "Zionist conspiracy."

At present the anti-Semitism in the Soviet Union and Eastern Europe has no government sanction. But a highly placed source within the Jewish community tells me that Soviet Jews are terrified that the wave of hatred there could at any time result in a full scale pogrom.

Up to 280,000 Soviet Jews are seeking to emigrate to Israel this year. This is a flood compared to 8,000, 12,000, and 28,000 in previous years. The government of Israel is estimating 4 billion dollars in resettlement costs. Jews in America have an emergency "Operation Exodus" fund-raising effort under way and are seeking 600 million dollars in supplemental aid from the United States government.

In recent months the United States Government has become more and more demanding in its pressure on Israel to reach an accord with the Palestinians. Clearly the Israelis are nervous about that, since the deeper implication is that the United States could withdraw both its financial and diplomatic support. There is also a fear that the bond between America and Israel may be weakening.

Articles have recently appeared in a number of magazines and journals asking if America has deserted Israel. Someone even raised the question on public radio a few months ago, what would George Bush say if you woke him at 3:00 A.M. and whispered the word, "Israel"? Would he respond "friend" or "foe"?

I don't know the answer to that, but I do know this. So long as this nation has any concern for God's favor, we cannot turn our backs on Israel. Throughout Scripture, the prophets warned that God will judge the nations that stand against Israel.

Intolerance in any quarter is wrong, but inasmuch as we are able, we must ensure that the trend throughout the 1990s remains in favor of a Jewish homeland in Israel and not for the elimination of the Jews.

THE FUTURE OF THE JEWS

Some sources have estimated that the total number of Jews coming to Israel from Russia could be well over a million people. If that is in fact the case, the burden on social and medical programs, not to mention the resettlement costs, are going to be enormous for the Israelis, as much as 16 to 25 billion dollars.

A massive influx of Jews will also exacerbate the tensions between the Jews and the Arabs because the Palestinians see the arrival of more and more Jews as a threat to their livelihood, to their national welfare, and to their prospects for an independent homeland of their own.

Population is key to the success of Israel, yet the demographics are clearly working against the Israelis, who have adopted the European and American custom of limited or childless marriages. The Arabs in Israel on the other hand have been exploding in population. The birthrate among Arabs is Israel is 31 per 1,000, the Israeli birthrate is 13 per 1,000.

According to the London *Economist* there are 3.5 million Jews in Israel and 822,000 Arabs. Palestinians living in the West Bank and Gaza number 1.7 million. At present birthrates, and with no major immigration, there will be 4.2 million Jews and 3.1 million Arabs in the area under Jewish control by the year 2000.

By the year 2020, at present birthrates, Arabs will be in the majority in the entire country.

It is obvious that the Israelis face a major problem. If they accept Palestinians as citizens of Israel, in a short while they will be a minority race in an Arab country. If they establish an Arab state of Palestine, they may be inviting a threat to their future security.

If they deport all the Palestinians, they will take the place of South Africa as the pariah nation of the earth. What they have now is a type of Apartheid, and it is only a question of time before the nations of "the new world order" begin to force Israel to abandon her settlements and give up the West Bank. When the demand by force extends to East Jerusalem there will be a nuclear war.

Perhaps the clearest answer to the Israeli problem, and one that would at least temporarily relieve world pressure, would be the arrival of one million or more Jews from the Soviet Union, despite the enormous costs involved.

Shimon Peres once told me a story about former Israeli Prime Minister David Ben-Gurion and the former President of France, Charles DeGaulle, walking along together, talking confidentially about the problems of Israel.

DeGaulle said, "Mr. Prime Minister, tell me frankly. What do you want? Do you want a larger army? Do you want more territory? Do you want a harbor? What do you want?" Ben-Gurion just looked at him and said, "I want more Jews!"

DeGaulle couldn't believe his ears, but Ben-Gurion realized that the success of Israel was going to depend not on military or technical achievements but on a vibrant population, and despite the potential cost of settlement, he wanted more Jews.

POPULATING ZION

Even though he died in 1973, Ben-Gurion is getting his wish. New settlers are coming in huge numbers. If the numbers they are projecting actually come, this will be the largest migration of Jews into Israel since the holocaust. They are mainly coming from Russia, from Eastern and Western Europe, and also from parts of Asia, though in much smaller numbers.

The greatest concentration of Jews in the world is still in the United States. It is not likely that many of America's Jewish families will volunteer to give up their secure lives here in order to go into that hotbed of racial tension and unrest, but I suppose it could happen.

I have been told that over the last 25 years more than 400,000 American Jews who immigrated to Israel have returned home. The problems there were just too great for them. In my estimation, nothing short of a holocaust or a global conflict will ever bring about a mass exodus of American Jews to Israel.

Jews have come to Israel from Iran, Iraq, and the rest of the Middle East; they have come out of North Africa, Europe, and to a lesser degree, South America, even though there never was a large Jewish population there.

Because of America's long-term commitment to and support of Israel, and because of our allegiance to the six million Jews in this country, the United States will in all likelihood continue to be Israel's strongest ally. That will likely keep America in the position of being the prime defender of Jewish interests in the Middle East.

Even though it seems inconceivable that anything will happen in the United States to cause an out-migration of the Jewish population here, it would be foolish to assume such a thing could not or will never happen. We trust it will not; but if it ever does, we will certainly know that the last days are upon us.

The fact that there are only two major populations of Jews in the world today is extraordinarily significant. In Isaiah 43, the Bible says, "I will bring your children from the east and gather you from the west. I will say to the north, 'Give them up!' and to the south, 'Do not hold them back.' Bring my sons from afar and my daughters from the ends of the earth." That seems to be what's happening now. This is a strong prophetic word which, in my view, is already being fulfilled.

Given the rise of anti-Semitism in the East bloc and the Soviet Union, and the pre-existence of strong anti-Semitic feelings in Western Europe (the bitterness in Germany has not gone away), there is a very real possibility that the United Nations may turn against Israel. The Arab-African non-aligned bloc has been anti-Israeli all along. The only defender of Israel besides the United States has been South Africa, and they have been made a pariah nation by these same people.

THE CHRISTIAN ALLIANCE

Even with some six million American-born Jews living in this country, we should not think that it is only the Jews in America who have supported Israel. Since the Reformation, Western Christians of all races and denominations have accepted the biblical teaching concerning the Jews as the "chosen people."

Yes, Christians believe that the Jews rejected their own Messiah, just as the Jewish prophets foretold they would. That rejection then brought about a **New Covenant** with God—succeeding the **Old Covenant** which God had given to Abraham—by which both Jews and Gentiles who renounced their sin and accepted Christ as the Messiah could inherit the promise of Salvation.

The obstinate denial of the Messiah by the vast majority of Jews has always concerned Christians. To anyone whose eyes are not closed, it seems so obvious that Christ fulfilled every single prophecy of the Scriptures! But the frustration and sorrow for these Jews does not, in any way, mean that Christians do not recognize the Jews as chosen of God and a special people. By and large Protestants and Catholics alike have upheld the Jewish nation throughout history.

A sad irony of the last 40 years, though, is the fact that the liberal Jewish population in America has been intent on diminishing Christian influence in the public life of America. They believe that Christianity is a threat to Judaism, and many recite the terrors of the Holocaust as evidence of the Christian "blood libel" against the Jews.

The crimes perpetrated against the Jews by the Nazis are an unspeakable horror. Christians are not guilty of that charge. The Nazis were guilty. Some of them may have claimed to be Christians, but everything in the New Testament condemns hatred, murder and revenge, especially against Jews. Anyone who believes Christianity is against Jews does not know the Bible.

Bible history tells us that because of their hardness of heart, God scattered the Jews time and time again. The Egyptians and the Babylonians and the Assyrians were allowed to make slaves of them. However, God eventually brought down His wrath upon those nations and eradicated their empires.

THE IMAGINARY ADVERSARY

Regrettably, the efforts of liberal Jews to destroy the Christian position in the world has, in fact, weakened the moral consensus that has supported Israel from the start.

About 30 years ago, futurist Herman Kahn, of the Hudson Institute in New York, warned Jewish leaders that Christians in America would not stand for the loss of their traditions. In forestalling the desires of certain Jewish leaders to denigrate and vilify Christian expressions and symbolism, Kahn said such behavior would bring inevitable reprisals against Jews.

Kahn was a brilliant man. His book, *Thinking the Unthinkable,* forced a generation to take a realistic look at some very serious issues concerning nuclear war and the welfare of the global community. Thinking people listened to him. But he is gone now. Those who advise restraint seem to be gone, and the assault against Christianity is on, and it is very strong.

Since the Christian Broadcasting Network and all our affiliates here and around the world are vitally concerned with issues concerning Christianity and the gospel of Jesus Christ, we get a lot of attention, not only from other Christians but from those who want to destroy our heritage and take away our freedom.

In recent months we have been involved in disputes with Hollywood executives over the defamatory film, *The Last Temptation of Christ,* with the anti-religious People for the American Way headed by Norman Lear, and with the agenda of the National Endowment for the Arts which has used taxpayers' money to support pornography, sacrilege, and blatant homosexuality. More and more we are in debates with writers and journalists who seem to be activists in the destruction of Christianity.

It has become perfectly clear over the past 20 years that any type of discrimination on the basis of race or gender or sexual preference will be condemned in this country. Blacks, Asians, Hispanics, and all other minorities are guaranteed equal rights under the law. Women are guaranteed rights in the workplace. Even homosexuals and Satanists are guaranteed certain rights.

But Christians are becoming fair game for the media, for authors and columnists, for filmmakers, for artists, for strident feminists, for abortionists, for drug pushers and their fellow travelers, for Marxists, for pornographers, for liberal politicians, for atheists, and even some who call themselves Christians.

A CONFLICT OF IDEOLOGY

The American Jewish community is not monolithic. Some are most sympathetic to the social concerns of Evangelical Christians. Some are indifferent. But the Liberal Jews have actually forsaken Biblical faith in God, and made a religion of political liberalism.

For example, they think government welfare somehow is Judaism. They think a pro-abortion stand and the absence of religious activity in the schools are Judaism.

If someone attacks abortion-on-demand or asks for prayer in the schools, the liberal Jewish community reacts as if this stand were somehow anti-Semitic. They have anti-Christian liberalism intermingled with Judaism to such a degree they can't distinguish anymore.

Liberal Jews are passionately in favor of the pro-choice, pro-abortion position—which doesn't make any sense, since the abortion position uses the same language and techniques that the Nazis used in exterminating Jews. Of all people, the Jews, who toast *LeChaim* ("to life") should be for life not death. They are dead set against prayer in the schools and public expressions of religion. Yet, anyone who has ever been to Israel knows that prayer is open and public in that nation. And why shouldn't it be?

The Jews in Israel are trying to build and populate a nation! There is no debate over prayer in the schools. People pray in the schools and read the Bible; so if anybody wants to pray in the schools, the Israelis don't care. They welcome religious expression.

So many of the political issues that the conservative evangelicals embrace in the United States are not even a debate in Israel—in fact they are very much in keeping with the feelings and beliefs of the Israelis.

The sabras—that is, those who were born and raised in Israel—don't have the same suspicions and animosities of their fathers and grandfathers. They were born free, born in their own nation, and they never knew the discrimination and the persecution of places like Germany.

So many of the Israelis I have met have been quite willing to talk about Jesus, to listen to the gospel, and to receive Christ as Messiah. I have talked to people in the army, I have been to meetings, I've met with people at all levels of society, and in every instance I have found a great openness and cordiality.

It is distressing that the situation is so different in the United States. While there is a great sense of unity between conservative Jews and the evangelical political position, liberal Jews feel threatened by Christians.

CRITICAL CONCERNS

Absolute liberty and unrestrained license have always been the slogans of the liberal; but even if that stance may work for the cosmopolitan, liberal, secular Jews, it does not work so well for the religious Jews. Religious Jews have always believed in ethical responsibility and moral restraint.

Perhaps the greatest irony of the liberal position is their split personality. They are outraged by anyone who would try to limit their own freedom of speech; but, on the other, they are absolutely insensitive to the rights of those they oppose.

Norman Lear wants unrestricted freedom for smut and pornography and the murder of the unborn, but anyone who speaks against kiddie porn or vulgarity on television is branded a reactionary and silenced without a hearing.

The part that Jewish intellectuals and media activists have played in the assault on Christianity may very possibly prove to be a grave mistake. It is beginning to appear that support for Israel in

America may already have been weakened in the political arena, and soon the Christians may be in no condition to help.

For centuries, Christians have supported the dream of Zion, and they have supported Jews in their dream of a national homeland. But American Jews invested great energy in attacking these very allies. That investment may pay a terrible dividend. If a shift should come in America's public opinion toward Israel, the Christians who have stood for them throughout the ages may not be able to reverse the trend.

This situation can also have dire consequences for our nation. Based on my understanding of the Scriptures, it is my conviction that if our nation turns against Israel, it will incur the wrath of God. This has happened in modern times to nations like Spain, England, and Germany when they have persecuted the Jews. And we as a nation will reap the same judgment if, in our public posture, we turn against Israel.

ISOLATION AND ATTACK

In this decade the isolation of the Jews will intensify. A world alliance is forming which is to become a new world order. The United Nations, without such an order, branded "Zionism as racism." The vast majority of the nations which make up the United Nations General Assembly have an almost pathological hatred of Israel.

If the Arabs are at the forefront of the movement against Israel, they will use their oil weapon to the maximum. The current president of the United States and his Secretary of State are both from the Texas oil industry. Israel is a secondary concern for people whose focus in private life has been petroleum and petro-dollars and whose personal friendships have for years been made with the rulers of the pro-Western Arab states.

We have mentioned the ongoing attempt of liberal Jews in America to undermine the public strength of Christianity. It should be equally clear that the liberal, wealthy Jews voted for Democratic candidates Carter, Mondale, and Dukakis, not Reagan and Bush. They have been on the losing side of the political battle for years and the present administration owes them no favors.

One day a vote against Israel will come in the United Nations when the United States neither abstains or uses its veto in the Security Council to protect Israel.

When that happens that tiny little nation will find itself all alone in the world. Then, according to the Bible, the Jews will cry out to the one they have so long rejected, and He will come in heavenly power to give them deliverance from the earthly power of all the nations of the earth.

Then we will have a reign of peace on earth known as "The Millennium." But more on that in the following chapter.

Saddam Hussein has set the machinery in motion which one day will bring the military force of world government against Israel.

12
Looking Ahead

The Bible promises a heaven-sent one world government to supersede the Gentile powers.

Attempts by the nations to establish by human effort a counterfeit millennium based on one world government will bring on an unspeakable nightmare.

To borrow a biblical phrase, America has long been in the world but not of the world. Since at least the mid-eighteenth century, the United States has maintained a position of isolationism and insularity, standing aloof from the global marketplace.

Even as we have sent armies, embassies, and missions abroad, we have stood back emotionally like stoic observers, protected to a large extent by our geography and our democratic individualism. But that era has now come to an end.

Suddenly the world has come to America and America must go to the world. Military and economic incursions abroad can no longer be construed as value-free operations. The world has grown too small, the interchange of ideas and ideologies has become the rule of the day, and every expression of American economy or foreign policy will henceforth be interpreted by the world as expressions of America's will and ideology.

In a recent column, Patrick Buchanan pointed out that America has participated in three great crusades in this century. First was

Woodrow Wilson's attempt to make the world safe for democracy. The failure of Wilson's "Fourteen Points" was demonstrated in the failure of the Treaty of Versailles. There was no enduring peace after the First World War. The subsequent war, World War II, was our second crusade. The third was the Cold War, the longest and costliest of the lot.

Today we are citizens of a new and different world. As we cast our eyes from East to West we see new allies and new adversaries on every horizon. Furthermore, we are no longer an island, for the world has come to our shores to buy and sell, to proselyte, and to live.

Tens of thousands of men, women, and children from the Third World have become citizens of our land, and they have helped to accelerate America's commerce with the world. Europe and Asia are no longer external and extraneous ideas. They have become as real to us as the cars we drive and the foods we eat. We are among them and they are among us.

The crusades of the past described in Buchanan's column were military and diplomatic incursions brought about by invasion, by conquest and surrender. The new crusades are invasions of population, not only here but around the world. Armies of immigrants from North Africa and the Middle East are swarming north and west into the homelands of the old colonial nations.

Hordes of Latins are moving north into the United States and Canada. The columnist suggests the question is not whether we will be invaded by warriors but whether our cultural identities will survive the immigrations from the Third World. Will the new invasions bring decline, or will they, perhaps, bring renewal?

Buchanan made one other observation which I believe to be not only true but very much a concern of this book. He quotes Albert Jay Nock who once wrote that, "We are in no danger whatever from any government except our own, and the danger from that is very great; therefore our own government is the one to be watched and kept on a short leash." How sad that Nock's observation remains so true.

At the conclusion of *Religion in American Public Life,* James Reichley writes that religion and the practice of democracy have been closely intertwined since the foundation of this country. Reichley believes that relationship will continue in the years ahead. George Washington certainly believed the two were inseparable and said so in his farewell address.

Washington said, "Of all the dispositions and habits which lead to political prosperity, religion and morality are indispensable supports. In vain would that man claim the tribute of patriotism, who should labor to subvert these great pillars of human happiness, these firmest props of the duties of men and citizens."

When we see the handiwork of the ACLU everywhere dismantling the traditions of a moral culture, can we believe that this nation remains committed to morality? When we see the work of the behaviorists who control the education establishment continuing to pollute the minds of our youth with deconstructionist rhetoric and anarchist ideologies, can we believe political prosperity is even a remote hope?

When we see the false religions of the New Age rising from the ruins of the rationalistic and humanistic culture, can we ever again hope that America will know itself to be "one nation under God"? If a moral democracy is the key to prosperity, what is our realistic hope for the future?

THE LAY OF THE LAND

As we move inexorably toward the dawn of the new millennium we ought to look back once again and review where we have come from as a civilization. To set the stage and to help us draw some conclusions about the broad range of issues we have considered in this book, I would also like to take a brief survey of some of the traditions of the modern age which have come down to us from the legacy of Rome and the Christian foundations laid down in Roman times.

Rome was the last major organizing unit of the old world. It was not only the greatest empire of its time, but the greatest of all the empires up until its time. The empire of the Caesars extended beyond any previous empire, to the ends of the known world. It brought about peace and a system of law and justice, and through the use of Greek, it gave the world a universal language.

This was a powerful empire. It extended from Turkey in the East to Great Britain in the West, and from the northern shores of Germany to the southern deserts of Ethiopia. The Roman Empire literally controlled the entire Mediterranean world.

When the empire finally collapsed around 476 A.D., there was a period of decline throughout Europe. By the year 600 A.D., the

Muslim world began to flourish. The religion of Mohammed spread rapidly into the gap left by Rome, and up until the Battle of Tours in 732, when the Franks under Charles Martel defeated the Saracens, the Islamic religion virtually engulfed Europe.

Later on we find the Mongol empires on the rise, Genghis Khan and others, who swept across the Steppes of Russia and came into what is now Hungary. Europe and the last vestiges of the Roman Empire were under assault by Islamic forces from the Middle East and the ravaging hordes coming out of Mongolia and China. The Europeans were frankly no match for these mighty armies.

But by 800 A.D., Charlemagne was beginning to unify the forces of Europe in what was called the Holy Roman Empire. Charles was made the Frankish king. By the time of the Renaissance, around 1500, Europe moved into the ascendancy in the world. In terms of economics and culture, and due in part to the spread of ideas brought about by the invention of the printing press in Germany, Europe entered the "Age of Exploration."

For the next 300 years, the European culture, which was now solidly Christian, was united first by the Church of Rome and subsequently by the Protestant churches. Colonists from Europe moved into India, Africa, and North and South America. They took possession of the Middle East and subjugated China. Although they didn't make China a possession, they nevertheless conquered it.

While Christendom was in the ascendancy, the Asiatic and Middle Eastern countries were in decline. That was the flowering of Western power and influence in the world.

The United States of America today is the last great expression of the triumph of Christendom. America has been the strongest of all the nations that came out of the Christian tradition extending from Charlemagne to the present.

But as we look back upon the vast sweep of history, it now appears that the end of this millennium will signal the end of a long and colorful cycle of history in which the Christian tradition had been the dominant moral and social force.

After World War II, America had more military might than any nation in history. It had more wealth and more global reach than any nation of this or any other time. The trouble was that America had never been prepared by its culture to assume the role of Empire.

Americans did not want overseas colonial possessions or empire, they merely wanted to help others to be free. Since the time of George Washington, the United States had been developing its tradition of isolation, so that it would not get involved in "entangling alliances" in Europe or other countries.

The role of global defender was alien to America, and yet after World War II—with all the nations of the world in chaos both in Asia and in Europe—the American dollar became the universal currency, and the American system of business (especially the mass production of goods) was the dominant system. American goods went everywhere, and America's share of the world's markets and the world's wealth was enormous.

So from its sleepy isolationism and 9 billion dollar annual budget, America set out to rebuild the world. We funded the Marshall Plan, sent industrial economists and engineers into Japan, built military bases around the globe, and began paying multiplied billions of dollars in aid to dozens of foreign nations on five continents.

THE MISSING MOTIVATION

But suddenly there was another problem. In the post-war era, America lost the things that had made us great: namely, our faith in God and our individual self-reliance. Although we continued to make enormous profits, we were consuming the spoils without any contingencies for the prospect of change in the future.

In essence, business leaders were doing what the British had done in the era just prior to World War II. They were milking their businesses and depreciating their plants and equipment without replacing them. They were consuming the future.

They were profit oriented, and in that era of monumental growth there was little or no competition in the world. American industries such as steel and automobiles had protected markets, and within a monopolistic, protective context, they could grant raises to workers and give financial concessions to the labor unions without any concern for the global consequences. We believed American products were just considered the best and everyone was copying us.

In this era Americans became "consumers." We had survived a period of decline during the Depression, we had won a war, and now we were exploiting this period of expansion to the limit. Homes were being formed; young people were getting married and starting families.

They were buying houses and automobiles and appliances, and there was enormous expansion of our economy and our society. But no one gave any thought to the possibility that someday we would have to be concerned about such things as inflation and domestic budgets.

During the Eisenhower years, things were kept pretty much in balance. But subsequently, the government began a process of rapid inflation, and during the tragedy of the Vietnam War, our society inflated rapidly without realizing that America's currency was the reserve currency, like gold, for the rest of the world.

By 1971 we had discarded the gold standard, and the dollar, at first, floated, then dropped in relation to other major currencies. So we exported American-style inflation overseas. Instead of being the stable, bellwether leader for the rest of the world, we became the irresponsible partner who inevitably earned the condemnation of our allies and trading partners.

We were still the strongest and had the nuclear umbrella. We still took the lead, but more and more our allies were reluctant to acknowledge our lead because of our irresponsible behavior. During this period we were still waging the false war—the so-called Cold War—and we wasted our resources on it in prodigal fashion.

It was as if somebody was intent on bringing America down from its pinnacle of world leadership. We were wasting our resources on an enormous arms build-up against an adversary that has later proven to be more illusory than real.

The Soviet threat perhaps was never as bad as we thought it was because their underlying economy was so terribly weak. In the last two years the Soviet Union has proven to be, in every meaningful respect, a Third World nation.

America has been drained of its resources and, to a degree, its resourcefulness. First in Korea, then in Vietnam, then in a cold war, we have been hamstrung and prevented from exercising our military strength. We have not been allowed to win a war or to defeat an enemy, but we've spent enormous amounts of money on an arms build-up, for a war we were never allowed to fight.

During the Vietnam war someone came up with the term "guns and butter." This was the idea that we would run a war and spend enormous amounts of money on the military while, at the same time, launch a costly war on poverty and social programs.

Thus we began a seemingly endless period of enormous domestic spending which sent us into a cycle of debt creation and inflation which has not ended to this day. It has, in turn, destabilized the entire world.

By 1966, the dramatic increase in the per capita income of the American worker in real, inflation-adjusted dollars simply stopped growing. By 1978 we had a trade deficit of 33 billion dollars, which climbed to 152.7 billion in the following decade; and by 1989 the federal debt surpassed the unbelievable 3 trillion dollar mark. The interest alone on the national debt is now 18 times the total national debt at the beginning of the Second World War.

A CRISIS OF CREDIT

The debt spiral and the mushrooming of consumer credit meant the creation of wealth through borrowing; but that wealth has not brought prosperity to the poorer nations. In fact, wealth creation through debt has impoverished countries like Nigeria and Brazil and the Congo and Mexico and the Argentine and Peru and many other countries that believed this American ideology would solve their domestic worries.

Yes, the game of debt creation has enriched those engaged in the money transfers to a degree beyond the wildest dreams of Croesus. But in the process, it has virtually crippled the economy of the entire world.

We are now at the end of a cycle of wealth creation through debt that has got to be worked out. In the process there may well be a massive economic collapse, and if not a collapse, at least a major slowdown.

Today the nations of Europe have forsaken Christianity, thus denying their spiritual heritage. They have moved into state socialism which, even in the most enlightened countries, consumes as much as 58 percent of the gross national product. The United States, too, is taking an increasingly large share of the people's income, but America has begun losing its competitive edge, just like Europe.

Today Japan is the largest creditor nation in the world while the United States has become the largest debtor. There was a time when American citizens had the highest standard of living in the world; today the Japanese and Germans surpass us in virtually every category, and the French, Danes, Swiss, and Italians are moving ahead as well.

It only takes a trip to Europe to see how weak the dollar has become. While Americans are shocked at the prices of food and hotels and incidental expenses, Japanese and European tourists are everywhere, buying up everything in sight. In the past 20 years the dollar has fallen from 350 yen to roughly 140, and from 4 German marks to roughly 1.5. In effect, that means Americans pay double for everything in Europe and Japan while the Germans and Japanese pay half price for American goods.

So, it seems as if we have come to the end of a major cycle, and as we look to the future, we see a revival coming out of the East. After some 500 years of decline, the East is coming back. Today the nations of the Orient are beginning to rise again, just as they did in the days after the Roman Empire, before the spread of Christendom.

They are flexing their economic muscles, taking a commanding position in world commerce, controlling the flow of capital in world markets. But it is not merely an economic revival, it is a spiritual revival as well.

In parts of Asia there is a spirituality custom designed for a new age, but it is clearly not compatible with the beliefs of Christianity. The beliefs—and the movement this revival entails—will most likely lead to the kind of poverty and misery associated with Bombay and Calcutta, and the desperation of the rigid caste system supported by adherents of Hinduism.

There is another system which features the kind of fanaticism that has been associated with the Shiite Muslims, the Ayatollah Khomeini, and those of his ilk who launch holy wars against infidels in order to bring about their own ends.

If the world's oil problems continue, we can expect more crises

like those in the mid-1970s when the energy supply was curtailed and manipulated for profit, for political advantage, or for harassment of the West.

The major supply of oil in the world is in the Saudi Peninsula, and in those nations that are predominantly Islamic. Many people have not stopped to realize that even the oil from Indonesia, Nigeria, and practically all the other sources is under Islamic control. Non-Islamic countries have a greatly reduced share of the petroleum that is vital to their existence, and that could easily become a major source of conflict in the immediate future.

In terms of trade imbalance, we know today that the United States has been running up a substantial deficit in trade equity with the Japanese, the Koreans, the Taiwanese, and the so-called "newly industrialized countries," called the NICs or the "Asian Tigers."

The growth rates of those nations, in terms of corporate earnings and individual savings alike, are dramatically ahead of the United States. One reason is that they have emphasized individual initiative, hard work, family values, and strong religious faith: all the things we used to have in America; the things that helped make us great.

THE NEED FOR RADICAL CHANGE

No one believes in some sort of blind determinism in history. No one is going to say that at the stroke of the year 2000 the focus changes and the world suddenly faces from West to East. Nevertheless, from a cyclical standpoint, it does seem that there is a definite shifting from West to East and a flow of wealth and technology and spiritual ideology to the East.

This does not mean that America is finished, but it does mean that unless we regain our roots, we in the West are doomed to fail. We need a radical change, in the original sense of the word "radical," meaning roots. Without a sense of our heritage, our democratic roots, we do not have a guiding ideology.

We cannot guide and motivate a society purely on the basis of politics or economics; and unless there is a spiritual revival of massive proportions, it seems to me that Western civilization, long range, will decline.

What could happen at the outset of such a time of decline? First of all, a political convulsion to bring forth a powerful charismatic leader, a dictator. In these cycles, as we have noticed, first the economics weaken, then comes a period of disarmament, then a dangerous autocratic leader.

We saw that in the 1920s. The economies of the major countries began to weaken so they decided it was in their best interest to cut back on arms, which they did, which in turn weakened the defenders of liberty and permitted one renegade in their midst to begin to arm dramatically.

By that time, the will of the people in Britain and France to use their might had been completely sapped by the post-World War I recovery. They had disarmed and did not have the military, financial, or spiritual will to rally against Adolph Hitler. As a result the world was plunged into war.

The early 1990s will certainly witness a period of dramatic disarmament. We have to stop spending so much on arms until we can get our budget balanced and begin to cut our national debt. That is a fact. But if it means that, in the wake of Vietnam we have lost our will to defend ourselves, then the chance that a person or nation might rise up as a result of an economic convulsion is a very real possibility.

If we have any kind of major economic crash in the 1990s, it could mean that the United States of Europe could fall into the hands of a demagogue, as I suggested earlier, who might well mobilize military power to go on a series of military adventures overseas in order to preserve his own dominion. In fact, it is not unrealistic to suppose that the Soviet Union might be the one: one last gasp as they are dying economically and being dismembered.

It is entirely possible that military rulers within that country might call a halt to *glasnost* and the dissolution of their empire and say since we do have this enormous arsenal, let's use it to reestablish once again Soviet hegemony, especially in the Middle East.

They could easily make a play for the oilfields in Iran, Iraq, and the Persian Gulf, and that in turn could trigger a war with a weakened United States—unless by that point the United States has already lost its will and would wait too late to intervene.

THE EASTWARD SHIFT

If the Lord doesn't return soon, and if there is not a major spiritual revival, we can expect the next hundred years to see a dramatic shift in wealth, in culture, and in military power from Western Europe and America into the nations of the Orient.

The Orient will have more active young people while the populations of Europe are growing older. By the year 2050, Western nations will likely have just over seven percent of the world's population. Their corresponding share of the world's wealth, power, and influence will be diminished accordingly. Trends are in progress which are irreversible without dramatic change.

These trends may or may not affect anyone alive today, but they will mean that the days of American ascendancy have come to an end. The Pax Romana, Pax Britannia, or the Pax Americana may well be a thing of the past. If we look at long-range trends based on demographics, economic flow, savings, competitive edge, education and other concurrent indicators, the prognosis for America in not terribly good.

That does not mean there cannot be a spiritual revival, or a renewal of education and the national will, or a curing of the moral rot in this country. It does not mean we cannot attack and eliminate the drug plague, the abortion plague, the divorce plague, and other forms of corruption in the land.

It does not mean that these social ills cannot be cured by an intervention of the hand of God. But absent that intervention, America is already in a state of decline which is going to accelerate. There is not a whole lot we can do to stop it *without* a revival.

I am not sure the trend is reversible even if there is a spiritual revival. If we lose our collective will to get our budgets balanced, to live within our means, and to return to a sense of individual self-reliance and faith in God, then the long shadows over this land are indeed dark and deep.

When I ran for the presidency in 1988, I campaigned on the premise that we have to restore the greatness of America through moral strength. If that moral strength is gone, then all the other things will disappear along with it. We are still the greatest nation on the face of the earth. We still have not lost the number one position.

We are much bigger and stronger than Japan. We may not be bigger and stronger than the collective United States of Europe, but we have a better long-term understanding of world economies, so we will continue to have economic advantages for a time.

And while we will not be nearly as big as a revived China—or especially a revived China combined with Japan, Southeast Asia, and the Pacific Rim—nevertheless, for at least this moment in history we are on the high ground. Where we go from here will make the difference in whether or not we can survive as a force in the world.

But America seems to be determined to destroy itself. While the Japanese have done everything they can to strengthen business, the liberal lobby in this country has done everything in its power to weaken business, to handicap government, business, and labor organizations, and to cripple the middle class with punitive taxation.

The major public institutions in Japan have worked in partnership to create a constructive economic environment. They see themselves as Japan Incorporated: they're all in it together. How can two such contrary systems truly compete?

In the United States, government has worked against business, business against labor, and all three have desperately worked to diminish the influence of the others. They say they can't trust each other. Yet we know that a divided nation cannot compete successfully in world competition.

The threat of a united Asia and a united Europe has opened our eyes, however, and perhaps we're beginning to get a little bit smarter, but we have a lot of learning yet to do.

The next ten years are going to be crucial in deciding the fate of this nation. If we don't surmount the moral problem, and if we don't meet the economic problems that Japan and the European Community are posing to us, we are going to find ourselves in an increasingly weak and defenseless posture.

GOD'S LOVE FOR THE FAMILY

There is a saying that a rising tide lifts all boats. When the tide rises there is more prosperity for everybody, and when the tide goes out, there is less. But whether or not we can anticipate an economic high tide in this nation in the near future, we know that God will care for those who honor Him. However desperate we may become, or however prosperous, God remains close by if we but seek Him.

During the Depression of the 1930s, 25 percent of the people in America were unemployed. That was a bitter and difficult time, but we often forget that 75 percent of the people were working. The vast majority of the people had jobs. Prices dropped dramatically, so a family with an income of just 10,000 dollars during the Depression could live very well, and could even afford domestic help.

God is able to take care of His people during a depression, just as He is during times of plenty. The average family does not feel the distress to any great degree, unless there is a military takeover, which is unlikely in this country. But that is not to say that there might not be a bondage of our national pride.

If our will remains weak and the Japanese boom continues, instead of working for American companies, we may well be working for Japanese companies before long. Instead of owing money to American banks, we will be owing money to Japanese banks. That means that ultimately the destiny of our nation is no longer in the hands of Americans but in the hands of foreign businessmen and bankers. That is not a very pleasant prospect, but, again, it isn't the end of the world.

The security for our nation does not depend on how many weapons we have stockpiled or how much wealth we have in reserve, but how strong is the family.

Jesus taught that love and self-sacrifice were among the greatest achievements in the kingdom of heaven. Instead of always looking out for number one, we must care for others, particularly those who look to us for affirmation and support.

I think it worthwhile to hear what the first lady, Barbara Bush, had to say at the Wellesley College graduation ceremonies in May 1990. After being slandered for her pro-family statements and threatened with boycott by militant feminists on campus, Mrs. Bush came and gave an eloquent address. Toward the end of that talk, she said,

> For several years you have had impressed upon you the importance to your career of dedication and hard work, and of course that's true. But as important as your obligations as a doctor, a lawyer, a business leader will be, you are a human being first and those

human connections with spouses, with children, with friends are the most important investment you will ever make.

At the end of your life, you will never regret not having passed one more test, winning one more verdict, or not closing one more deal. You will regret time not spent with a husband, a child, a friend, or a parent . . . .

Whatever the era, whatever the times, one thing will never change: Fathers and mothers, if you have children, they must come first. You must read to your children and you must hug your children, and you must love your children. Your success as a family, our success as a society, depends not on what happens in the White House but on what happens inside your house.

What a moving and important statement! Through whatever times of struggle may lie ahead, the ability to believe in the future of such families, and on homes built upon the premise of mutual support and love, takes the apprehension out of the future and the potential changes ahead.

Beyond any doubt, we are in for a period of turmoil for the individual family. We must acknowledge that. The decade ahead will be a period of economic turmoil, which means that caution should be the rule of the day, not wild optimism. We should be cautious in terms of investment policies and in terms of debt accumulation, whether for housing, automobiles, school tuition, or any other activity. But there is long-term hope, and there are ways to ensure our peace of mind and survival through these times.

First of all, every worker should be sure that he or she has marketable skills. The best investment anybody can make is in education, to ensure that they and their children have skills and abilities others will pay for. Women need to have that assurance, just as men do.

Nobody should feel that because today there's the promise of a pension guarantee from some corporation, or that they have put away a sizable economic nest egg, that it will be there forever. In uncertain times, we need to have available reserves that we can get our hands on, the short-term obligations of the United States Government. Yet, in the final analysis, only our investment in the kingdom of God will survive the ravages of inflation or depression.

THE TRENDS

As we look back at the trends we have discussed, we can see that the future promises many revolutionary changes, but it also offers the hope of a profound revival and renewal in the world, from West to East. We know that Christians will play a much larger role during the coming decade but that our beliefs and our perspectives will be challenged on many fronts.

Nevertheless, we will prevail, for we have the assurance of God's love, and we have confidence in His plans for us. As written in Jeremiah, "I know the plans I have for you," says the Lord, "that they are plans for good and not for evil, that you may have a future and a hope."

So here, then, are the issues we have explored:

1. The collapse of world communism

2. The rise and fall of secularization in the West

3. The surge of interest in the supernatural

4. The shift of influence from the West to the East

5. The deliberate undermining of America

6. The continuing assault on the traditional family

7. The boom in technology and environmental issues

8. The growing importance of global economics

9. Anti-Semitism and the meaning of Saddam Hussein

10. The challenge of the new millennium

These issues will loom large in the next ten years, and how successful we are in dealing with them—both individually and as a nation—will depend not only on our intellectual and professional skills, but on our spiritual depth.

We have come to a time and place in history when human intellect alone is no match for the problems we must confront. If we are to win the race for survival, we will need super-human powers. We will need the help of a loving and powerful God.

Collectively as Christians in America, each family, working together, can do two very important things. They can continue in prayer, asking that God will heal this land, and they can contribute their time and talents to the work of revival.

As we continue in steadfast prayer and contribute to the cause of Christ through our own efforts, we can bring about a spiritual revival in this nation. Now is the greatest opportunity in the history of the world to get the gospel out. We should be willing to spend and be spent in the service of the Lord.

The Bible talks about a time when the night comes when no man can work. What is down the road none of us can say with absolute certainty, but we can say that now while we are in the daylight, and now while there is receptivity to the gospel all over the world, we can help to shape the future that we and our children are going to live in by bringing the gospel to those nations who don't know our Lord.

If Japan is a Christian country which shares our values, then it is really of no great consequence whether they succeed economically or not. If Germany, England, France, Spain, and Italy share our values, then the fact that they invest huge sums in our country and employ American workers is not something to be feared: it can be something good rather than bad. It is only a thing to be feared if we are going to be dominated by those who worship the devil, who are malicious, or who only desire to hurt people.

Each individual family—in our neighborhoods and across this land—must use our wealth and our energy wherever we can to help spread the gospel around the world. Personally, I believe we have a two-year window in the East bloc countries and the Soviet Union when the opportunities will be beyond anything we ever dared to believe possible. But now is the time to work. A night will come when those opportunities are no longer there.

MAKING A DIFFERENCE

We cannot sit by and wring our hands and say, well it would be nice if those people in the Congress and the Legislature would vote laws that we like. Waiting around won't make it happen. We must be prepared to vote and to join with our neighbors, especially with our Christian neighbors, in influencing the laws under which we live. We must become involved.

The way we do that is by writing to our legislators, by calling our congressmen and senators, by visiting with them and talking to them, by explaining our issues, and by supporting candidates who have pledged themselves to issues we support.

The oft-quoted statement of Edmund Burke is certainly true, "All that is necessary for evil to prevail is for good men to do nothing." For too long the Christian people of America have done nothing, so it is absolutely imperative that we learn about the structure of our local precincts, about political organizations, and the formation of our parties.

We should attend party caucuses, and if we have the leadership skills, stand for election as precinct chairmen. We need to get out and knock on doors and ring telephones and send letters on behalf of candidates, and give money to them, and let our voices be heard.

With the apathy that exists in our nation, a small, well-organized minority can influence the selection of candidates of both major parties to an astonishing degree.

In the past, hippies, radicals, feminists, and deconstructionist liberals have had a field day with that fact. Now it is our turn to monopolize the system, to demand a place of political involvement, and to have a say in what happens in this country. In essence, the destiny of this nation is in the hands of the Christians.

I love the old story about the two young men who came up to the ancient Chinese sage to try to stump him. One had a bird clasped is his hand and he said, "Old man, tell me about this bird. Is it alive or dead?"

Now, if the old man said the bird was alive, the young man planned to close his fist and kill the bird; but if the sage said it was dead, the youth would open his hand and let the bird fly away. But the old man, perceiving the plan, said, "As thou wilt, young man. As thou wilt."

In the United States right now, it is very much as we will. The opportunity is ours to fashion a just society based on biblical principles which can endure strong and proud and free well into the twenty-first century.

BIBLICAL CERTAINTIES

As we look ahead to the fulfillment of the decade of the nineties and the beginning of the next millennium I would like to lay out in very concise form some of the biblical certainties which may impact your life and mine in the days ahead.

I would like also to engage in some speculation about future events which these biblical certainties may have foretold. If you happen to be one who dislikes a bit of intrigue and speculation, this section of this chapter is not for you. For others I hope you enjoy this section but please feel free to judge carefully and critically.

To me the most powerful word in the scripture concerning the present course of the nations of the world is found in chapter 21 of the Gospel of Luke, where the Lord Jesus Christ says, "And Jerusalem shall be trodden under foot of the Gentiles until the times of the Gentiles are fulfilled."

The "times of the gentiles" refers to the ascendancy of the great world powers from Assyria to Babylon to Alexander to Rome and to the offshoots of Rome. According to Jesus, Jerusalem would not be under the control of the Jews until the ascendancy of the Gentile powers was at an end.

This prophecy was literally fulfilled in June of 1967 at the end of the Six Day War, when a Jewish nation, for the first time since 586 B.C., had gained military control over all of Jerusalem. When that event took place a clock began to tick that signaled the downfall of the great Gentile powers, the last and greatest of which is the United States of America. It also began the rise of Israel. What we would like to learn now is, very simply, how long will the clock be ticking?

We do not know for sure, but here is one speculation. A biblical generation is 40 years. If June 1967 began the "generation" of the end of the times of the Gentiles, then 40 years takes us to the year 2007.

In Biblical numbers 10 is the number of completion. Usually the completion of provocation, sins, and judgment. Forty, a generation, times 10 is 400, the number of years that God, for instance, permitted the Amorites living in Canaan to sin against Him before He gave their land to the nation of Israel. The Bible tells us that God told Abraham that his descendants would sojourn for 400 years in Egypt and then would inherit the holy land, because "the iniquity of the Amorites is not yet full."

In the city of Virginia Beach, where I live, is a point of the Atlantic shore called Cape Henry. The United States Interior Department erected a sign at this place reading, "Act 1, Scene 1 of the unfolding drama which became the United States of America."

History tells us that the first official act of the first permanent English settlers at the beginning of America took place on April 29, 1607 when the settlers planted a seven-foot oak cross in the sand, then knelt in prayer and claimed this new nation for the glory of God and His Son Jesus Christ. In God's eyes the United States of America did not begin on July 4, 1776, but on April 29, 1607.

Four hundred years from the beginning of America—ten full biblical generations—takes place on April 29, 2007. By some amazing coincidence—or might we not say foresight of God—the 400th anniversary of the greatest Gentile power that the world has ever known coincides precisely with the 40th year conclusion of the generation of the "end of the Gentile power."

More remarkably the anniversary dates of the two events—Cape Henry and the taking of Jerusalem by the Israelis—(if my calculations are correct) are 40 days apart within the calendar year. (The spring of that year, I might add, this observer of events will have turned exactly 77 years old.)

Could this be a time of collapse of the Gentile powers? None of us knows the times and seasons which God has reserved for Himself, but this scenario is fascinating to contemplate. If correct, it reinforces some of the other conclusions of this book that indicate the long cycle of Western European ascendancy has come to an end.

The year 2007 is only 17 years away. But we should remember that an incredible number of convulsing events can take place in 17 years. In 1933 when Germany was prostrate economically Adolf Hitler came from nowhere and seized power.

In just seven years from that time he had plunged Europe into a devastating war. In only twelve years his evil had brought devastation to the entire globe and he lay dead as a suicide. Seventeen years can be a very long time if a demonic dictator is let loose on the earth.

An economic collapse in Germany set the stage for Hitler. An economic collapse of worldwide proportions could set the stage for some leader equally bad.

The second scriptural event which impinges on our understanding of the future course of nations is found in the book of the prophet

Daniel in the Old Testament. On successive raids against Judah which finally culminated in the sack of Jerusalem in 586 B.C., Nebuchadnezzar, King of Babylon took Jewish hostages to Babylon so that he could indoctrinate them in the culture of his country.

One named Daniel showed such wisdom that he was given a prominent place among Nebuchadnezzar's spiritual advisors. The Bible tells us that Nebuchadnezzar had an alarming dream, promptly forgot it, then demanded upon pain of death that the Chaldeans, astrologers, and soothsayers who were advising him should tell him what the dream was and what it meant.

God revealed to Daniel both the dream and its meaning. Nebuchadnezzar had seen a large statue of a man. The head was gold, the torso and arms were of silver, the thighs and belly were bronze, the legs were iron, and the toes were iron mixed with clay. Then a stone, not cut by human hands, fell upon the toes, crushed them and the rest of the statue, and then became a mountain filling the whole earth.

The interpretation given to Daniel is clear to us who live today. The head of gold was Nebuchadnezzar who had absolute authority. The silver torso represented the Persian Empire, where the King was bound by laws which he himself had made. The bronze thighs represented the Macedonian empire of Alexander where even the powerful world ruler could not stop a near mutiny of his army.

The next empire of Rome had a fighting machine of steel, but was governed, at least early on, by a senate and a clear rule of law. Finally, the ten toes represent the successors to Rome where the central authority has been mixed more and more with and derived from popular democracy and representative parliamentary government.

If we understand Daniel on this point, a government instituted by God will arise to supersede all of the previous world empires. But the specific group of nations then in existence which are to be superseded by God's kingdoms are those ten or more successors of the Roman Empire which are governed by a combination of strength, possibly socialism, and democracy.

The kingdom of God which crushes the preceding empires will "fill the earth," so it is not merely a European or a Middle East phenomenon but a worldwide kingdom.

King Nebuchadnezzar took Jerusalem away from the Jews in 586 B.C. They got it back in 1967. Jesus' prophecy concerning the end of the times of the Gentiles was made around 30 A.D. It seems to me that Nebuchadnezzar's dream and Jesus' prophecy are two sides of the same thing. It also seems that since Nebuchadnezzar was the one who conquered Jerusalem, his dream would span the period of empires and nations that existed during the time of conquest until Jerusalem was restored.

What then is the rock cut without hands that crushes the nations and fills the earth? Jesus told His disciples that "this gospel of the kingdom shall be preached in all the world for a witness, and then the end shall come."

Clearly, Jesus who said, "My kingdom is not of this world," intended that there would be a spiritual expansion of His kingdom into all the earth. In fact most Bible scholars agree that the one clear sign of the end of this age will be a vast worldwide proclamation of the good news of Christ's kingdom, not unlike the events described in chapter four.

But Nebuchadnezzar's dream was about earthly kingdoms, not spiritual kingdoms. Certainly the rise of the Roman Catholic church in 453, the Holy Roman Empire in 800, and the worldwide victory of Christendom during the post Reformation period could clearly satisfy what Nebuchadnezzar saw. But it does not satisfy Jesus' prophecy for two reasons.

First, from 453 A.D. on, though the Roman Empire was in decline, Gentile powers were in ascendancy somewhere in the world until the present day. Although Christian in name, it is hard to believe that nations who fought successively bloody wars against one another up through World War I and World War II were Christian in spirit.

Never in its history was this mass of ignorance, treachery, intrigue, greed, and oppression to be considered the "Kingdom of God." Many representatives of Christ's invisible kingdom lived in Christendom, and Christian principles were clearly the basis of its legal and social organization, but Christendom was not God's ultimate plan for earth.

Secondly, it is equally clear that during the entire period from 453 A.D. until 1967, Gentile powers—Romans, Turks, Arabs, British—controlled Jerusalem. Only at the end of Christendom did the Jews take back Jerusalem.

What then is the worldwide kingdom of God to be like— this mountain not cut with hands—that will supplant the Gentile

Kingdoms? Certainly the tiny nation of Israel does not have the population, the wealth, or the military power to become a world power. Here again the Bible gives us a clue. The prophet Micah has this to say:

> And it will come about in the last days
> That the mountain of the house of the Lord
> Will be established as the chief of the mountains
> It will be raised above the hills, And the peoples will stream
>   to it.
> And many nations will come and say,
> "Come and let us go up to the mountain of the Lord
> And to the house of the God of Jacob
> That He may teach us about His ways
> And that we may walk in his paths."
> For from Zion will go forth the law,
> Even the word of the Lord from Jerusalem.
> And he will judge between many peoples
> And render decisions for mighty, distant nations.
> Then they will hammer their swords into plowshares
> And their spears into pruning hooks;
> Nation will not lift up sword against nation,
> And never again will they train for war.
> And each of them will sit under his vine
> And under his fig tree,
> With no one to make them afraid . . . and the LORD will
>   reign over them in Mount Zion.
>
> Micah 4:1–4

This is the government that God Himself will institute from the city that Jesus Christ and Abraham before Him, hallowed by supreme acts of faith and obedience to God.

There will then be a one world government, headed by Jesus Christ, and there will be one system of laws for all of the inhabitants of the earth based on righteousness, justice, and fairness. The hard cases will be settled by the Lord Himself with absolute wisdom.

There will be no more war anywhere because all residents of the earth will agree to abide by the total wisdom and justice of the Lord. The military academies will all be closed, and the enormous worldwide expenditure for arms will be diverted to peacetime use.

The right of private property will be respected, and no man need feel threatened in the enjoyment of his possessions by his fellow citizens or by his government. There will be no oppression of the rights of any group by any other.

The power and cost of individual governments will dramatically decrease and under the new system of law people will be citizens of the world with the greatest individual freedom that people have ever enjoyed since the Garden of Eden.

The reason is simple. All people will be directed by an inner code of conduct whose basis is the golden rule, "Do unto others as you will have them do unto you." External restraints on the citizens will be unnecessary for all people will have the benevolent law of God written in their hearts.

The standard of living, the technological advances, the freedom from stress and disease, and the happiness of the people will be beyond calculation. Not only will men live at peace with one another, but the Bible says that even the animals will live at peace with man and with one another to such an extent that a little child can play safely at the den of a venomous cobra. The *Lex Talionis*, the law of the jungle, will be a thing of the past.

Wouldn't it be wonderful to be alive to see such a day? Some, in fact, want this day so badly that they have decided that they will help God out and bring it in for Him. Marx wrote of a classless society of such equality and bounty that soon struggle would be over and governments would become unnecessary and fade away. The Marxist Utopia brought on a hell on earth for two billion people. Millions died as central planners tried to force "heaven" upon them.

Hitler wrote of a 1000 year (a millennium) kingdom, the Third Reich, which would bring splendor, majesty, and happiness to the German people. His Utopia ended in the bombed out destruction of his nation and the death from war of 50 million people.

Now the Utopian vision of the people of wealth and power is for a "New World Order" in which there is such a strong central authority that individual nations will not dare to engage in war or to violate international norms.

On their part, the New Age believers yearn for a brotherhood of man and a one world government under a counterfeit Christ whose wisdom comes from demons they call "ascended masters."

With all of the strength at my command I warn the readers of this book that a one world government which tries to be a counterfeit of the millennial government that Christ will establish will become the most hellish nightmare this world has ever known.

> Fortunately for us all the Utopian schemes of men, despite the damage they can do, must fall. The glorious kingdom of Jesus Christ is certain. It may appear in our lifetime with the return of Jesus Christ to earth. When it comes, the earth will know a thousand years of peace and joy.

> May the new millennium be the Millennium of the rule and reign of Jesus Christ.

Bibliography

Allen, Frederick Lewis, *Only Yesterday: An Informal History of the 1920s* (New York: Harper & Brothers, 1931, rev. 1962).

Amos, Gary, *Defending the Declaration* (Brentwood, TN: Wolgemuth & Hyatt, 1989).

Barna, George, *The Frog in the Kettle: What Christians Need to Know about Life in the Year 2000* (Ventura, CA: Regal, 1990).

Billingsley, K. L., *The Seductive Image: A Christian Critique of the World of Film* (Westchester, IL: Crossway, 1989).

Billington, James, *Fire in the Minds of Men: Origins of the Revolutionary Faith* (New York: Basic Books, 1980).

Bloom, Allan, *The Closing of the American Mind* (New York: Simon & Schuster, 1987).

Blue, Ron, *The Debt Squeeze: How Your Family Can Become Financially Free* (Pomona, CA: Focus on the Family, 1989).

Blumenfeld, Samuel, *NEA: Trojan Horse in American Education* (Boise, ID: Paradigm, 1984).

Bosworth, Barry P., et al., *Critical Choices: What the President Should Know about the Economy and Foreign Policy* (Washington, D. C.: Brookings Institution, 1989).

Bozell, L. Brent and Brent Baker, eds., *And That's the Way It Isn't* (Alexandria, VA: Media Research Center, 1990).

Brooke, Tal, *When the World Will Be One: The Coming New World Order in the New Age* (Eugene, OR: Harvest House, 1989).

B'Tselem, the Israeli Information Center for Human Rights in the Occupied Territories, *Annual Report 1989* (Jerusalem: B'Tselem, 1989). Includes April 1990 Update.

Bureau of Justice Statistics, *Drug Use and Crime* (Washington, D. C.: U. S. Department of Justice, 1989). Plus reports of the National Institute of Justice.

Carlson, Allan C., *Family Questions: Reflections on the American Social Crisis* (New Brunswick, NJ: Transaction, 1988).

Chandler, Russell, *Understanding the New Age* (Dallas: Word, 1988). Chubb, John E. and Terry M. Moe, *Politics, Markets, and the Organization of Schools* (Washington, D.C.: Brookings, 1989).

Crane, Edward H. and David Boaz, *An American Vision: Policies for the '90s* (Washington, D.C.: Cato Institute, 1989).

Cromartie, Michael ed., *Evangelicals and Foreign Policy: Four Perspectives* (Washington, D. C.: Ethics and Public Policy Center, 1989).

Crosson, Russ, *Money and Your Marriage* (Dallas: Word, 1989).

Davidson, James Dale and Sir William Rees-Mogg, *Blood in the Streets: Investment Profits in a World Gone Mad* (New York: Summit, 1987).

FRC Publications, *Cultural Trends and the American Family* (Washington, D.C.: Family Research Council, 1987).

Golitsyn, Anatoliy, *New Lies for Old: The Communist Strategy of Deception and Disinformation* (New York: Dodd, Mead, 1984).

Groothius, Douglas R., *Unmasking the New Age* (Downers Grove, IL: InterVarsity, 1986).

Hart, Benjamin, *Faith & Freedom: The Christian Roots of American Liberty* (San Bernardino, CA: Here's Life, 1988).

Henry, Carl F. H., *Twilight of a Great Civilization: The Drift Toward Neo-Paganism* (Westchester, IL: Crossway, 1988).

Herman, Victor, *Coming Out of the Ice: An Unexpected Life* (New York: Harcourt Brace Jovanovich, 1979).

Hirsch, E. D., *Cultural Literacy: What Every American Needs to Know* (New York: Houghton Mifflin, 1987).

Hitchcock, James, *What Is Secular Humanism?* (Ann Arbor, MI: Servant, 1982).

Hufbauer, Gary Clyde, *Europe 1992: An American Perspective* (Washington, D. C.: Brookings Institution, 1990).

Johnson, Paul, *A History of the Jews* (New York: Harper & Row, 1987).

Johnson, Paul, *Intellectuals* (New York: Harper & Row, 1988).

Johnson, Paul, *Modern Times: The World from the Twenties to the Eighties* (New York: Harper & Row, 1983).

Kimball, Roger, *Tenured Radicals: How Politics Has Corrupted Our Higher Education* (New York: Harper & Row, 1990).

Kurtz, Paul, ed., *A Secular Humanist Declaration* (New York: Prometheus Books, 1980).

Kurtz, Paul and Edwin H. Wilson, *Humanist Manifesto* (1933), and *Humanist Manifesto II* (1973), published jointly (New York: Prometheus Books, 1984).

Lacey, Robert, *The Kingdom* (New York: Harcourt Brace Jovanovich, 1981).

Lockerbie, Bruce, *Who Educates Your Child?* (Garden City, N.Y.: Doubleday, 1980).

McElvaine, Robert, *The Great Depression* (New York: Times Books, 1984).

Medved, Diane, *The Case Against Divorce* (New York: Donald I. Fine, 1989).

Muggeridge, Malcolm, *The End of Christendom* (Grand Rapids: Wm. B. Eerdmans, 1983).

Morken, Hubert, *Pat Robertson: Where He Stands* (Old Tappan, NJ: Revell, 1988).

Neuhaus, Richard John and Michael Cromartie ed., *Piety & Politics: Evangelicals and Fundamentalists Confront the World* (Washington, D. C.: Ethics & Public Policy Center, 1987).

Office of National Drug Control Policy, *National Drug Control Strategy, 1990 and 1989 Reports* (Washington, D. C.: Executive Office of the President, 1989, 1990).

Peters, Tom, *Thriving on Chaos: Handbook for a Management Revolution* (New York: Alfred A. Knopf, 1987).

Reichley, A. James, *Religion in American Public Life* (Washington, D. C.: Brookings Institution, 1985).

Robertson, Pat, *The Secret Kingdom* (Nashville: Thomas Nelson, 1982).

Rothman, Stanley and S. Robert Lichter, *Roots of Radicalism: Jews, Christians, and the New Left* (New York: Oxford, 1982).

Slosser, Bob and Cynthia Ellenwood, *Changing the Way America Thinks* (Dallas: Word, 1989).

Smith, Page, *Killing the Spirit: Higher Education in America* (New York: Viking, 1990). Sykes, Charles J., *Profscam: Professors and the Demise of Higher Education* (Washington, D.C.: Regnery-Gateway, 1988).

Tocqueville, Alexis de, *Democracy in America,* trans. Henry Reeve, rev. Francis Bowen and Phillips Bradley (New York: Alfred A. Knopf, 1956.)

U. S. Department of Health and Human Services, *Annual Data from the Drug Abuse Warning Network* (Rockville, MD: National Institute on Drug Policy, 1989).

U. S. Department of Health and Human Services, *Drug Use, Drinking, and Smoking: National Survey Results from High School, College, and Young Adult Populations 1975–1988* (Rockville, MD: National Institute on Drug Policy, 1989).

U. S. Department of Health and Human Services, *National Household Survey on Drug Abuse* (Rockville, MD: National Institute on Drug Policy, 1989).

Vaughan, John N., *Church Growth Today* (Bolivar, MO: Southwestern Baptist University, series vol. 4 no. 4 1989—vol. 5 no. 1 1990).

Vertefeuille, John N., *Sexual Chaos: The Personal and Social Consequences of the Sexual Revolution* (Westchester, IL: Crossway, 1988).

Walters, Philip, ed., *World Christianity: Eastern Europe* (Eastbourne, Sussex, U.K.: MARC, 1988).

Wattenberg, Ben, *The Birth Dearth* (New York: Pharos, 1987).

DATE DUE

NOV 0 9 1995			

124896